Getting Started in

FUTURES

The Getting Started in Series

Getting Started in

FUTURES

FIFTH EDITION

Todd Lofton

John Wiley & Sons, Inc.

For general information on our other products and services or for technical support, please contact our Customer Care Department within the United States at (800) 762-2974, outside the United States at (317) 572-3993 or fax (317) 572-4002.

Wiley also publishes its books in a variety of electronic formats. Some content that appears in print may not be available in electronic books. For more information about Wiley products, visit our Web site at www.wiley.com.

Library of Congress Cataloging-in-Publication Data:

Lofton, Todd.
    Getting started in futures / Todd Lofton. — 5th ed.
      p. cm. — (Getting started in . . .)
    Includes index.
    ISBN-13: 978-0-471-73292-1 (pbk. : alk. paper)
    ISBN-10: 0-471-73292-3 (pbk. : alk. paper)
    1. Futures market. I. Title. II. Series.

HG6024.A3L64 2005
332.64'52—dc22   2005048620

Printed in the United States of America

10 9 8 7 6 5 4 3 2 1

To Beth, James, Christine, and Margaret, whom I love more than they know.

And, to the incandescent minds at Apple Computer, to me anonymous, from which sprung my marvelous Macintosh iBook. Without it I would be mute, engaged in a mind-numbing spiral of writing and rewriting. Without it, this book would not exist.

Preface

I f you would like to know how futures markets can help you reduce risk or earn greater profits, you have come to the right place. Futures enable you to:

- Set now the purchase price of a financial instrument that you'll buy later
- Protect a foreign currency bank balance from changes in the exchange rate
- Reduce the market exposure of a single-stock or a large stock portfolio
- Benefit from a favorable change in interest rates without owning the cash instruments
- Protect an inventory of an actual commodity against a decline in its cash price
- Make a bet on the price trend in any traded commodity, from corn to the Canadian dollar

This is the fifth edition of *Getting Started in Futures*, and a lot of the information is new. But our goals have not changed. Our first goal is help you understand how futures markets work. Our second goal is to show you how you can use these fast-moving marketplaces to your own personal economic advantage.

And we do it all in simple, easy-to-read prose, with lots of examples.

Begin at the Beginning

We begin by introducing you to the basics using the traditional commodity markets as examples. Then we move on to financial futures, the newest and fastest growing futures markets in the world. These include futures and futures options in interest rates, equities, and foreign currencies. Finally, we talk about the modern marvels that the personal computer has wrought: rock-bottom commission costs, lightning-fast online trading, and the ability to get up-to-the-minute market information at the touch of a computer key.

In between, you'll learn how to set yourself up for trading online, where to dig when you're mining the Internet, ways to forecast prices, and how day trading works.

What's New

A modern Rip Van Winkle who had snoozed for the past 20 years would barely recognize today's futures markets. What began 150 years ago as relatively simple local trading in grains, meats, and metals has evolved into an international world marketplace where millions of dollars worth of financial futures and options are traded every day.

The most recent innovation are futures contracts on single stocks, and a new chapter in this edition is devoted to the subject. (If single-stock futures are what have drawn you to this book, you might read Chapter 13 first. It is designed to stand alone; it refers you to earlier chapters, when necessary, to explain basic concepts.)

There are also several other new futures contracts, especially in the financial futures. We tell you about the ones that are catching on.

Options on futures (puts and calls) offer special advantages, and they behave differently than futures. We'll explain.

Finally, we've taken care of the nits: We've verified that any phone number that we give you still works; that the market reports mentioned are still available; and that the Suggested Reading section at the end of each chapter lists the most up-to-date books.

What's Not New

This is still the most readable book ever published on the subject of futures. There's no gobbledegook. There's no higher math. Everything is written in simple English, and there are lots of everyday examples, to make sure that you understand.

When you've finished reading this book, you'll have the know-how to get started in futures. That's a promise.

Thanks

Christopher Lown is the editor-in-chief of Commodity Research Bureau (CRB) in Chicago, which has been producing price charts, price forecasting tools, and market research reports for its subscribers since 1934.

Mr. Lown and CRB graciously provided all of the charts that we have used as illustrations. We thank CRB and Mr. Lown, personally.

One final word: To avoid repeating the phrase "(or she)" throughout the book, we have restricted our use of the singular personal pronoun to "he." It is not intended as a slight. We are fully aware of the increasing presence of successful women in every aspect of futures: as owners of brokerage firms, brokers, exchange members, market research analysts, and private traders.

Errata

If you run across any mistakes in these pages, I request your patience. There's no one to blame but me.

TODD LOFTON

McLean, Virginia
July 2005

Contents

Chapter 20

Getting Started in

FUTURES

Introduction

Suppose that you and I lived in rural Iowa. I raise beef cattle. You raise corn 15 miles down the road. Each fall, when your corn comes in, you truck the entire crop to me, and I buy it to feed to my steers. To make things fair, we agree that I will pay you the cash price for corn on the Chicago Board of Trade on the day I take delivery.

Corn is important to both of us. It is your principal crop; it is my main cost in feeding cattle. I hope for low prices. All summer long you are praying that something benign—an unexpected Russian purchase, for example—will send corn prices up.

One spring day you come to me with a suggestion. "Let's set our corn price now for next fall," you say. "Let's pick a price that allows each of us a reasonable profit and agree on it. Then neither of us will have to worry about where prices will be in September. We'll be able to plan better. We can go on about our business, secure in the knowledge of what we will pay and receive for the corn."

I agree, and we settle on a price of $3.00 a bushel. That agreement is called a forward contract—a "contract" because it's an agreement between a buyer (me) and a seller (you); "forward" because we're going to make the actual transaction later, or forward in time.

It's a good idea, but it's not without flaws. Suppose the Russians did announce a huge surprise purchase, and corn prices went to $3.50. You would be looking for ways to get out of the contract. By the same token, I would not be too eager to abide by our agreement if a bumper crop caused corn prices to fall to $2.50 a bushel.

1

There are other reasons why our forward contract could fail to be met. A hailstorm could wipe out your entire corn crop. I could sell my cattle-feeding operation, and the new owner not feel bound by our agreement. Either one of us could go bankrupt.

Futures contracts were devised to solve these problems with forward contracts, while retaining most of their benefits. A futures contract is simply a forward contract with a few wrinkles added.

Chapter

Basic Terms and Concepts

There are some basic concepts that you should understand if you are going to deal with the futures markets. The first is the futures contract itself. In the Introduction we stated that a futures contract is simply a forward contract with some added wrinkles. One of those wrinkles is *standardization*.

A forward contract can be written for any commodity. It can also be written for any amount or delivery time. If you want to make a deal to buy 1400 bushels of silver queen corn for delivery to your roadside stand next July 2, you can do it with a forward contract. You can't in the futures market.

A futures contract is for a specific grade, quantity, and delivery month. For example, the futures contract for corn on the Chicago Board of Trade (CBOT) calls for 5000 bushels of No. 2 yellow corn. Delivery months are March, May, July, September, and December. There are no other delivery months. All futures contracts are standardized in this way. That's done to make specific futures contracts interchangeable. Grade, quantity, and delivery months are specified by the exchange when they design the contract. Only the price is left to be determined.

Smart Investor Tip

A futures contract is a standardized forward contract that can be broken by either party with simply an offsetting futures market transaction.

Another difference is where business may be done. A forward contract can be drawn up anywhere. Futures contracts are bought or sold only on the exchange trading floor by members of the exchange.

Money

Three other differences between a forward contract and a futures contract involve the important matter of money. If two parties make a forward contract, no money need change hands until the cash transaction is completed at a later date. If you buy a futures contract, you will have to put up *margin* money. This is not a down payment, and no money is borrowed, as in stocks. It is a good-faith deposit, or "earnest money," to demonstrate your intention to pay for the commodity in full when it is delivered.

If you buy a futures contract and cash prices go up, so will the price of your futures contract, as they tend to move together. In that event you would have an *unrealized* profit in your futures account. Without closing out the futures position, you may withdraw this profit in cash and use it for whatever you wish. This is not possible with a forward contract.

You will have to pay your broker a *commission* for handling the futures transaction for you. There is no commission in a forward contract.

An Exit

One of the most important qualities of a futures contract is its *escapability*. If you enter into a forward contract and later decide you want out, the other party would also have to agree to break the contract. If he won't, you're stuck. If you buy a futures contract and later decide that you don't want to be a party to it anymore, you can close out your position and wipe the slate clean by simply selling the same futures contract. (Now you can see why it is important that individual futures contracts be interchangeable.)

Futures provide other, broader economic benefits that probably won't affect you directly. Because they trade actively, futures markets are constantly "discovering" the current price for the particular commodity. These prices are disseminated around the world within seconds. If you want to make a futures transaction, there's no need to search for a buyer or seller. There are virtually always buyers and sellers (or their representatives) waiting on the exchange trading floor; the only question is price. Most futures markets, by providing for alternate delivery of the actual cash commodity, also provide a safety valve for producers who for some reason cannot deliver their actual commodity through normal supply channels.

The Long and Short of It

Before we talked only about buying a futures contract. That's known as being *long*, or having a *long position.* The holder of a long futures position may receive delivery of the actual commodity if he holds the futures position into the delivery period.

You may have also heard the term *short.* The rules surrounding futures trading allow you to sell a futures contract before you buy it. When you do, you are said to be short futures, or have a *short position.* You will be expected to deliver the actual commodity if you hold a short futures position into the delivery period. To close out a short futures position, you buy an identical futures contract on the exchange. You would then be out of the market altogether.

The idea of a short position may be confusing because it involves selling something you don't have. Actually, you may already have participated in a short sale without being aware that you were doing so. If a car dealer doesn't have the car you want on his lot and orders one for you from the factory, he has sold the car short. Furniture is often sold (short) by a retail store before the items are manufactured.

Smart Investor Tip
In futures, there is a short position for every long position.

Why would someone want to sell a futures contract short? To establish his selling price, because he believes the market is headed lower and that he will be able to buy the futures contract back later at a lower price. Regardless of which transaction came first, the profit or loss in a futures trade is the difference between the buying price and the selling price.

Who's long and who's short is one of the biggest differences between the futures markets and the stock markets. Most stock investors buy shares. They hold them for dividends and price appreciation. Only the most sophisticated investors sell stocks short. It is conceivable, therefore, that everyone who owns a certain stock has a profit in it. For example, let's say that General Motors stock advanced from $68 to $69 in today's trading. If there are no short positions in the stock and no present stockholder paid more than $68 a share, everybody involved with GM stock would have a profit. And they would all have just seen their profits increase by $1 per share.

That's not true in futures. In futures, there is a short position for every long position. If you are out of the market and decide to buy a futures contract, another market participant must take the other side and sell it to you. If you sell a futures contract short, somebody somewhere must take the other side and buy it from you. That's the only way a futures contract can be created. Gains on one side of the futures markets therefore come out of the pocket of someone on the other side of the market; what the longs win, the shorts lose, and vice versa. It may serve as a sobering thought: If you take money out of the futures markets, it's not coming out of thin air; you're taking it from another player.

Smart Investor Tip

If you gain a profit in a long futures position, a short somewhere has lost the same amount.

Prices

Cash versus Futures

The *cash* or *spot* price of a commodity is the price at which the actual commodity is currently being bought or sold in the marketplace. The *futures* price is the price at which futures contracts are changing hands. Cash and futures prices for a particular commodity do not stray too far from each other. If the cash price of a commodity goes up or down, its futures prices tend to follow. But cash and futures prices do not all necessarily move together penny for penny. The reason is that different forces are at work on the two prices.

Cash prices respond to the present supply of and demand for the actual commodity. If there is an immediate shortage of a certain commodity, its price will be bid up by processors, distributors, and others who use it in their course of business. If the commodity is in abundant supply, its cash price will fall.

Futures prices respond to changes in the cash price. The futures price most affected by a change in the cash price is that of the nearest delivery month because it will soon be virtually the same as the cash price. Distant futures months are less responsive, perhaps because traders feel that whatever is affecting the cash price now may not be a factor later.

Smart Investor Tip

Cash prices respond to the supply of and demand for the actual commodity. Futures prices respond to changes in the cash price and to traders' expectations.

These are not the only winds blowing on futures. Futures prices are also driven by traders' *expectations*. The mere threat of drought or crop disease or labor strike can send futures prices up long before the actual event materializes.

An example of the power of traders' expectations can be seen in Figure 2.1, which is a price chart for November soybeans on the CBOT.

Price Charts

The chart in Figure 2.1 is called a *bar chart*. Figure 2.2 is a more complete example; it shows daily price action, volume, and open interest for December New York gold futures over a 7-month period.

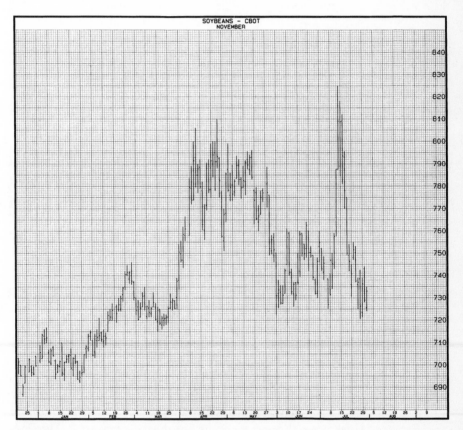

Figure 2.1 The power of traders' expectations can be seen in this price chart for November soybeans. Small carryover and rumored low yields for the current crop sent prices skyrocketing in mid-July. When the dangers were discounted, the market fell straight back to earth. What traders thought might happen triggered a round trip of $2.00 a bushel—$10,000 per contract—in only 7 trading days.

Chart courtesy of *CRB Futures Perspective*, a publication of Commodity Research Bureau.

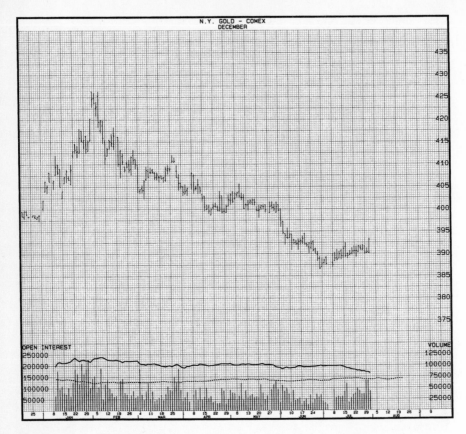

Figure 2.2   A typical bar chart, the most widely used chart. It shows several months of price activity, enabling a comparison between present and past price levels. Shown at the bottom of the chart are daily trading volume and open interest, analysis of which can reveal who's doing the buying and selling.

Chart courtesy of *CRB Futures Perspective*, a publication of Commodity Research Bureau.

Each day's price activity is represented by a vertical line; the top of the line marks the day's high price, the bottom of the line the day's low price. The closing or settlement price is denoted by a short "tick" mark extending to the right of the vertical line. Futures prices are on the right-hand scale.

The calendar across the bottom shows only weekdays; that is, the weekends are omitted, so the price action has a continuous appearance. The vertical bars extending upward from the bottom are daily trading volume, read on the lower right-hand scale. The two horizontal lines meandering across the chart from left to right represent open interest (the number of outstanding futures contracts) and are read on the lower left-hand scale. The broken horizontal line is the 5-year average open interest in New York gold futures. The solid horizontal line above it shows current daily open interest.

Price charts are economic shorthand, enabling you to compare several weeks or months of past price action at a glance. Most traders use price charts at one time or another, and some key their entire trading strategy to the interpretation of price movements.

The Necessary Arbitrage

For a futures market to do its job, the cash price and the futures price of a given commodity must meet during the delivery period. If the two prices did not come together, hedging—the economic reason for all futures markets—would be impossible.

To ensure that cash and futures prices are virtually equal when the futures contract matures, the exchanges have historically provided for delivery of the actual commodity in satisfaction of a short futures position. Then, if cash prices should range too far above nearby futures prices, for example, arbitrageurs in the trade would buy the nearby futures, take delivery against the futures contract, and sell the cash commodity thus received in the spot market for a certain profit. This action by arbitrageurs would put downward pressure on cash prices and upward pressure on futures, moving the two prices back together again.

Conversely, if nearby futures prices move far enough above the cash price to make it profitable, arbitrageurs would sell the futures, buy the cash commodity, store it, and deliver it against the futures contract. This action would continue until cash and futures prices moved closer together, erasing potential arbitrage profits.

Volume and Open Interest

Trading volume is the number of futures transactions that took place during a certain period. For example, if you bought a futures contract today, you would add 1 to today's trading volume. One contract would have changed hands, from the seller to you. If later today you decided to sell it, you would add another unit to today's trading volume. When you pick up the newspaper tomorrow morning and see that trading volume in that commodity was 4105 contracts, you know that you were personally responsible for two of them.

Open interest is the number of *outstanding* futures contracts, or the total of short and long positions that have not yet been closed out by delivery or by offsetting futures markets transactions. Your two transactions could have changed the open interest, but not necessarily. As you will see later, it depends on which player took the other side of your trades. The idea of open interest is unique to the futures and options markets. There's nothing comparable in stocks or bonds.

The Clearinghouse

Each futures exchange has its own clearinghouse. Some are separate and distinct from the exchange itself; others are departments within the exchange. Membership is available only to members of the exchange. In addition, clearinghouse members must meet very strict financial requirements.

The functions the clearinghouse performs are vital to the efficient operation of the futures markets. It is the clearinghouse that makes it possible to close out a futures position with simply an offsetting futures market transaction. It does so by breaking the tie between the original buyer and seller. At the end of every trading day, the clearinghouse becomes the buyer to every seller and the seller to every buyer. Either party can therefore close out his futures position through the clearinghouse, without having to locate and obtain the agreement of the original second party.

Smart Investor Tip

The clearinghouse makes it possible to close out a futures position with simply an offsetting futures market transaction.

The accounts of the clearinghouse show the numbers of long and short positions held by each clearing member, not by individual customer name. If you sell to get out of a long position, the clearinghouse balances your sale with a purchase made that day. You'll never know (and don't care, really) who was on the other side of your transaction.

The clearinghouse also has other important responsibilities, including supervising the delivery of actual commodities against a short futures position and guaranteeing the financial integrity of each futures contract it clears.

We take a closer look at open interest and the operation of the clearinghouse in later chapters.

Suggested Reading

Introduction to Futures and Options. Futures Industry Association, Washington, DC, 2003.

Chapter 3

Futures
Markets Today

There is a wide variety of futures markets today, many of them for "commodities" that could not possibly have been envisioned when the first futures contract for corn was traded on the Chicago Board of Trade in the mid-1800s. The two biggest differences between now and then are (1) the preponderance of financial futures and (2) the number of new futures and option exchanges around the world.

As for the markets themselves, the leader in futures trading volume in 2004 was stock index futures. The next most popular underlying instruments were interest-rate securities, such as U.S. Treasury notes or Eurodollars. These are followed by single-stock futures and options. Last year, these three categories comprised 85 percent of the total worldwide trading volume in futures and futures options.

The remaining 15 percent comprised the more traditional futures markets in agricultural products, energy products, foreign currencies, and metals.

Following is a list of the active futures markets in the United States:

Grains: wheat, corn, oats, soybean complex (soybeans, soybean oil, soybean meal)

Meats: live cattle, feeder cattle, lean hogs, pork bellies

Metals: platinum, silver, high-grade copper, gold

Foods and fibers: coffee, sugar, cocoa, orange juice, cotton

Interest-rate futures: Treasury bonds, Treasury notes, Eurodollars, 30-day Federal Funds, London Interbank Offered Rate

Foreign currencies: Swiss franc, British pound, Japanese yen, euro, Canadian dollar, Mexican peso, Australian dollar

Index futures: S&P 500 Index, S&P MidCap 400 Index, Nikkei 225 Stock Average, Goldman Sachs Commodity Index, U.S. Dollar Index

Energy futures: light sweet crude oil, heating oil No. 2, unleaded gasoline, natural gas

Wood: lumber

There are also e-mini futures contracts for the Japanese yen, euro, gold, silver, natural gas, light sweet crude oil, and hard red wheat. These are smaller than regular futures contracts, and they are traded only electronically. On the overseas futures exchanges, foreign stocks and interest-rate instruments predominate. Foreign futures exchanges and their principal markets are described in Appendix G.

Reading Prices. Following is a typical report of one day's trading in one futures market, such as you might find in the financial section of your daily newspaper. As you can see, it contains a great deal of information:

Wheat (CBOT); 5000 Bushels; Cents per Bushel					
Delivery	*Open*	*High*	*Low*	*Settle*	*Change*
December	338½	341	338¼	340	+2½
March	343½	346	337	336½	+3
May	339½	341½	339½	340¾	+2¼
July	328	329½	327	317¼	+1¾
September	332½	332¾	332	332	+1¾
December	338¼	340	338¼	340	+1¾

Est. sales 26,000; Prev. sales 28,473; Open int. 68,816; Change +897

The top line identifies the commodity and provides information about the futures contract. It shows the exchange where the futures contracts are traded (CBOT stands for the Chicago Board of Trade). It also shows the size of the futures contract (5000 bushels). The last item in that line explains that prices in the table are expressed in cents per bushel.

The second line identifies the columns. In the far left column are the delivery months. Chicago wheat futures are traded for delivery in March, May, July, September, and December. Notice that delivery months extend out to 1 year ahead. The delivery months are established by the exchange where the commodity is traded and vary from market to market.

The second column shows the opening price for each contract that day. In the next four columns are the day's high price, the day's low price, the day's settlement price, and the change from yesterday's settlement price.

The bottom line shows today's estimated trading volume; yesterday's actual trading volume; yesterday's total open interest in Chicago wheat; and the change in open interest from the previous day.

To interpret the prices, you add a decimal point. A price of 340, for example, means $3.40 per bushel. The minimum price change is ¼ cent per bushel. To calculate a change in equity caused by a price change, you must take into consideration the contract size. For example, if you had been long one futures contract of nearby December wheat that day, the value of your equity would have increased 2½ cents per bushel; 2½ cents × 5000 bushels = $125.00. If you had been short one futures contract of December wheat, you would have had an unrealized loss of $125.00. If it's easier for you, you can simply remember that 1 cent = $50.

The size of the futures contract for all grains and for soybeans is 5000 bushels. Prices of all grains and soybeans are expressed in cents per bushel, and 1 cent equals $50 in equity.

Let's take a look at the meats:

Cattle (CME); 40,000 Pounds; Cents per Pound					
Delivery	Open	High	Low	Settle	Change
December	75.30	75.57	74.95	75.42	+1.35
February	72.00	72.57	71.87	72.47	+1.35
April	74.50	75.00	74.35	74.67	+.80
June	74.40	75.15	74.40	74.72	+.62
August	72.10	72.65	72.00	72.07	+.45
October	71.50	71.90	71.30	71.40	+.45
December	72.45	73.00	72.45	72.90	+.60

Est. sales 19,858; Prev. sales 16,260; Open int. 77,110; Change –748

The cattle futures contract on the Chicago Mercantile Exchange (CME) is for 40,000 pounds of live cattle, and prices are expressed in cents per pound. A price of 71.87, for example, means 71.87 cents per pound. If you had been long one contract of February cattle that day, you would have had an unrealized profit of 1.35 cents per pound, or $540 ($.0135 × 40,000 pounds). For shorthand, simply remember that a 1 cent change in cattle futures prices causes a $400 change in equity.

Futures prices for live cattle, feeder cattle, lean hogs, and pork bellies—which comprise the meat futures—are all expressed in cents per pound. However, the minimum "tick" (price change) is $2\frac{1}{2}$ cents per pound. The prices of 75.52 and 75.57 are really $75.52\frac{1}{2}$ and $75.57\frac{1}{2}$. The "$\frac{1}{2}$" is omitted in the table to reduce clutter. The last digit of all meat futures prices is therefore always 0, 2, 5, or 7.

Following are prices for the most well known of the metal futures contracts:

Gold (COMEX); 100 Troy Ounces; Dollars per Troy Ounce					
Delivery	*Open*	*High*	*Low*	*Settle*	*Change*
December	361.00	362.30	357.00	358.50	−1.60
February	366.30	367.40	359.80	360.40	−1.60
April	373.50	374.00	366.50	367.10	−1.50
June	379.80	381.00	374.00	374.60	−1.40

COMEX stands for Commodity Exchange, Inc., which is a division of the New York Mercantile Exchange. The futures contract calls for delivery of 100 troy ounces of pure gold, and prices are expressed in dollars per troy ounce. A futures price of 358.50 thus means $358.50 per troy ounce. The minimum price change is 10 cents per troy ounce, which represents a change in equity of $10 per futures contract ($.10 × 100 = $10).

Metal futures contract sizes and prices are not uniform, as the following list shows:

Copper: 25,000 pounds; cents per pound.

Platinum: 50 troy ounces; dollars per troy ounce.

Palladium: 100 troy ounces; dollars per troy ounce.

Silver: 5000 troy ounces; cents per troy ounce.

Prices for futures in U.S. Treasury bonds are expressed in an entirely different way:

Treasury Bonds (CBOT); $100,000; Points and 32nds of 100%					
Delivery	*Open*	*High*	*Low*	*Settle*	*Change*
December	94-20	95-07	94-20	95-05	+14
March	93-19	94-07	93-16	94-05	+14
June	92-19	93-09	92-19	93-07	+14
September	91-29	92-13	91-27	92-12	+13

Treasury bond futures are traded on the CBOT. The asset underlying the futures contract is $100,000 worth of T-bonds. T-bond futures prices are expressed in points and 32nds percent of par. The digits after the dash are therefore not decimals but the number of 32nds. A price of 93-20, for example, means 93 percent of $100,000 plus $\frac{20}{32}$ of 1 percent of $100,000.

The minimum price change of $\frac{1}{32}$ of 1 percent equals $31.25 ($1000 divided by 32). A trader with a long position in CBOT March T-bonds, for example, would have had an unrealized gain of $\frac{14}{32}$ on this day, or $14 \times \$31.25 = \$437.50$. A short somewhere would have had a mirror image unrealized loss of $437.50. Prices for municipal bond index futures are expressed in the same way. The shorter term Treasuries (2-, 5-, and 10-year notes) have different futures contract sizes and minimum tick values.

Foreign currency futures are also irregular. The active foreign currency futures and their specifications are:

Currency	Contract Size	Prices Expressed in
Swiss franc	125,000 francs	Dollars per franc
British pound	62,500 pounds	Dollars per pound (sterling)
Canadian dollar	100,000 dollars	Dollars (U.S.) per dollars (C)
Mexican peso	500,000 new pesos	Dollars per peso
Australian dollar	100,000 dollars	Dollars (U.S.) per dollars (A)
Euro	125,000 euros	Dollars per euro
Japanese yen	12.5 million yen	Dollars per yen (.00 omitted)

Of these, the last could give you trouble in interpreting, so let's take a closer look. The following are representative futures prices for the Japanese yen:

Open	High	Low	Settle	Change
.7608	.7637	.7600	.7603	−.0010

In Japanese yen futures prices, two zeros are omitted right after the decimal point to keep the numbers manageable. The approximate cost of 1 Japanese yen in U.S. currency is not 76 cents, but 76/10,000 of a cent, or $.0076. The change of .0010 that day was really a change of $.000010 per yen. That number multiplied by the contract size of 12.5 million yen equals a change in equity of $125 that day, a modest move.

The final prices we will show you in this chapter are for S&P 500 Stock Index futures:

S&P 500 Index (CME); $250 Times Index					
Delivery	Open	High	Low	Settle	Change
December	1475.40	1484.40	1475.20	1484.00	+8.55
March	1475.90	1485.00	1475.90	1484.80	+8.65
June	1477.05	1487.25	1477.05	1486.35	+9.05

Futures contracts in the S&P 500 Stock Index are traded on the CME. Because all stock index futures are settled in cash, the size of the futures contract is not fixed but is equal to $250 times the present value of the index. Each 1.00 change in the futures price therefore represents a $250 change in the total value of the futures contract.

This table shows volatile price activity. A speculative long position in the March delivery month, for example, would have earned an unrealized gain of $2162.50 that day.

The futures contracts presented in this section are those that represent large groups of futures or those that are irregular. There are several other futures contracts that we have not considered here, including the several e-mini contracts traded on the CBOT, the CME, and the New York Mercantile Exchange.

Minicontracts are a fraction of the size of the standard futures contract, are traded on electronic markets, and are fungible with their larger siblings in offsetting existing market positions.

Normal and Carrying Charge Markets

Futures prices for all delivery months of a particular commodity tend to move together. After all, the same commodity underlies December T-bills and March T-bills, February cattle and April cattle, March corn and May corn.

Smart Investor Tip
Futures prices for different delivery months of the same commodity do not always move together. Although there are other causes, the major reason for the divergence is seasonality.

Nevertheless, different delivery months of the same commodity do not always move in lockstep. One reason for the difference is seasonality. For example, the harvest for winter wheat in the United States takes place in late May and June. May wheat futures contracts mature before the harvest, when cash prices depend on old-crop supplies; July wheat futures mature after the harvest, when a new supply of the actual grain will be on hand. As a result, a rally in the May wheat might not be matched in the July wheat.

Petroleum futures provide another example. Because the demand for heating oil is greater in winter, cash prices tend to firm then; futures traders anticipating this effect may drive the prices for January and February futures contracts up above those for the warmer months.

Livestock are a special case. Live cattle and hogs cannot wait around long after they have reached marketable weights; they must be sold. The futures price for each delivery month in these two markets therefore anticipates the pending supply of live animals for that particular time period. A delivery month with a large pending supply will tend to be relatively weaker than one with a fewer number of animals in the pipeline.

Trading tactics may also cause a divergence. Some traders buy one delivery month of a commodity and simultaneously sell another delivery month of the same commodity. Their actions cause the delivery month bought to gain on the delivery month sold.

Certain delivery months of a commodity simply attract a large following. December cotton shows high volume and open interest even in the spring, when December is a distant month. The U.S. Treasury refunding cycle can make certain delivery months of Treasury bond futures more in demand than other delivery months.

Normal Market

Futures prices are considered to be "normally" arrayed when each succeeding delivery month is higher priced than the preceding delivery month. A normal futures market in wheat, for example, might look something like this on any given day:

Wheat Futures Contract	Price (per Bushel)
September	$3.25
December	3.35
March	3.42
May	3.42
July	3.24

Smart Investor Tip

Futures prices are considered to be "normally" arrayed when each succeeding delivery month is higher priced than the preceding delivery month.

December wheat is higher priced than the September, the March higher priced than the December, and so on until anticipation of the coming harvest pushes July wheat below all the other delivery months.

The difference between the price of September wheat and December wheat is 10 cents. That difference represents the cost of carrying the actual wheat for that 2-month period. It includes, among other things, the cost of warehouse space and the cost of insurance against loss from dampness or rodents.

If the price difference between the two delivery months were to become much greater than the actual carrying charge, arbitrageurs in the trade would see a sure profit. They would buy the (lower-priced) nearby future and sell the (higher-priced) distant future. When the nearby future matured, they would take delivery. They would store the grain and deliver it against the most distant futures contract when it matured. In effect, the futures market would pay them more for storing the wheat than it actually cost them to do so. Their actions would put upward pressure on the nearby futures price and downward pressure on the more distant futures price, driving the two prices back into line.

Smart Investor Tip

Arbitrage brings cash and futures prices together in or near the futures delivery period.

This phenomenon requires that the commodity concerned be storable because storage is necessary to make the strategy work. It also requires that there be a good supply of the commodity on hand.

Inverted Market

When an agricultural commodity suffers from short supply, people do what they have done for centuries: They hoard it. This causes the cash price of the commodity to rise. Nearby futures prices are also affected, for reasons we have already seen, and an "inverted" futures market develops, where succeeding delivery months are lower in price.

An inverted market in soybean meal, for example, might look like this:

Futures Contract	Price (per Ton)
July	$201.20
August	196.50
September	192.70
October	190.70
December	188.20
January	186.00

August meal is lower than July, September is lower than August, and so on. There is virtually no limit as to how far the cash and nearby futures price can go above the price of the more distant futures contract. The arbitrage possible in a normal market doesn't work in an inverted market; to buy the (higher-priced) cash commodity and deliver it against a (lower-priced) distant futures contract would lock in a loss, not a profit.

Smart Investor Tip

If futures prices become successively lower as they go out in time, the market is said to be "inverted."

The situation is different in the financial futures. No warehouse is needed to store a Treasury security or a foreign currency bank balance. The carrying charge for these cash assets is figured in a different way, and the price relationship between delivery months depends on different factors. We will talk more about this subject later, when we take a closer look at the financial futures.

Suggested Reading

How the Futures Markets Work, Jacob Bernstein. New York Institute of Finance, New York, 2000.
Fundamentals of the Futures Markets, Donna Kline. McGraw-Hill, New York, 2001.

The Speculator

Commodity speculators get blamed for many of the economic ills that befall humanity. Speculators cause runaway high prices and prices so low that agricultural producers cannot survive. Gluts are their doing, as are shortages. They are accused of manipulating markets, fixing prices, and disrupting normal supply channels, all for their own nefarious ends.

Most of these accusations arise from a lack of understanding. Futures markets are complicated mechanisms, and how they work is not common knowledge.

A futures market without speculators would be like a country auction without bidders—and would work just about as well. In most markets, speculators are many times more numerous than any other participants. It is the speculators who create a liquid market. Their activities cause prices to change often, and by small increments, enabling relatively large orders to be filled without sending prices sharply higher or lower.

When a speculator buys or sells a futures contract, he is voluntarily exposing himself to the risk of price change. The speculator accepts the risk because he expects to profit from the price change.

Here's an example of a successful speculative trade:

			Margin
May 15	Bought 1 contract December copper at	90.25	
			$1,500
June 21	Sold 1 contract December copper at	<u>96.70</u>	
		+6.45	

The speculator made a profit of 6.45 cents per pound, or (6.45 × $250 =) $1612.50, less commissions. That's a gain of 107 percent on his original margin of $1500, and it was earned in about 5 weeks. However, losses can accrue equally fast:

			Margin
May 15	Bought 1 contract December copper at	90.25	
			$1,500
June 21	Sold 1 contract December copper at	84.25	
		−6.00	

The decline of 6 cents caused the loss of $1500, or 100 percent of the original margin.

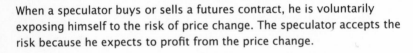

Smart Investor Tip

When a speculator buys or sells a futures contract, he is voluntarily exposing himself to the risk of price change. The speculator accepts the risk because he expects to profit from the price change.

Most speculators have no truck with the actual commodity. In fact, inadvertent delivery of the commodity against a long futures position—which, despite the stories you may have heard, rarely happens—would be a financial gaffe for most speculators. This would be particularly true in the agricultural markets. You can imagine someone who wouldn't know soybeans if he saw them being told by his broker that he is now the proud owner of 10,000 bushels in a grain elevator in Illinois.

Speculators are drawn to the futures markets by the opportunity for profit and by the game itself. It is not unusual for $20,000 equity in a futures trading account to become $50,000—or $5000—within a few months. The game is not difficult to play. An account can be opened in a few minutes; after that, your telephone or computer connects you indirectly with every futures exchange in the world. It's certainly not dull. As a speculator, you are pitting your judgment and trading skill against some of the best financial minds in the world.

Smart Investor Tip

In a simple spread, the prices of the two futures contracts tend to go up and down together. Gains on one side of the spread are therefore offset by losses on the other.

Speculators come from every walk of life. They may be private individuals, informal groups like commodity trading clubs, or corporate members of the trade. Their goals are the same: to earn trading profits from futures positions by being long when prices are rising and short when prices are falling.

Speculators also use *spread* positions. A simple spread involves two positions, one long and one short. They are taken in the same or economically related commodities. Prices of the two futures contracts therefore tend to go up and down together, and gains on one side of the spread are offset by losses on the other. The spreader's goal is to profit from a change in the *difference* between the two futures prices. He is virtually unconcerned whether the entire price structure moves up or down, just so long as the futures contract he bought goes up more (or down less) than the futures contract he sold.

Smart Investor Tip

The spreader's goal is to profit from a change in the *difference* between the two futures prices.

One of the most popular agricultural spreads involves the end of the crop year in wheat. As we mentioned earlier, May wheat is the last futures contract before the harvest, and July wheat is the first futures contract after the harvest. Prospects for a good harvest will therefore weigh more heavily on July wheat than on May wheat.

A spreader who expected a bumper crop would buy the potentially stronger contract (May) and sell the potentially weaker contract (July). Some time later he would "unwind" the spread (close out both positions) by selling the May and buying back the July.

The following example will help you understand how the spread works:

May Wheat			*July Wheat*	
Buy a	$3.85 per bushel	February	Sell at	$3.80 per bushel
Sell at	4.20 per bushel	April	Buy at	3.90 per bushel
Gain	+$ .35		Loss	−$.10

Net result +$.25

The spread was put on in February and taken off in April. During that time, the effect of the coming harvest held the price of July wheat down, while May wheat registered a fair gain. The end result was a profit for the spreader because the futures contract he bought went up more than the futures contract he sold.

Prices don't have to go up for the spread to earn profits. Suppose that right after the spread was established, Brazil and Canada announced unexpectedly large wheat crops:

May Wheat		*July Wheat*
Buy at $3.85 per bushel	February	Sell at $3.80 per bushel
Sell at 3.35 per bushel	April	Buy at 3.10 per bushel
Loss –$ .50		Gain +$ .70

Net result +$.20

Both futures prices went down in expectation of the flood of wheat. The long side accrued losses; the short side earned profits. But the short position lost more ground than the long position, so the spread still generated gains.

A spread incurs market losses when it moves in a direction opposite to that which the spreader anticipated:

May Wheat		*July Wheat*
Buy at $3.85 per bushel	February	Sell at $3.80 per bushel
Sell at 4.20 per bushel	April	Buy at 4.25 per bushel
Gain +$ .35		Loss –$ .45

Net result –$.10

Although both prices advanced, the long position went up less than the short position. This resulted in a net loss.

The same principle works in financial futures. For example, a long position in Swiss franc futures and an opposing short position in Euro FX futures would qualify as a spread. It would be put on by a speculator who believed that the Swiss franc is undervalued relative to the euro. A long T-bond/short 5-year T-note is another example. It would generate profits if long-term interest rates gained ground on short-term rates.

Examples of other spreads would include:

Long wheat/short corn

Long hogs/short pork bellies

Long gold/short silver

Long cattle/short hogs

In each case, the prices of the two commodities tend to go up and down together, and that's a basic requirement for a spread. Long silver/short coffee and long cattle/short cotton are examples of multiple positions that do not qualify as spreads because the two commodities are not economically related. The two prices move independently.

Because a loss on one side tends to be offset by a gain on the other, the market risk in a spread is categorically less than the risk in a net short or long position. This fact, coupled with relatively low margin requirements, makes the spread an attractive trading vehicle to smaller traders. However, it is still possible, by taking on too many contracts, to establish a total spread position with overall market risk just as high as that of a single net long or short position.

Figure 4.1 is a spread chart. It depicts 7 months in the life of an intermarket spread comprising long Chicago wheat and short Kansas City wheat.

The chart shows the difference between the two wheat prices, determined by subtracting the Kansas City Board of Trade price from the Chicago Board of Trade price. Because Kansas City wheat is at a premium to Chicago wheat, the value of the spread is a negative number.

This particular spread has been volatile, ranging over 40 cents in the 7 months shown. The 15-cent price move in late October, from –35 to –50, is particularly unusual. Most spreads, by their very nature, have very low volatility.

A spread trader might see this situation as an opportunity. If a long-term spread chart showed that –50 cents is an unusually low value for this spread— that it normally hovers around, say, –20 cents—a spread trader would give thought to putting the spread on now, in the hope of its returning to its historical norm.

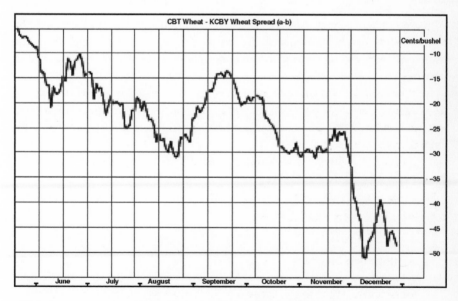

Figure 4.1 A spread chart shows the difference between the two sides of a spread, not the actual prices of each contract. This intermarket wheat spread (long Chicago wheat/short Kansas City wheat) displays unusual volatility, moving from minus 10 to minus 50 in just 6 months.

Chart courtesy of *CRB Futures Perspective*, a publication of Commodity Research Bureau.

Do Speculators Succeed?

How well do speculators do? That depends on to whom you talk. The conventional wisdom is that some 95 percent of private individual speculators lose. A more reliable indication may be found in a study done by Thomas A. Hieronymus, an agricultural economist at the University of Illinois. He analyzed 462 speculative trading accounts of a major brokerage firm over a period of 1 year (1969). The accounts traded the full gamut of commodities at the time. Over the year, 164 accounts showed profits, and 298 accounts showed losses; or, nearly twice as many people lost money as made money.

On the assumption that one trade does not a speculator make, Hieronymus then divided the accounts into two groups: those who entered the market, made one or two trades, and went away; and those who stayed to play the game. The latter group he called *regular* traders; a regular trader was defined as one who made at least 10 trades or who had made or lost $500.

Here the results were different. Forty-one percent of the regular traders made money during the year. Most won or lost $3000 or less, although a few made or lost substantial sums. For the group, net (after commission) profits were about the same as net losses.

Among the one-time traders, some 92 percent lost money.

His conclusion from the 1-year sample: The game is played and won by some people; but, for the most part, the regular players take money from the nonregular players and give it to the commission house to pay for the cost of playing.

Granted, the evaluation was made more than 35 years ago, and there have been many new futures markets added since then. But human nature has not changed.

Suggested Reading

Commodity Spreads: Analysis, Selection, and Trading Techniques, Courtney D. Smith. Traders Press, Greenville, SC, 1988.

The Commodity Futures Game: Who Wins? Who Loses? Why? R. J. Teweles and Frank J. Jones. McGraw-Hill, New York, Rev. 1998.

Trading in Futures: An Introduction for Speculators. Chicago Board of Trade, Chicago (online only).

Chapter

The Hedger

Y ou've heard the phrase "hedging your bet." If you put $100 on the Los Angeles Lakers to win tomorrow night and later find out that two of their starters have the flu, you could hedge your bet by putting $100 on their opponents.

A hedge in the futures markets operates on the same general principle. A hedge is a futures position that is roughly equal and opposite to the position the hedger has in the cash market. A better definition may be that of Holbrook Working, a Stanford University economist. He defines a hedge as a futures transaction that acts as a substitute for a later cash transaction.

Smart Investor Tip

A hedge is a futures position that is roughly equal and opposite to the position the hedger has in the cash market. It is also defined as a futures transaction that acts as a substitute for a later cash transaction.

What makes a hedge work is the fact that cash and futures prices for the same commodity tend to go up and down together, so the losses on one side are canceled out by gains on the other. If you are long (own) the cash commodity, your hedge would be a short futures position. If prices decline, the money you lose on the cash commodity would be offset by the profits in your short position.

Short Hedge

Assume you are a dealer in Treasury bonds. You buy them and sell them at a markup. Between the time you buy the bonds and the time you find a customer, the bonds are, in effect, sitting on your shelf. If bond prices go down while you are holding them, you would have a loss on your inventory.

You do not want to assume the risk that the bonds will lose value while you hold them. You know that a short position in Treasury bond futures would accrue gains if prices decline, offsetting the loss. So as soon as you buy the cash Treasury bonds, you sell Treasury bond futures short as a hedge.

Let's assume that bond prices did indeed fall before you found a customer for your bonds. The outcome would look something like this:

Short Hedge in T-Bond Futures

Cash Market			Futures Market	
Buy cash bonds at	105-07	Now	Sell T-bond futures at	105-17
Sell cash bonds at	104-18	Later	Buy T-bond futures at	104-28
Loss	0-21		Gain	0-21

Net gain or loss = 0

This example is oversimplified, but it demonstrates the point. If the bond dealer had not hedged his inventory, he would have lost $^{21}/_{32}$ ($6.56) on each $1000 worth of bonds. The gain of $^{21}/_{32}$ on the futures position fully offset the decline in the market value of the cash bonds while he held them.

Smart Investor Tip

Short hedgers comprise those who grow, store, process, or distribute a cash commodity and who would be hurt by a decline in the cash price.

Another example: It is fall, and a farmer plans to plant his winter wheat soon. It will be harvested next May. The price for cash wheat now is $3.85 per bushel. He'd like to be able to lock in that price for his wheat next May. With futures, he can:

Short Hedge in Wheat Futures

Cash Market			Futures Market	
Wheat price	$3.85	Fall	Sell wheat futures at	$3.90
Sell wheat at	3.44	Next May	Buy wheat futures at	3.49
Opportunity loss	$ .41/bushel		Gain	$ .41/bushel

Net gain or loss = 0

In May, the farmer received $3.44/bushel for his actual wheat plus a 41-cent gain in his futures hedge. The sum of $3.44 and $.41 is $3.85, which is the cash price he wanted. If it were not possible to hedge, or if for some reason he had chosen not to hedge, the farmer would have gotten only $3.44/bushel as the fruits of his labors.

In this case, the loss on the cash side is referred to as an "opportunity loss," which means that it's not actually money removed from the farmer's pocket, but what he might have earned under other circumstances (e.g., if he had had the cash grain in the fall and sold it then).

There's something else different about this particular example. Notice that the farmer put the hedge on (took the short futures position) even before he planted the wheat. An anticipated position in the cash commodity can be hedged just as effectively as an existing position.

Short hedgers comprise those who grow, store, process, or distribute a cash commodity. A U.S. oil importer with a tanker of crude on the high seas would use a short hedge to protect his cargo from a price decline. General Mills would use a short hedge for the wheat stored in its warehouses. The common denominator is risk of loss due to a decline in the cash price.

For the short hedge to be effective, the hedger has to be dealing with the basic commodity, or something very close to it. A manufacturer of cotton shirts, for example, would probably find hedging in cotton futures of limited value because there are so many other, more important costs in the making of a shirt.

Long Hedge

It is also possible to use a long hedge in futures. To help you understand it, bear in mind Holbrook Working's definition: a futures transaction that substitutes for a later cash transaction.

Smart Investor Tip

A long hedge would be taken by someone who has promised to deliver the cash commodity later and is concerned that cash prices will go up in the interim.

Let's assume you are an exporter of grains. You have sold 1 million bushels of corn to China for delivery 3 months from now. The agreed price is today's cash price in Chicago—$2.85 per bushel. You could buy the cash corn today, store it for 3 months, and then deliver it. But you have no warehouse. Instead you buy corn futures:

Long Hedge in Corn Futures

Cash Market		Futures Market
Cash corn at $2.85/ bushel	Now	Buy corn futures at $2.96/bushel
Buy cash corn at $3.10/ bushel	3 Months Later	Sell corn futures at $3.21/bushel
Opportunity loss $.25/ bushel		Gain $.25/bushel

Net gain or loss = 0

You paid $3.10 per bushel for the cash corn to ship to China; however, the gain of $.25 in your long futures position lowered your effective cost to only $2.85 per bushel, which is the price on which you planned.

These examples do not reflect brokerage commissions or certain other costs such as storage and insurance. These costs are intentionally omitted to keep things simple. Also, you may have observed that each hedge we described worked perfectly, which is seldom true in actual practice. We'll take a closer look at these important financial transactions in a later chapter.

Suggested Reading

The Business of Hedging: Sound Risk Management Without the Rocket-Science, John Stephens. Wiley, New York, 2000.

Chapter

6

The Green Stuff

We mentioned earlier that the margin for a futures position is not a down payment, as in stocks. A futures position confers no rights of ownership to the underlying asset. The owner of a futures position does not gain any income or benefits from the asset. A futures contract is really just a pair of promises: one to deliver the underlying commodity and another to receive and pay for it.

Futures margin is a good-faith deposit. The balance of the value of the futures contract is not borrowed, so no loan interest is paid by the holder of a margined futures position.

The purpose of futures margin is to ensure contract performance and to protect the financial integrity of the marketplace. Margin is required of both the buyer and the seller of a futures contract. Each futures contract has its own minimum margin levels, set by the exchange where the contract is traded. The margin put up when a futures position is first opened is called *original* margin. Depending on the requirements of the particular exchange, original margin may comprise cash, a transfer of funds from another one of the customer's accounts, U.S. government securities, a letter of credit, or a negotiable warehouse receipt.

Smart Investor Tip

The purpose of futures margin is to ensure contract performance and to protect the financial integrity of the marketplace.

If a futures position generates unrealized losses as a result of adverse price movement, additional margin may be called for. This is referred to as *maintenance* margin. Its purpose is to restore the financial protection that margin provides, so the amount of maintenance margin required is that needed to build the margin back up to the original level. The requirements for maintenance margin are more stringent, requiring either (1) deposit of the necessary cash or (2) a reduction in the number of futures positions held.

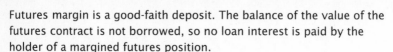

Smart Investor Tip

Futures margin is a good-faith deposit. The balance of the value of the futures contract is not borrowed, so no loan interest is paid by the holder of a margined futures position.

In addition to prescribing minimum margin levels, the exchange sets the levels at which maintenance margin will be called for. This varies from exchange to exchange, but the 75 percent level is a common benchmark; that is, if the margin level drops below 75 percent of its original value, a margin call would be triggered.

Delivering margin calls to market participants and following up to see that they are met is the responsibility of the futures broker (technically, an *associated person*). If you receive a margin call and for some reason do not meet it within a suitable period of time, the brokerage firm is empowered to raise the necessary cash by (1) closing out the position that created the margin call, (2) closing out any other futures position you might have, or (3) transferring funds from another of your accounts that the firm holds—your money market account, for example—into your futures account to cover the shortfall. This authority is given to them by you in the forms you sign when you open your futures account.

Capital Leverage

Futures prices have a generally undeserved reputation of wild volatility. There are common stock issues that fluctuate more in price than many commodities. The apparent volatility of futures prices is derived; it is the result of extremely low minimum margin requirements.

Most futures margins range from a fraction of a percent to 10 percent of the value of the underlying futures contract. A small change in the value of the commodity therefore causes a big change in the equity in the futures account.

Example

Cash cotton and cotton futures are both 80 cents a pound. You are long one contract of cotton futures. Your original margin is $2000. The contract size for cotton is 50,000 pounds, so the total value of the cotton itself is 50,000 pounds × 80 cents = $40,000.

Cash and futures price of cotton both advance 1 cent, from 80.00 to 81.00 cents a pound. The value of the cash cotton has thus gone up $500 ($.01 × 50,000 pounds), or from $40,000 to $40,500; that's an increase of 1¼ percent. The value of your equity in the futures contract has also gone up $500; but that's from $2000 to $2500, a jump of 25 percent.

This effect is called *capital leverage*, and it is a two-edged sword. If cotton prices were to fall, your losses would be magnified on the same scale. If cotton prices fell 3 cents per pound, for example, three-fourths of your original margin would be wiped out:

	Old Price	New Price	Percentage Change in Price	Change in Value	Equity	Percentage Change in Equity
Cash cotton	80.00	77.00	–3.75%	–$1500	$40,000	– 3.75%
Futures contract	80.00	77.00	–3.75%	–$1500	$ 2,000	–75.00%

Margin

The setting of margin levels is a chain reaction that begins with the exchange. The exchange sets the *minimum* amounts required to support a futures position. Next in the chain is the clearinghouse. It is responsible for the financial integrity of the market and may ask more margin from its clearing members than the exchange minimums. The final link in the chain is the brokerage firm (technically, a *futures commission merchant*, or *FCM*). If the FCM considers it necessary, it may ask more margin from its public customers than the exchange minimum requirements.

The flow of actual margin money is the reverse. The public customer writes a check to cover his margin requirement and gives it to his FCM, who holds the funds in the customer's name in a segregated account. The FCM posts margin with the clearinghouse for the FCM's open positions. In most exchanges, the FCM's countervailing long and short positions are offset, and only the net exposure is margined. The balance of the customers' funds are retained by the FCM.

Original and maintenance margins may be changed at any time by the appropriate exchange. In the past, exchanges have used changes in margin levels as an effective means to control price volatility. When a futures market becomes overheated, margin levels are raised significantly. Fewer futures positions can then be supported with any given amount of capital, and trading slows. Margin requirements may also be routinely increased during the "spot month," or the period of time when delivery of the actual commodity can be made against the futures contract.

On most exchanges, changes in margin levels are retroactive. That is, the changes apply immediately to both old and new futures positions. If margins are raised and the new maintenance level is above the old maintenance level, the change could trigger margin calls in existing positions. If margins are lowered, capital committed to existing positions would be freed and the owner of the futures accounts could withdraw the excess funds in cash or use them to margin additional futures positions.

Only funds in excess of the original margin level are free and available for withdrawal or other use. That increment of margin between the original level and maintenance level is part of the original margin and must be on deposit as long as the futures position is held.

For example, suppose you buy one contract of gold futures at 383.00. Your required original margin is $2700; the margin maintenance level is $2100. The transaction plays out as follows:

End of Day	Gold Futures Price	Equity in Account	Remarks
1	383.00	$2700	Opening transaction.
2	379.00	2300	Equity has been eroded, but margin is still above the maintenance level.
3	374.50	1850	Margin below $2100 maintenance level. Margin call would be issued for $850, to build margin back up to original level of $2700.
4		2700	$850 margin called deposited in a.m.
4	384.10	3660	$960 ($3660 – $2700) is now available for withdrawal in cash or to use to margin other futures positions.
5	393.90	4640	$1940 ($4640 – $2700) is now available for withdrawal in cash or to use to margin other futures positions.
6		3640	You withdraw $1000 in cash in a.m.
6	390.70	3320	No change in status.
7	384.20	2670	Margin is below original level but still above $2100 maintenance level; no action required.
8	385.70	2820	You close out the position at end of trading day.

Your accounting in the preceding transaction works in this way: You paid an original margin of $2700 plus maintenance margin of $850. That totals $3550. You withdrew $1000 on Day 6 and had an equity of $2820 after the closing transaction. That totals $3820. You therefore received $270 ($3820 – $3550) for your efforts.

Smart Investor Tip
Only funds in excess of the original margin level are free and available for withdrawal or other use.

A shorter route to the same answer is simply to compare the opening and closing gold futures prices. The closing price of 385.70 minus the opening price of 383.00 equals $2.70 per ounce. For 100 ounces, that's $270.

When setting minimum margin levels, the exchange also countenances the kind of futures position involved. Speculative short or long positions present the highest risks and so have the highest margins. At the other end of the spectrum are hedges, which generally have the lowest margins. The reason is that hedgers hold offsetting cash and futures positions in the same (or similar) commodity, making the overall economic effect similar to a spread.

Daily Mark to Market

The clearinghouse member deposits original margin with the clearinghouse when the opening transaction is cleared. Outstanding futures contracts are marked to the market by the clearinghouse at the end of each trading day. That is, gains are credited and losses are debited on all open positions. The settlement price is used as the benchmark for these calculations.

If a clearinghouse member's account has a credit balance as a result of the daily marking to market of his positions, he may withdraw that amount of cash overnight. If the clearing member owes money, it must be deposited before the opening of trading the next business day. This is called *variation* margin.

Exchanges are also empowered, during times of emergency, to call for variation margin during the trading day. This is generally due in the clearinghouse within 1 hour. On October 19, 1987, the day the Dow Jones Industrial Stock Average fell more than 500 points, the Chicago Mercantile Exchange made two such extraordinary calls for variation margin for long positions in S&P 500 Stock Index futures.

Commissions

The FCM performs a variety of services for its public customers. These services have historically included safekeeping their funds; apprising them of current market conditions; taking their orders and reporting back the fill prices; issuing periodic written statements of trading activity, profit and loss, and account balances; and publishing market research reports. For providing these services, the FCM charges a commission on each trade its customer makes.

Futures commissions are not uniform. They vary from commodity to commodity, with the type of futures position, and from one FCM to another.

The lowest commission is for a position that is opened and closed during the same trading session because it does not have to be taken up fully into the FCM's accounting system. Also at the low end of the scale are commissions on spreads, which are less than the commissions would be on the two positions if they did not comprise a spread. Commissions are highest on net long or short positions that are held overnight.

The greatest difference in commissions is between FCMs. A household-name brokerage firm may charge a commission several times larger than the same trade through a discount broker.

Smart Investor Tip

In most markets there is a limit on how far prices can move in one day. The daily limit is measured from the previous day's settlement price and applies in both directions.

There are several large discount futures brokerage operations in the United States. Some of them specialize in futures only. Many have no research departments and acknowledge that they are for the person who makes his own trading decisions. Others have become more competitive, providing personal brokers for their clients and written market research reports. Virtually all of them are available online.

Smart Investor Tip

The daily price limit is set for each commodity by the exchange on which the commodity is traded.

Price Limits

From time to time, unexpected news galvanizes a futures market, sending prices up or down sharply. In most markets, there is a limit on how far prices can move in one day. The purpose of these daily price limits is to force a "cooling-off" period, to allow market participants time to reevaluate the news and its impact on their holdings.

The daily limit is measured from the previous day's settlement price and applies in both directions. It is different for each commodity. For soybeans, for example, the normal daily price limit is 50 cents. If beans close at 6.50 today, their maximum trading range tomorrow would be 6.00 to 7.00. If they closed at 6.48 tomorrow, their maximum trading range the next day would be 5.98 to 6.98.

When the price reaches a limit during a trading day, market activity tends to slow, and may even stop, because of the same economic forces that caused the price move. If prices have hit limit up, for example, it means there are many buyers and few sellers. If there are no sellers at the limit price, trading could literally cease in that market. However, no one goes home. Transactions may still take place at or within the limit. It is even possible that later news or a reevaluation could bring sellers suddenly back into the market, prices could back away from the limit, and active trading could resume.

The daily price limit is set for each commodity by the exchange on which the commodity is traded. Exchanges also have standing rules to deal with exceptionally strong or weak markets. Limits are, after all, artificial constraints. Despite their benefits, they block the free operation of economic forces in the marketplace. In an effort to mitigate the adverse economic effects of limits, exchange rules allow for automatic expansion of price limits when prices have closed at the limit on consecutive days. There are also standing rules for returning the daily price limit to its normal value when the market has quieted down again.

Suggested Reading

Commodity Trading Manual. Chicago Board of Trade, Chicago, 1998.
Come Into My Trading Room: A Complete Guide to Trading, Alexander Elder. Wiley, New York, 2002.

Chapter 7

The Orders

A futures market order always consists of five elements:

1. Whether to buy or to sell.
2. The quantity.
3. The delivery month.
4. The commodity, including the exchange if the commodity is traded on more than one exchange.
5. Any special instructions, such as a time or price limit.

The first element—whether to buy or to sell—is not as self-evident as it might seem. You and your local broker are aware of whether your order is for an opening or closing transaction. It's not an issue after that. The floor broker who executes your order doesn't know or care. To the clearinghouse, your trade is just another purchase or sale to be processed.

Except in a few instances, it is not legal to be both long and short the same futures contract in the same account. When you buy a December T-bond, for example, your broker's computer checks your account to see if you are already short a December T-bond. If you are, the trade is treated as a closing transaction. If you are not currently short the December T-bond, your trade is logged in as an opening transaction.

The rule against being both long and short the same futures contract is quite specific. Chicago wheat and Kansas City wheat are not considered the same; nor are New York silver and Chicago silver, even though the underlying commodities are the same: refined silver of not less than .999 fineness.

The exceptions to the general rule are day trades, where you open and close the transaction within the same trading session; a futures position taken to meet the exercise of a futures option you have sold short; a bona-fide hedge; the sale of futures during the delivery period for the purpose of making delivery; and in certain circumstances where different independent money managers control separate accounts for the same investor.

The delivery month must be included in your order because, as we will see later, different delivery months of the same commodity may vary considerably in liquidity and price behavior. The year should also be specified in the order if there is any possibility of confusion between a nearby contract and the same delivery month a year away. Likewise, it may be necessary to indicate the exchange on which the commodity is traded.

Smart Investor Tip

A market order authorizes the floor broker to take the best price he is offered, without qualifications. In a thinly traded market, that price could be several cents away from the previous price.

Futures market orders differ most in the possible contingencies they may contain. We will discuss these in the context of actual representative orders.

Smart Investor Tip

A limit order to buy may be filled only at or *below* the limit price.

Market Orders

The simplest order is called a *market order*. It would take the form of:

"Buy one June cattle at the market."

This order would be filled by the floor broker at the best price obtainable at that moment he receives it. The price you paid for your June cattle will not be known to you until the actual fill is reported back to you.

The market order is executed without delay and is used in situations where that is desirable. For example, suppose that you had been short June cattle for 3 weeks, had a trading profit, and felt that the market was about to rally sharply. You would not be interested in finesse but would want to be out as soon as possible. You would use a market order in this instance.

The price you get on a market order depends largely on the liquidity of that particular futures contract. Futures markets are very efficient. The spread between the bid price and the asked priced in an active futures trading pit may be as little as one-tenth of 1 percent. By comparison, the bid/asked spread for most common stocks is about one-half of 1 percent; in real estate, it is not unusual for a buyer to bid 15 to 20 percent below the original asking price.

Care must be taken, however, in futures markets where there is little trading activity. A market order authorizes the floor broker to take the best price he is offered, without qualifications. In a thinly traded market, that price could be several cents away from the previous price. You have no recourse if the price you receive on a market order is an unpleasant surprise.

Smart Investor Tip
A limit order to sell may be filled only at or *above* the limit price.

Contingent Orders

All other futures market orders are contingent orders; that is, they contain some condition that must be satisfied before the order can be executed. The most commonly used is the *limit order*. It would take the form of:

"Buy one June T-bond at 103-20."

This is called a limit order because you have placed a limit on the price you will pay. It resolves the biggest problem with the market order, that of price vulnerability. The floor broker can fill your buy order at less than 103-20 but not at more than that price. The words *or better* are sometimes added to the limit order, but they are unnecessary. If the market is trading below 103-20 when your order reaches the floor, the floor broker will get you the best price he can. With a limit order, however, you have no assurance of execution. If the limit price is never reached, your order will never be filled.

Orders that are placed at prices well away from the current market are defined broadly as resting orders. There are two kinds: *stop orders* and *market-if-touched* (MIT) orders.

An MIT order is used to enter or leave a market at a price somewhat more favorable than the present price. An MIT buy order is therefore placed below the current price, and an MIT sell order is placed above the current price. To take an example, suppose December euro futures were trading at 1.2925. You want to take a new long position in that futures contract and want to pay about 1.2911. You would tell your broker:

"Buy one December euro at 1.2911 MIT."

Smart Investor Tip

Orders that are placed at prices well away from the current market are defined broadly as resting orders. There are two kinds: *stop orders* and *market-if-touched* (MIT) orders.

When this order reaches the trading floor, the floor broker puts it in his deck of resting orders, which are organized by price. If December euro futures later trade at 1.2911, your order would become a market order at that instant and would be treated by the floor broker like any other market order.

At what price would you buy your December euro future? It depends. Remember that an MIT order becomes a market order when the specified price is hit, and market orders are filled at the best price obtainable at that moment. If the market rallied after touching 1.2911, you could legitimately pay 1.2920 or even more for your December euro futures contract.

MIT orders are used when there is no urgency to enter or leave a market. As with all orders that specify price, however, there is the chance that the MIT order will not be filled. In the specific example just given, if December euros never traded at 1.2911 but instead rallied to 1.2930 and beyond, the resting MIT buy order would remain unexecuted. Some experienced traders with a knack for forecasting daily price trading ranges are willing to risk the chance of not getting filled to try for the possible price advantage.

Stop orders may also be used to enter or leave a market, but they perform a different function from MIT orders. The simplest way to avoid confusion between the two is to remember that the most common use of stop orders is to curtail losses. If you are long, falling prices generate losses; any resting sell order intended to curtail those losses must therefore be *below* current price levels. Conversely, any buy order to curtail losses in an existing short futures position must rest *above* current price levels.

Let's take a specific example. Suppose you have held a long position in December S&P 500 Index futures for a month. You bought it at 1345.70, and it is now trading at 1374.10. You have a good gain, but you feel prices may not go much higher; you decide that if the market falls below 1372.50, you will get out. The order you would give your broker is:

"Sell one December S&P 500 at 1372.45 stop."

The December S&P 500 is trading at 1374.10 when you place this order. If prices continue to advance, the stop price will never be touched, and your order will not be executed. However, if you were correct in your assessment of the market and prices start to slip, your stop order automatically converts to a market order when the stop price of 1372.45 is reached, and your long position will be closed out.

To understand the significance of the word *stop* in the order, look at what happens if you take it out:

"Sell one December S&P 500 at 1372.45."

If this order were entered when December S&P 500 futures were trading at 1374.10, it could legally be executed immediately, as the price limit is long since passed. As a practical matter, a floor broker who received such an order would most likely suspect a mistake and query the brokerage firm before he acted on it.

As with the MIT order, there is no guarantee of receiving the stop price when the order is filled. The stop order becomes a market order when the stop price is hit; if prices are moving quickly at that time, the price you receive could be several "ticks" away from the stop price.

The *stop limit* order combines the qualities of both the stop order and the limit order. It would take the form of:

"Buy one September British pound at 1.8618 stop, limit 1.8620."

Nothing would be done on this order until the stop price is reached. At that point, however, it becomes not a market order but a limit order. The floor broker can legally fill it only at a price of 1.8620 or lower. If prices were to jump above 1.8620 immediately after the stop price was hit, the order could remain unexecuted.

The purpose of the stop limit order is, of course, to preclude the possibility of getting an unfavorable price. The stop limit order is not widely used. It is employed mainly in thinly traded markets or those that, even though liquid, are quite volatile.

Many practitioners feel that the closing prices at the end of the trading day are the best consensus of the market. After all, these are the prices that buyers and sellers are willing to take home for the night. There is a futures market order designed to obtain the closing price. It takes the form of:

"Sell one March Eurodollar MOC."

MOC stands for "market on close." This order would be held by the floor broker until a minute or two before the closing bell, at which time he will treat it as a market order. The price you receive will not necessarily be the exact closing or settlement price, but it will be somewhere in closing range, which is loosely defined at the last 60 seconds of trading.

Orders may also be executed at the opening of the market. The letters *MOO* would be added to the order; they stand for "market on opening." MOO orders can be utilized to take advantage of the overnight buildup of market orders. For example, if a short-term trader suspected that there was a bulge of overnight orders to buy and that once these orders were assimilated the market would settle back, he might sell short on the opening in the hope of buying his contracts back at a lower price later in the day. MOO orders are not as widely used as MOC orders.

Any order that does not mention time is considered a day order. That is, it will expire at the end of the trading session during which it was entered. GTC stands for *good 'til canceled* and may be added to any resting order. Most brokers prefer to use day orders, reentering the order each morning if necessary. There isn't a broker who has been in the business more than a few years who hasn't returned from vacation or a business trip to learn that a forgotten GTC order was triggered in his absence. The resulting position is rarely a gain.

We talked about commodity spreads in Chapter 4. A spread involves a long position in one commodity and an offsetting short position in the same or economically related commodity. There is a special order that can be used to establish these dual positions. Because a spread trader is interested only in the price difference between the two sides of the spread, he loses nothing by placing his order in that context. For example:

> "Spread buy 1 Chicago May wheat/sell 1 Chicago July wheat, May 5 cent premium."

Smart Investor Tip

Any order that does not mention time is considered a day order.

An order entered in this fashion gives the floor broker latitude. He can elect to execute each side separately, taking whatever prices are available, or he can deal directly with a floor trader who specializes in spreads. If the same order were entered as two separate transactions—for example, buy 1 Chicago May wheat at 3.95 and sell 1 July wheat at 3.90—your floor broker would be handcuffed. He has two orders, with two different limits, and somehow has to execute them both at the proper time.

There are other possible orders that can be used in the futures markets. They are known more for their exotic qualities than their value in obtaining a desired price or time of execution. The exchanges publish lists of orders that they will accept. Generally, no contingent orders are accepted on the last day of trading in a futures contract because trading activity may be too hectic to allow their orderly handling.

Suggested Reading

Commodity Trading Manual. Chicago Board of Trade, Chicago, 1998.

Chapter

The Arena

There are three major organizations involved in futures trading: the exchange, the clearinghouse, and the futures commission merchant (FCM).

The Exchange

There are a half a dozen or so major future exchanges in the United States. Most are private, nonprofit organizations owned by their members. The oldest futures exchange in the United States is the Chicago Board of Trade, founded in 1848.

The exchange provides the arena where buyers and sellers of futures contracts meet to conduct business. The trading floor, where the actual buying and selling takes place, is divided into several large circular trading "rings" or "pits." Each pit is designated as the trading site for one or more commodities, depending on the level of activity. If a commodity trades only a few hundred contracts a day, it may share a pit with another relatively inactive market. If a commodity has a large following, the entire pit will be devoted to it.

Historically, trades have been executed by open outcry in the pits. That is, orders to buy or to sell have been shouted out by floor brokers for anyone in the crowd who might be interested in doing business.

This situation is changing. Led by the successful new exchanges in Europe and Asia, futures exchanges in the United States seem to be gradually moving toward electronic trading. There are several U.S. futures contracts now that are traded both by open outcry and electronic means, side-by-side or at different times.

Only exchange members may buy and sell futures contracts on the trading floor. Persons in the pits break down into two broad categories: *floor brokers* and *floor traders*. Floor brokers are agents; they transact trades for third parties, for which they receive a small commission. Virtually all floor brokers are affiliated with one or more FCMs.

A floor trader uses his exchange membership primarily to buy and sell futures contracts for his own account. His advantages over off-floor trading include immediate access to new market information and very small commission costs. Historically, members have been able to act alternately as a floor broker and floor trader at any time, under regulations to preclude their taking advantage of a public customer.

Smart Investor Tip

Only exchange members may buy and sell futures contracts on the trading floor.

The exchange determines, with approval of the Commodity Futures Trading Commission (CFTC), what futures contracts will be traded on its floor. The exchange specifies the underlying commodity, the contract size, delivery months, how prices will be expressed, and daily price limits. The exchange also sets original and maintenance margin levels for its futures contracts.

The exchange establishes and enforces the rules under which its futures contracts may be traded. The rules are designed to ensure free and orderly markets and to protect both the public customer and the commodity professional from damage. The exchange does not own any commodities.

Exchange memberships are sold by the exchange when it is first established and whenever new memberships are made available, which is not often. Otherwise, a new member must buy his "seat" from a present member.

The Clearinghouse

Each exchange has its own clearinghouse. At the end of each trading day, the clearinghouse takes the other side of every trade it clears. This action breaks the link between the original buyer and seller, making it possible for a trader to close out a futures or options position with simply an offsetting market transaction. There is no need for the original two parties to relocate each other or for both original parties to agree to undo the trade.

The clearinghouse serves two other vital functions: It warranties the financial integrity of each futures contract it clears, and it supervises deliveries made against futures contracts by holders of short positions.

To create the funds necessary to guarantee the financial stability of the futures markets it clears, the clearinghouse requires that each of its clearing members posts a guaranty deposit. The amount required is substantial. It may be in cash or letter of credit. If a member defaults, these funds may be drawn on to ensure that no public futures customer loses money as a result of the default. If the total of the guaranty deposits on hand is still not enough to cover a defaulting member's debits, the clearinghouse is authorized to levy a special pro-rata assessment on its members to make up the difference.

Mark to Market

Rules for the payment of variation margin to the clearinghouse are quite strict. There is no maintenance level or trigger point. Clearinghouse members' accounts are marked to the market at the end of each trading day, and all deficits must be covered before a certain time the next business morning. The clearinghouse is also empowered to issue calls for additional margin during the trading day if market conditions warrant and has done so on occasion.

Smart Investor Tip

Traders who hold futures positions beyond the last trading day must settle their futures contracts by delivery or cash.

Delivery

The last day of trading in a futures contract is specified by the exchange; it will be a day during the delivery period, which is usually a calendar month. The last day of trading in December T-bond futures on the Chicago Board of Trade, for example, is the seventh business day from the end of December. After that date, the December T-bond futures contract for that year expires and is gone forever.

Traders who hold futures positions beyond the last trading day cannot close out their futures contracts with an offsetting futures transaction. Shorts will be expected to deliver the actual commodity to an exchange-designated delivery point; longs will be expected to take ownership of the actual commodity and pay for it in full. In cash-settled markets, the trader must at settlement pay or receive the difference between the cash price and the futures price.

The delivery process differs from exchange to exchange, but it generally starts when the short asks his broker to prepare a delivery notice. This notice is presented by the broker to the exchange clearinghouse, which assigns it to one of its clearing members with a long position still open on the clearinghouse books. The clearing member in turn assigns the notice to one of its customers who is still long.

Smart Investor Tip

The delivery process is generally initiated by the short position holder, who may choose any day during the delivery period.

On some exchanges, the assigned long may decline the notice by selling the equivalent number of new futures contracts short and passing the notice along, via the clearinghouse, to another long. On others, a delivery notice cannot be passed along; it must be accepted and the cash commodity received and paid for.

Smart Investor Tip

Only individuals may be members of a futures exchange.

The form of delivery varies with the commodity. Evidence of delivery in the grains may be a warehouse receipt for actual grain stored in some distant location. Cotton can be delivered into any licensed southern warehouse. "Delivery" of stock index futures involves only the transfer of cash. Delivery against a short position in T-bond futures results in a book-entry transfer of ownership of the cash bonds; no actual bond certificates change hands.

In some instances, more than one grade of the commodity is deliverable against the futures contract. The exchange where the futures are traded specifies the alternate deliverable grades. The epitome is the T-bond futures contract. Much has been written on the selection of the optimum cash bond to deliver because it may be chosen from among all outstanding Treasury bonds with at least 15 years to maturity.

Delivery against a futures contract was a relatively rare occurrence in the past. Producers, processors, and distributors of foods, metals, and fibers used the futures markets to hedge against price risk but continued to conduct their normal day-to-day cash business with their regular customers. With the advent of financial futures, delivery against futures contracts has become more common. In fact, some financial futures traders take their positions for the express purpose of making or taking delivery.

The Futures Commission Merchant

The FCM is the private individual trader's link to the futures and option markets. The FCM carries the public customer's account. It accepts and holds margin money for the customer. It provides for the execution of his trades and maintains a complete record of his open positions, cash balance, and profit and loss. It provides current market information and research reports on historical price activity.

Merrill Lynch, Salomon Smith Barney, and Prudential are old-line FCMs, and their names are familiar to many investors. The new breed are the discount FCMs, which offer futures traders very low commissions and online access.

Opening an Account

When you open a futures or options account with an FCM, you will be required to fill out and sign several forms. One form is personal information. Another concerns your income and net worth and asks many of the same questions you would find on a loan application. Your broker is required by law to have these data, because it is his responsibility to qualify you under a "know-your-customer" rule. If he considers that you do not have the financial wherewithal to take on the risks associated with futures or options trading, he should refuse to open your account.

The most important form, from the standpoint of your broker, is called something like "Commodity Account Agreement." It identifies whether the account is for hedging or speculating. It identifies the owner of the account, which can be a single individual, two or more parties in joint form, a partnership, or a corporation.

The Commodity Account Agreement also contains a "Transfer of Funds Authorization." This paragraph gives your broker an advance okay to move your money around if you are on margin call and for some reason do not meet it. The actions he is authorized to take include closing out the futures position that created the margin call or transferring money from another of your accounts with the firm to your commodity account to cover the shortfall.

Suggested Reading

Futures 101: An Introduction to Commodity Trading, Richard E. Waldron. Squantum Publishing Company, Quincy, MA, 2000.

Chapter

Fundamental Analysis

I f you could buy a copy of next week's *Wall Street Journal*, there would soon be buildings with your name on them. Correctly assessing where prices will be in coming days or weeks is an important element in successful futures trading. No player is exempt. Price increases generate gains for the longs and losses for the shorts. When prices decline, the shorts gain what the longs lose.

If you exclude tea leaves and fortunetellers, there are two approaches to futures price forecasting. The first involves evaluating the supply of and demand for the actual commodity, on the premise that a short supply or high demand will cause prices to rise, and vice versa. This approach is called *fundamental analysis*.

The other major school of thought is referred to as *technical analysis*. The pure technical analyst disregards any information about the supply of and demand for the actual commodity. He focuses his attention instead on the futures market itself, on the assumption that no matter what the fundamentals portend, the effects will show up in the behavior of price, trading volume, and open interest.

We'll look at both approaches.

Fundamental Factors

Every significant commodity price move in the history of futures trading has been rooted in fundamental factors. Unless there is a true shortage or surplus of the actual commodity, unusually low or high prices cannot be maintained. Remember the soybean futures chart we showed you in Chapter 2; prices rocketed upward and then, a few days later, were right back where they started. That was an example of a price move fueled entirely by traders' expectations.

There have been some spectacular sustained futures price moves when fundamental factors were the engine. Blight sent corn prices from $1.40 to $3.90 a bushel in 1973 and 1974. Bumper corn crops in the following 3 years finally drove prices back down to $1.80 again.

Smart Investor Tip
Every significant commodity price move in the history of futures trading has been rooted in fundamental factors. Unless there is a true shortage or surplus of the actual commodity, unusually low or high prices cannot be maintained.

After hovering between 2 cents and 10 cents a pound for 9 years, sugar prices responded to a worldwide shortage by soaring to 67 cents a pound in 1974.

The combination of reduced world supply and growing industrial demand propelled copper futures prices from 60 cents to $1.70 a pound in 1988. More recently, grain and soybean prices soared to 9-year highs on small current supply and prospects for modest yields in the coming crop year.

Japanese yen futures staged a virtually unbroken rally from early 1990 to mid-1995, more than doubling in price. The cause: not short-term expectations but an inexorable world demand for the foreign currency.

Supply and Demand

The fundamental analyst tries to estimate how much of the commodity will be around in coming months and how much demand there will be for it. The supply of a commodity comprises imports, current production, and any carryover from previous years. Consumption is the sum of domestic use and exports.

For example, for an agricultural field commodity, the fundamental analyst would consider planting intentions, yield per acre, forecast weather in growing areas, probability of crop disease, the prices of competing commodities, government loan levels, and current supplies on hand. These same data would also be considered for foreign growing areas, to evaluate potential U.S. exports.

Smart Investor Tip

The fundamental analyst tries to estimate how much of the commodity will be around in coming months and how much demand there will be for it.

Fundamentals for cattle, hog, and pork belly futures include farmers' farrowing intentions, expected litter size, the number of animals currently on feed, prices for competing red meats, trends in consumption, and the present status of the livestock price "cycle."

A trader of copper futures would be interested in the level of mining activity, housing starts, the amount of copper resting in the London Metal Exchange (LME) and other storehouses around the world, and the potential for political unrest in foreign producing areas. Platinum traders keep an eye on automobile production. Gold has a dual role: in jewelry and as a worldwide store of value when rampant inflation or armed conflict creates a temporary mistrust of paper currencies.

Frozen concentrated orange juice (FCOJ) is the futures market most susceptible to weather. Even the hint of a coming winter freeze in the Florida growing area will send prices soaring. Less violent fundamental factors include the anticipated size of the orange crop in the United States and other orange-growing nations, yield, and crop disease.

Coffee has less of a reputation as a weather-driven market, but it can be just as violent. As Figure 9.1 shows, in late June and early July (their winter, our summer), a hard freeze sent prices limit up for 13 out of 14 days, literally doubling the price of coffee futures.

Fundamental analysis of the financial futures requires a somewhat different approach. In some instances, the supply is virtually unlimited. In others, there is no tangible asset underlying the futures contract, and settlement is by cash only.

Smart Investor Tip

The supply of a commodity comprises imports, current production, and any carryover from previous years. Consumption is the sum of domestic use and exports.

The most popular financial futures market is that for 3-month Eurodollar deposits. (Eurodollars are U.S. dollars on deposit in banks outside the United States.) Next in activity (in the United States) are 10-year T-notes and the E-mini S&P 500 Index.

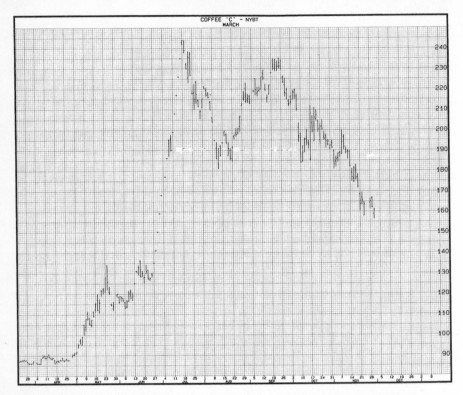

COFFEE 'C' – NYBT
MARCH

Figure 9.1 In July, coffee reminded traders that frozen concentrated orange juice is not the only weather market; a deep freeze in coffee-growing areas drove prices limit up for almost 2 weeks. By the time the rally ended, prices had gained 80 percent from their spring trading range.

Chart courtesy of *CRB Futures Perspective*, a publication of Commodity Research Bureau.

Prices in all markets for fixed-income securities are tied directly to interest rates. If interest rates rise, the prices of these securities go down. If interest rates fall, the prices of these securities rise. Fundamental analysis therefore is directed at projecting the course of interest rates; that involves many complex economic variables, including the demand for loans, interest rates on other instruments such as commercial paper and certificates of deposit (CDs), the prime rate, the discount rate, prevailing interest rates in other nations, current policies of the Federal Reserve Board, and the general health of the U.S. economy.

Stock index futures were the first futures markets based on an intangible asset. The "delivery unit" underlying the futures contract is the value of the index, not actual shares of stock, and settlement is by cash only.

Because each index represents a large number of different stocks, fundamental analysis involves not the assessment of individual stocks but the factors that contribute to overall market movement. These include the present state of the business cycle, interest rates, the relative strengths of U.S. and foreign currencies, the amounts of money available for investment, and investor confidence in the U.S. economy.

Demand for foreign currencies is based largely on a nation's shopping habits. If a U.S. retailer imports watches made in Switzerland, he must pay for them with Swiss francs. He buys the Swiss francs with U.S. dollars. This action causes the value of the Swiss franc to rise relative to the U.S. dollar. An American manufacturer who sells products in England would receive British pounds in payment. He would buy U.S. dollars with them because he can't use pounds to buy materials and pay workers in the United States, and that would have the opposite effect; it would cause the value of the U.S. dollar to rise relative to the pound.

There are other reasons that currencies flow from one nation to another. An unusually high rate of interest or a strongly bullish stock market will attract foreign capital; investors from other nations buy U.S. dollars with their currencies, then use those dollars to buy stocks or bonds in U.S. markets. Tourists buy foreign currencies to spend for hotels, meals, and shopping overseas. When the United States grants economic aid to a foreign nation, the U.S. dollars granted must be converted to that nation's currency before the money can be put to work there. Some developing nations park their cash reserves in one or more foreign currencies.

Note that the examples in the preceding paragraph all relate to demand. The supply of a foreign currency is not a price factor. Except in unusual cases where the government steps in to curtail the movement of its currency in foreign markets, the supply is virtually unlimited.

Commodities whose principal source is overseas present special problems for the fundamental analysts. Sugar, cocoa, coffee, and petroleum are subject to international commodity agreements about price controls and production quotas. Reliable information may be difficult to come by. Nations take steps to protect their own currencies or economies and may not be open and aboveboard about their activities. The briefing sheets in Chapter 17 list some of the public sources of information on foreign commodities that have proven reliable over the years.

The Importance of Perspective

Suppose you saw in the newspaper that the U.S. trade deficit last year was $460 billion. Is that bullish or bearish for the major foreign currencies? Will it affect interest rates? Could U.S. exports of commodities be curtailed as a result?

If you are long copper futures and read a report that 1.4 million new housing starts are expected next year, what does that mean? Is that a lot of starts? Is the news likely to affect copper prices?

You can't answer fundamental questions like these without more information. You have to be able to make comparisons between today's situation and prior situations—to see, for example, where prices were the last time these particular supply and demand conditions prevailed. Projected housing starts of 1.4 million may be bullish for copper prices if the starts constitute an increase of 20 percent over last year; the same housing report could have a depressing effect on the price of copper tubing and wire if 1.4 million was a surprisingly low number of starts.

It's also important that you evaluate any long-range trends in price, consumption, and usage. This leads to still more questions. Is aluminum wiring replacing copper? What is the projected rate of new family formation next year? What kinds of homes will be built? Do they use more or less wire and tubing than the standard detached single-family dwelling?

These are factors that affect copper prices. But you don't own copper. You own copper futures, and there's a subtle difference. It's possible that a fundamental report that looks bullish on its face could turn out to be neutral or even negative for futures prices. The reason would be that the futures price had already discounted the report; the report was already "in the market." The bulk of traders had expected a sharp increase in projected housing starts and had bought futures contracts in anticipation. The publication of the expected numbers caused no new buying.

Disappearing Qualifiers

You may have played this game when you were younger. Participants sit in a circle. The one who starts the game writes a simple message down, so it can be later verified, and then relates it verbally to the person sitting next to him. That person repeats it to the next person, and so on, until it gets back to the one who started it. What comes back is compared to the original written message, and the results are often surprising. What happens invariably is that the qualifiers disappear. What began as "Tom may have almost twenty dollars by next Friday" comes back as "Tom has twenty dollars."

The same pitfall awaits the fundamental analyst. Many assumptions will have gone into the final conclusion that, say, gold should reach $425 an ounce by next spring. But the longer you look at the number "425" the easier it is for you to forget about the "guesstimates" that were made in arriving at that number. The number, viewed alone, implies arithmetic precision and accuracy.

Some fundamental analysts try to elude this trap by avoiding single numbers in any of their data. If they were analyzing hog prices, for example, they would translate the number of hogs and pigs on farms, stated farrowing intentions, expected pigs per litter, and the resulting price estimate into probable ranges. This approach to fundamental analysis has been refined by Jack Schwager, whose book is referenced at the end of this chapter.

Finding the Information

The data you need for effective fundamental analysis are not easy to find, at least, not all in one place. The U.S. Department of Agriculture is a repository of vast amounts of background information on the agricultural commodities, and much of it is published in periodic reports. Likewise, the U.S. Geological Survey is a good source of data on the production and consumption of metals; the Federal Reserve keeps track of a large number of economic indicators and measures that bear on the future course of interest rates; the Department of Commerce has information to help you determine the health of the U.S. dollar.

There are many journals, newsletters, and charting services that deal with futures price forecasting. Some are purely technical, some are purely fundamental, and some combine both kinds of analysis to arrive at their conclusions.

There are also private or nongovernment sources of fundamental data. The most notable is *Commodity Year Book*, referenced below, which contains historical charts and tables for more than 100 commodities, including all of the major futures markets.

That's all we are going to say about fundamental analysis here. Individual briefing sheets in Chapter 17 contain a description of each commodity, where it is grown or produced, pertinent fundamental factors, data on the futures contract, and where you can find out more about that commodity.

Suggested Reading

Commodity Year Book. Commodity Research Bureau, Chicago (annual).

Fundamental Analysis, Jack Schwager. Schwager on Futures Series, Wiley, New York, 1995.

Chapter

Technical Analysis

There are two important differences between fundamental and technical analysis. Fundamental analysis of futures markets is characterized by a great deal of subjective information; it is used to forecast price movement over several weeks or months. The technical analyst deals with only three pieces of data: price, trading volume, and open interest. He evaluates them to form an opinion on the likely direction of prices over the next several days.

The complete analyst looks at the fundamentals to decide whether a significant price movement is in the cards and employs technical analysis to determine the most propitious time to enter the market.

As we saw earlier, financial periodicals report four prices for each day's activity in a futures contract: the day's opening price, high, low, and settlement or closing price. (Some newspapers omit the opening price.) Of the four, the closing price is generally considered to be the most meaningful, as it represents the day's final verdict. The opening price is the least significant because it is often distorted by the overnight buildup of market orders.

In the simplest context, a rise in prices reflects growing demand for the futures contract. If the trading volume increases when prices rise, it is a sign that there is interest in the rally—that the price increase is attracting followers. That's a bullish omen. Rising open interest would further strengthen the technical picture, as it would indicate that new buyers are entering the fray.

There are several other combinations of these three factors, and each holds a different meaning for the technical analyst. We'll see how they work. But first there are some other things you should know.

Price Trend

A trend is the tendency for prices (or any other value) to move more in one direction than the other. A number of years ago, when gasoline supplies were short and prices soared, increasing numbers of light, fuel-efficient automobiles were made. There was a trend toward small cars. If you wanted to place a bet that tomorrow's outside temperature would be higher than today's, you would choose the springtime to do so (in the Northern Hemisphere), because temperatures are trending higher at that time of year. If you have ever sat on an ocean beach and watched the tide come in, you have observed an uptrend. Each wave tends to lap a bit higher on the sand and to recede a bit less.

An uptrend on a price chart looks very much like an incoming ocean tide. Each peak is higher than the previous peak, and each valley is higher than the previous valley. Figure 10.1 is a good example. The series of higher highs and higher lows in March corn lasted from January through most of July. The resulting price gain of 35 percent qualifies this as a major uptrend.

Smart Investor Tip
A trend is the tendency for prices (or any other value) to move more in one direction than the other.

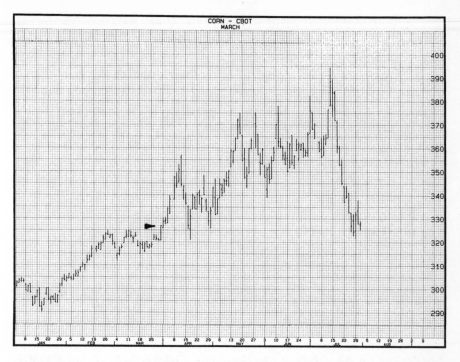

Figure 10.1 A chart uptrend is identified by climbing "stairsteps." At least four points are required: a low, a high, a higher low, and a higher high. An upward trend in this market began with the low of $2.90 on January 19; however, the trend could not be confirmed until March 31 (arrow), when prices closed above the peak reached on March 11.

Chart courtesy of *CRB Futures Perspective*, a publication of Commodity Research Bureau.

A downtrend in prices is characterized by a series of lower highs and lower lows, as shown in Figure 10.2. The lower trend was confirmed on June 2, when the closing price for December soybean oil fell below the watermark set the previous week. This particular trend lasted about 2 months, when dry weather and reported shortages of soybeans in storage triggered an explosive rally.

When prices have no apparent direction, as they did for 3 years in Figure 10.3, the trend is referred to as sideways or neutral.

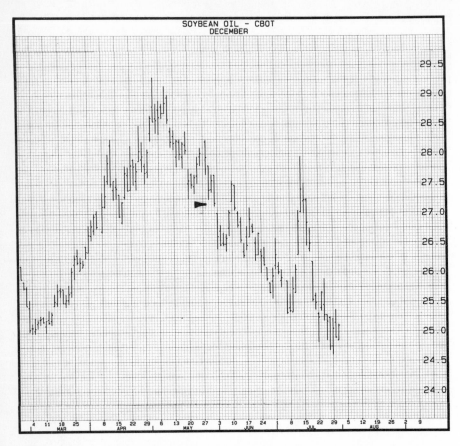

Figure 10.2 In a chart downtrend, the same rules as for uptrends apply, but the stairsteps go down. The four points are the high on May 4, the low on May 20, the lower high on May 30, and the lower low on June 2 (arrow), which officially confirmed that the chart trend was downward.

Chart courtesy of *CRB Futures Perspective*, a publication of Commodity Research Bureau.

History has shown that established price trends in futures markets tend to persist; that is why they fascinate traders. The existence of a trend increases the probability that tomorrow's price will be higher or lower than today's, and a trader can use that information to very good advantage.

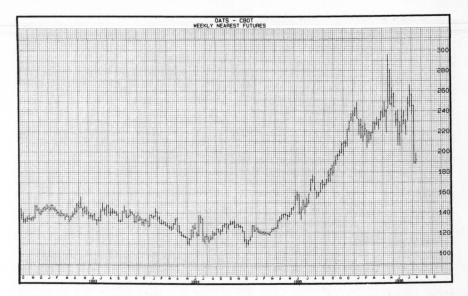

Figure 10.3   Extended up- or downtrends are not commonplace. Futures prices spend most of their time in trendless price action. Prices in this market, for example, wandered aimlessly between $1.20 and $1.50 a bushel for many months before starting to trend higher.

Chart courtesy of *CRB Futures Perspective*, a publication of Commodity Research Bureau.

Trendlines

Technical analysts often draw a straight line through the extreme lows in an established chart uptrend (Figure 10.4). This is called an *up trendline* and is used as a reference. A *down trendline* is drawn through the extreme highs, as shown in Figure 10.5.

Trendlines serve several purposes. One purpose is for warning. If prices break through a well-established trendline, it is an indication that the ongoing trend is losing its force. Figure 10.4 provides an example. After trending higher for 4 months, prices suddenly broke down through the trendline at $1920, flashing the signal that the uptrend had run its course.

Figure 10.4 An up trendline is drawn across the extreme lows. A minimum of two reference points is required. In this chart for crude oil, they were in place in early June. Further reference points, like the lows in July, serve to strengthen the trendline's credibility. Breaking of an established trendline, as happened here on August 5, is a sign that the trend is faltering and may be about to change. It was true in this case.

Chart courtesy of *CRB Futures Perspective*, a publication of Commodity Research Bureau.

A trendline can also be used to enter a market. In Figure 10.6, for example, if you were convinced in January or February that the uptrend was well established and that prices were headed a great dealer higher, pullbacks to the trendline (as in mid-April) would have provided logical points to take your long position. The probability of short-term adverse (downward) price movement would be minimized, because to do so would require breaking the trendline.

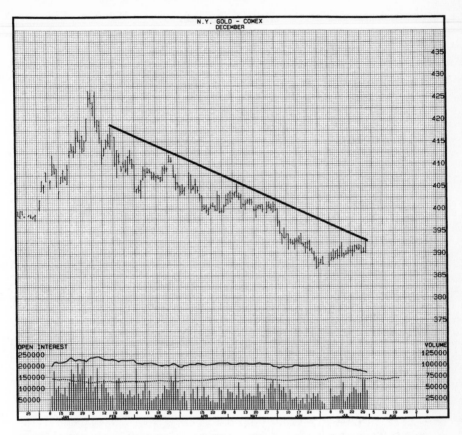

Figure 10.5 A typical down trendline, drawn across the extreme highs.
Chart courtesy of *CRB Futures Perspective*, a publication of Commodity Research
Bureau.

And you can place a sell stop order just below the trendline to get you out of the
market immediately if prices did continue to fall and the trendline was broken.

Breaking of a trendline means the current trend is losing its zip; it does not
mean that the opposite price trend has begun. Few trends change course
abruptly. There is almost always an interim period of trendless activity before
any new sustained upward or downward price movement begins.

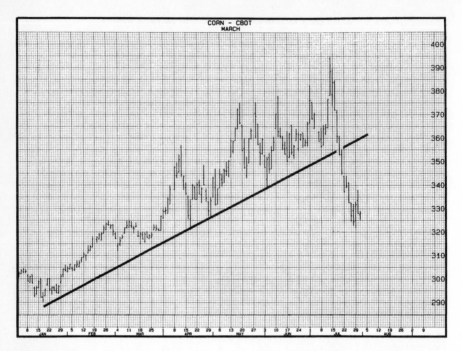

Figure 10.6   When prices approach an established trendline, a good case can be made for choosing that site to enter or leave a market. This chart provides an example. The higher trend was in place in March. In the following weeks, prices returned to the trendline on several occasions, offering bulls an opportunity to take long positions with relatively low technical risk.

Chart courtesy of *CRB Futures Perspective*, a publication of Commodity Research Bureau.

Support and Resistance

"Prices met support and closed higher for the day." You've probably heard or read a statement something like that. If you didn't know what the word *support* meant, you probably shrugged the comment off as market doubletalk.

Smart Investor Tip

The price level where a decline may be expected to stop is called a *price support level*.

The fact is, prices tend to stop where they have stopped before.

A rally will tend to fade and prices turn back down again near the point where the previous rally ended. A decline will tend to stop at or near the price where the previous decline stopped.

The price level where a decline may be expected to stop is called a *price support level.* Prices receive support from below. The price level where a rally can be expected to run into trouble is called a *price resistance level.* Sellers there resist any further advances.

The rationale for support and resistance levels is found in human nature. When prices move, three groups of participants are affected. Traders on the right side of the market begin to accrue profits. Traders on the wrong side of the market watch uncomfortably as their paper losses mount. And traders who had intended to be on the right side of the market but who never got around to acting on their beliefs are kicking themselves.

Smart Investor Tip

The price level where a rally can be expected to run into trouble is called a *price resistance level.*

Now what happens if prices return to the point where they started? Traders on the right side of the market consider adding to their positions because the market has demonstrated its ability to move in their direction. Traders on the wrong side of the market, after sweating through a period of paper losses, heave a sigh of relief as they close out their positions with small debits. And the intended, who missed the boat the first time, make sure they won't miss it again.

That is a lot of kinetic energy, and it's all pointing in the same direction.

To take a specific example, suppose copper futures prices had been declining for several months. The decline stopped around 83.50 cents per pound; prices milled about for several weeks and then rallied sharply to 90.00 in what looked like the beginning of a sustained upward move. The longs are smiling, the shorts are looking for an exit, and the bulls in the wings are wondering why they didn't take their long positions last week.

When copper futures prices retreat to 84.00, all three groups are galvanized into action—the longs to add to their positions, now that the market has demonstrated its buoyancy; the shorts to close out their losing positions; and the intended bulls, who now have an unexpected second chance to get aboard. The buying of these three groups stops the decline near the point where it started, the previous low. Prices have found support at that level.

Price resistance involves the same psychology but with the picture inverted. Sellers are waiting overhead to roadblock a rally.

Figure 10.7 provides examples of both of these technical phenomena in the lean hogs futures market at the Chicago Mercantile Exchange.

Other Locations

Price support and resistance are found at locations other than previous highs or lows. When prices move within a narrow range for several weeks, they form what is called a *price congestion area*. This area will provide support when prices approach it from above and resistance when prices approach it from below. An example of the former is shown in Figure 10.8.

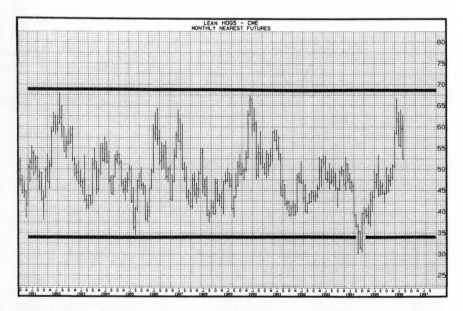

Figure 10.7 The persistence of price support and resistance levels can be seen in this monthly futures chart for lean hog futures. During the 16 years shown in the chart, the band of resistance between 65 and 67 cents stopped rallies on five occasions; the 37-cent level provided support seven different times.

Chart courtesy of *CRB Futures Perspective*, a publication of Commodity Research Bureau.

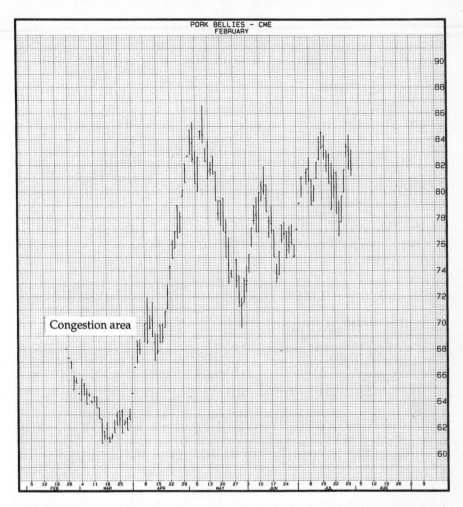

Figure 10.8 Congestion areas, where prices have traded in a relatively narrow range for several days, can later act as roadblocks. In this example, a 3-week congestion area was formed between 67 cents and 72 cents in early April. When prices returned to that area in late May, support there not only halted the decline, it provided the foundation for a strong rally.

Chart courtesy of *CRB Futures Perspective*, a publication of Commodity Research Bureau.

To see another example, flip back to Figure 9.1, where we showed you a runaway coffee market. The chart is on page 56. As you can see, coffee prices paused for just 2 days on their vertical ascent to 8-year highs. Yet that small congestion area blocked declines on five separate occasions before giving way in mid-November.

Somewhat weaker support and resistance are also found at price *gaps*, which are simply areas on the chart where no trading took place.

Role Changing

An established support level, once broken, will often reverse its role and act as resistance the next time prices approach it from below. A resistance level that has been surpassed will provide support if prices should later fall back to that level. An example of this chameleon-like change from support to resistance is shown in Figure 10.9.

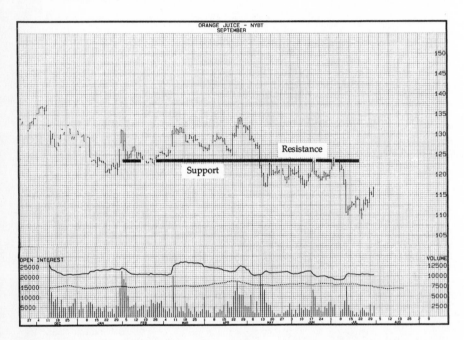

Figure 10.9   Support and resistance often swap roles. Support near $1.23 per pound, which had twice stopped declines in FCOJ early in the year, finally yielded in mid-May. In the following weeks, that same level acted as resistance on four occasions.

Chart courtesy of *CRB Futures Perspective*, a publication of Commodity Research Bureau.

Chart Patterns

A table of commodity prices in the newspaper is a snapshot of price action. A price chart is a moving picture of the conflict between the bulls and the bears. A chart provides a valuable perspective. It permits comparison between today's price action and previous action. It enables the technical analyst to spot when prices have moved into new high or low ground.

Certain chart patterns have over the years become associated with particular kinds of price behavior.

Rectangles

Many technical analysts consider the rectangular price pattern the most meaningful. The pattern is formed by trading for several weeks or even months in a relatively narrow horizontal price range. It is completed when prices then suddenly break out.

Some technical analysts refer to this chart pattern as a "coil," in the sense that prices are coiling to strike sharply higher or lower. It is true that an extended price move in the direction of the breakout usually follows. An example of a rectangular price pattern is shown in Figure 10.10.

This phenomenon makes sense if we look at the rectangle in the same way as we did support and resistance levels. As depicted along the bottom of the chart, total trading volume during the 6 months while this rectangle was forming was 1.62 million futures contracts. That means there were 1.62 million new short positions and 1.62 million new long positions established during the period. Even after allowing for multiple contract positions and traders who were in and out and back in again, the great majority of the traders in this market had a vested interest in the narrow price range.

When prices leave that range, market participants will behave characteristically. If the breakout is to the upside, longs will add to their winning positions; bulls on the sidelines, seeing the breakout, will start to buy. Most important, however, are the existing shorts, who represent a large reservoir of potential buying power. As prices move higher, their losses mount; gradually they will give up hope and buy futures to cover their short positions, adding more fuel to the rally.

Rectangles may be found at major price turning points. They may also represent price consolidation; that is, sometimes prices will wander around inside a rectangle for several weeks and then resume their previous trend. It is difficult to tell before prices break out of a rectangle just which direction the next move will

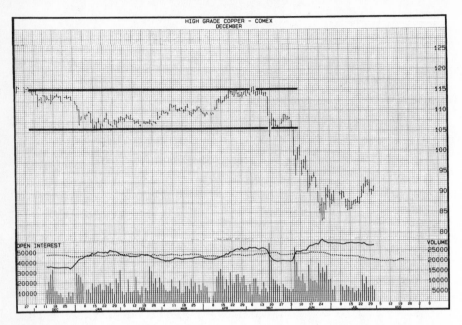

Figure 10.10   A rectangular price pattern is formed when overhead resistance and underlying support trap prices in a narrow horizontal trading range for several weeks or months, as in this copper chart. The pattern ends when one or the other—bulls or bears—finally prevails. The ensuing price move is often extensive.

Chart courtesy of *CRB Futures Perspective*, a publication of Commodity Research Bureau.

be, but there may be hints. If prices are historically high when the rectangle forms, the probabilities would favor a downside breakout. The opposite would be true if prices were at 10-year lows.

Anthony Reinach writes that prices tend to leave a rectangle through the boundary where they have lately spent the *least* time (*The Fastest Game in Town*, Commodity Research Bureau, New York, 1973). To put it another way, if price action has been concentrated in the bottom half of the rectangle during the most recent trading activity, the odds favor an exit through the top and vice versa. As you can see, this thesis was borne out in Figure 10.10.

There are several other bar chart patterns that technicians recognize, in addition to rectangles. Some patterns contain forecasting power; others are noncommittal. If the subject has caught your interest, you will find them discussed in Appendix A.

Failed Signals

If prices fail to follow through—if they break out of an established pattern and immediately stall—it is a sign that the breakout was counterfeit and that the most likely course of prices in coming days is *opposite* to the breakout. This doesn't happen very often, but some chartists consider this particular event one of the most important chart signals.

Candlestick Charts

Candlestick charts originated in Japan more than a century ago. They derive their name from their appearance: Each day's price action looks like a candle with a wick sticking out of one or both ends.

Construction of a candlestick chart is not complicated. As in a bar chart, each day's high and low price is marked by the top and bottom of a single vertical line. In a candlestick chart, however, there is a narrow cylinder wrapped around the line. This cylinder (the candle) provides two pieces of information. Its *color* shows where that day's closing price was in relation to the opening price. If the closing was higher than the opening price (a bullish portent), the candle is left white; if the close was lower than the open (indicating a bearish tone), the candle is colored black. The candle's overall *length* represents the distance between the opening and closing prices. (See Figure 10.11.)

Because bearish days have black candlesticks and bullish days have white candlesticks, it is possible to tell at a glance which kinds of days dominate the chart.

There are many chart phenomena common to both bar charts and candlestick charts, and they are interpreted in similar fashion. There are also candlestick patterns that have no counterpart in bar charts; they are strictly candlestick patterns and are interpreted according to the special rules surrounding this Oriental discipline. Some of the latter are shown in Figure 10.12.

As with most technical tools, candlestick charts are of greatest value when used in conjunction with other indicators of market strength or weakness.

For more on building and interpreting candlestick charts, *Candlesticks Explained*, referenced at the end of this chapter, is an excellent source.

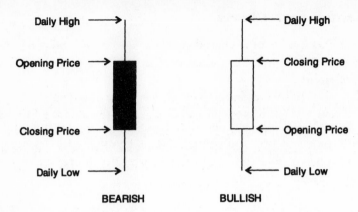

Figure 10.11 Depicted are two representative days of candlestick chart price action. In the presentation on the left, the day's closing price was below the day's opening price, indicating a bearish undertone; the candlestick is colored black. In the presentation on the right, the situation is reversed. The closing price is higher than the opening price, evidence of a strong day. The candlestick is left white.

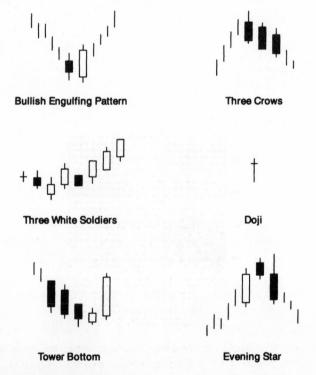

Figure 10.12 Candle price patterns are associated with the reversal or weakening of the current trend. Shown here are some of the patterns unique to candlestick charting.

Point-and-Figure Charts

There is another kind of price chart that technicians use. It is called a point-and-figure chart, and it is more than a record of prices. It comprises a well-defined trading method.

The point-and-figure chart is typically hand-drawn and posted daily by the chartist. Figure 10.13 shows a typical example. Prices are on the left-hand scale, in the spaces between the lines. There is no calendar across the bottom; point-and-figure charts are kept without regard to time. The X symbol is used to record rallies and the O to record declines. Each time the chartist shifts from one symbol to another, he begins a new column to the right.

Smart Investor Tip

If a price breakout is immediately followed by stalling price action, the breakout was false, and price movement in the *opposite* direction is more likely.

The size of each "box" is chosen by the chartist. It is generally some conveniently divisible number. For example, if you were constructing a point-and-figure chart for lean hog futures, you might assign each box the value of 20 points. If a rally were underway and Xs were being plotted, a new X would be

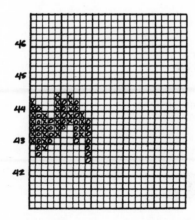

Figure 10.13 A typical point-and-figure chart. Prices are in the spaces rather than on the lines. Xs are used to record advances, Os to record declines; a new column to the right is started when the trend reverses. More than a record of prices, the point-and-figure chart is a complete trading method.

added to the top of the column with every 20-point gain. If prices were falling and Os were being plotted, a new O would be added to the bottom of the column each time the price fell by another 20 points.

Shifting from Xs to Os (or vice versa) is called reversal, and the chartist has to decide how far prices must move against the prevailing trend before he shifts to the next column to the right and starts plotting the other symbol. A "three-box" reversal criterion is common; that is, if prices would fill three or more boxes in the direction opposite to the direction you have been plotting, you move one column to the right and shift symbols.

Appendix B presents further information about these unusual charts, including how to get a point-and-figure chart started, how to recognize "buy" and "sell" signals, and how to select the most effective box size and reversal criterion.

Moving Averages

Moving averages are among the oldest trading tools. The purpose of the moving average is to smooth out short-term ups and downs in prices, to reveal the underlying trend. Use of a moving average has been likened to turning down the treble on your high-fidelity sound system, to suppress the higher-frequency cycles.

To take an example, assume that the closing prices for copper futures over the past 3 days were 109.50, 108.70, and 107.25:

Day 1	109.50
Day 2	108.70
Day 3	107.25
	325.43 ÷ 3 = 108.50

The total is 325.45. The average price over the 3 days was 325.45 ÷ 3 = 108.50. (Actually it was 108.48, but we rounded.) The next day's close is 106.40. We add that to the bottom of the column and delete the oldest price:

	~~109.50~~
Day 2	108.70
Day 3	107.25
Day 4	106.40
	322.35 ÷ 3 = 107.45

The new total is 322.35 and the new 3-day average is 107.45. The decline in the closing price caused the moving average to fall. The 3-day average is now moving forward in time; hence its name. The next day's close is 107.40:

	~~108.70~~
Day 3	107.25
Day 4	106.40
Day 5	107.40
	321.05 ÷ 3 = 107.00

The new total is 321.05, and the new 3-day moving average is 107.00. Here you see an important feature of moving averages demonstrated. The daily closing price went up by 100 points, while the moving average continued to decline. The moving average filtered out the rise in the closing price. It said, in effect, "If I'm going to recognize a gain, it will have to be bigger or more sustained than that."

The closing price for copper on the following day was 107.70, another daily gain:

	~~107.25~~
Day 4	106.40
Day 5	107.40
Day 6	107.70
	321.05 ÷ 3 = 107.15

On this day, the moving average increased from 107.00 to 107.15, finally recognizing that the minor price trend had reversed from down to up.

If prices on Day 6 had gone down instead of up, resuming the previous lower trend, the brief rally would never have shown up in the moving average. This is the smoothing action we mentioned. To demonstrate, substitute a price of 106.65 for 107.70 on the last day:

	~~107.25~~
Day 4	106.40
Day 5	107.40
Day 6	106.65 (substitute price)
	320.45 ÷ 3 = 106.80

If we substitute a closing price of 106.65 for 107.70 on Day 6, the moving average on Day 6 is 106.80, a decline from its Day 5 value of 107.00; the rally in the closing price on Day 5 is obscured.

Putting all the days together will give you a clearer picture:

Day	Closing Price	3-Day Moving Average
1	109.50	
2	108.70	
3	107.25	108.50
4	106.40	107.45
5	107.40	107.00
6	107.70	107.15

From Day 1 through Day 4, both the closing prices and the 3-day moving average are going down. On Day 5 an upturn in the closing prices began. However, the moving average continued to decline on Day 5, not turning up until Day 6, a lag of one day.

This lag is both the cost and the benefit of using a moving average, as it delays a decision about market direction until more data are available.

Selecting the Number of Days

Any number of days can be used to build a simple moving average. We used 3 days in our example, but there's no magic to that number. The key is the market where the moving average is to be employed.

The shorter the moving average, the more sensitive it will be to price changes. The longer the moving average, the slower it will be to respond. Early signals from a moving average run the risk of being false; late signals may give up too much of the trend. The technical trader tries to strike the optimum balance between the two.

As we saw, with the 3-day moving average, the lag between the upturn in the price and the upturn in the moving average was only 1 day. That would not provide adequate filtering action in a volatile market. Trading decisions based on turns in the moving average would cause a trader to jump in and out of the market frequently, creating not only frustration but high commission costs. A longer moving average would reduce these so-called whipsaws.

By the same token, a long moving average in a very quiet market would not provide very satisfactory results; by the time a new trend showed up in the moving average, the price move could be over. Given these trade-offs, experienced traders generally consider the longer moving averages as more dependable.

Appendix C presents more information about moving averages. It covers linearly weighted moving averages, exponential moving averages, and how moving averages are used in a trading program.

Trading Volume and Open Interest

We briefly mentioned trading volume and open interest in Chapter 2. Trading volume is the number of futures contracts that changed hands during a specific period, usually a day. Open interest is defined as the number of outstanding futures contracts, or those that have not yet been closed out by offsetting futures transactions or delivery of the actual commodity.

To help you understand the nature of open interest and how it changes, let's take an example. Suppose there were a brand-new futures market in bananas, with nobody in it yet. Mr. A, who has been a student of bananas for some time, believes banana prices are headed lower. So he sells short one futures contract. Mr. B holds the opposite opinion; he expects higher banana prices in coming weeks. He buys the futures contract from Mr. A. The buying and selling is done, of course, through their respective brokers.

Those two positions—one long and one short—together comprise one unit of open interest.

Now the banana market starts to attract attention. Mr. C buys a futures contract from Mr. D; open interest increases to 2. Mr. E buys a futures contract from Ms. F; open interest increases to 3.

Mr. G also decides to go long bananas, but something different happens this time. Instead of buying from another new player, Mr. G buys a futures contract from Mr. B, who was long and has decided that he doesn't want to be in the market anymore. Mr. G takes over Mr. B's long position; he replaces Mr. B in the standings, and open interest therefore does not change.

The next buyer and seller to step up are Mr. C and Mr. D, both of whom already hold positions in the market. (Mr. C is long; Mr. D is short.) They close out their positions by reversing their original futures transactions: Mr. C sells and Mr. D buys. The market has now lost two previous players, and open interest decreases by one. (Remember, one long futures contract and one short futures contract together comprise one unit of open interest.)

From this sequence you can see that:

- Open interest increases when a new long buys from a new short.
- Open interest decreases when an old long sells to an old short.
- Open interest does not change when a new long buys from an old long or a new short sells to an old short, as the new player simply replaces the old player.

Measuring Trends

Data on trading volume and open interest can be used to evaluate the status of the current price trend. The simplest gauge is trading volume. The axiom is that the volume should "follow" the trend. If an uptrend is healthy, for example, trading volume should increase on rallies and dry up when prices set back temporarily. If these conditions do not prevail, a shadow of doubt would be cast on the current trend. The converse would be true in a bear market. Trading volume would tend to increase on declines and fall off when prices staged minor rallies.

Smart Investor Tip

When price, volume, and open interest rise together, the market is considered technically strong.

Open interest is a bit more complicated, but it is also a more valuable diagnostic tool. The character of open interest and its change in relation to price changes provide insight into why the market is moving. For example, suppose that during the past 2 weeks both prices and open interest had risen sharply. The price rise means that aggressive buying is coming into the market. The rise in open interest tells you that the buying is coming from new longs rather than old shorts who are closing out their positions. Why? Recall how open interest changes. If the buying were coming from departing shorts, open interest would be flat or going down. Ergo,

Thumb Rule 1

When price and open interest rise together, the market is considered to be technically strong.

A price rise accompanied by flat or falling open interest is, for the same reason, suspect. The rally is being sponsored by shorts who are buying to leave the market and will last only as long as they last. If no new factor enters the picture in the meantime, the rally will end when the last short has bought.

Thumb Rule 2

When prices rise on falling open interest, the market is considered technically weak.

A price decline that is accompanied by falling open interest also suggests a temporary condition. Sometimes referred to as a "liquidating market," the situation implies that the selling pressure is coming mainly from existing longs and that it will subside when all the longs have sold out.

Thumb Rule 3

When prices fall on declining open interest, the market is potentially buoyant.

If prices are falling while open interest is increasing, the presumption is of a legitimate bear market. A lot of selling is going on. The rise in open interest tells us that the selling pressure is coming from aggressive new shorts, who have suddenly been drawn into the market. The lower price trend is therefore on a relatively sound technical footing.

Thumb Rule 4

When prices decline on rising open interest, the market is considered to be technically weak.

These four rules of thumb may be further distilled into two general observations:

> *When price and open interest go up or down together, the current price trend is given a vote of confidence; when prices and open interest diverge, the market may be about to change course.*

We have called these "rules of thumb" because they are not hard and fast. They are guidelines, to be applied in concert with other technical indicators to develop a rounded picture of the status of that particular market.

Stochastics

The word *stochastic* came originally from the Greek, where it meant "good at conjecturing." In modern market analysis, a stochastic is a mathematical oscillator that measures the relative location of the closing price in the daily trading range.

The idea behind stochastics is that horses pull in the direction the stagecoach is moving. If the market is in an established uptrend, daily closing prices tend to fall at the high end of that day's price range. In bear markets, prices tend to close at the low end of the daily trading ranges. A stochastic expresses this idea in mathematical terms. It gives meaning to the location of the current closing price by comparing it to the highest high and the lowest low in the past several days. Changes in the oscillator's value become the basis for entering or leaving a market.

Close kin of the stochastic is the *momentum* oscillator, which is used to measure the rate at which prices have been changing. The simplest and most widely known momentum oscillator is probably the Relative Strength Index (RSI), devised by J. Welles Wilder, Jr. and published in 1978 in his book, *New Concepts in Technical Trading Systems.*

The RSI begins by developing a ratio of the number of "up" days to the number of "down" days. The period Wilder studied was the past 14 trading days, but a greater or lesser number of days may be evaluated. This ratio of up to down days is then taken through several mathematical steps. The final result is an index number between 0 and 100 that stands for current market strength.

The RSI can be put to work in several ways. A high RSI value connotes a market that is "overbought" and vulnerable to a setback. A low RSI signals the converse. How high is high? A study done by Peter W. Aan ("How RSI Behaves," *Futures* magazine, January 1985) showed that the average RSI value for a market top then was 72, and the average value for an RSI bottom was 32.

A divergence between the RSI and the prices on which it is based also signals change. For example, if the RSI fails to follow the most recent price gains in a sustained bull move, the uptrend would be viewed as faltering.

Finally, some of the technical phenomena found in bar charts—for example, support and resistance levels—may also be applied effectively to charts of the RSI.

Descriptions of the calculation and use of stochastics and of Wilder's Relative Strength Index may be found in Appendix D and in Perry Kaufman's book, referenced at the end of this chapter.

Contrary Opinion

There are just so many futures traders. They are not easy to count, as futures commission merchants are reluctant to reveal the identity of their customers; but estimates range in the hundred thousands. By comparison, some 50 million investors are said to be involved in the securities markets.

If there is a finite number of futures traders, they can be exhausted. That is, it is possible that a particular futures market could literally run out of new players.

To take an example, suppose prices in a certain market have been advancing for several months. Open interest has also been increasing and now stands at a record high. Given this scenario, it is conceivable that virtually everyone who ever intended to buy one of these futures contracts has already bought. That leaves the market in a precarious balance. The bulls are fully committed, and the bears are watching. Positive news, which helped fuel the rally, now has little or no effect on prices. However, it may take only a scrap of negative sentiment to tip the scale, sending the longs packing and bringing in the short sellers.

An extended advance or decline in futures prices thus may contain the seeds of its own demise.

This philosophy goes under the name of contrary opinion and is based on the observation that markets look most bullish near their tops and most dismal just about the time they are ready to turn up again. Traders who espouse this philosophy attempt to measure the extent to which futures markets have become overloaded to one side or the other and to use these evaluations in making their trading decisions.

Informed Opinion

There are other ways to consider open interest. Suppose you learned from a reliable source that many of the large speculators in wheat had just moved from the long side of the market to the short side. You could draw conclusions from that. Large speculators are supposed to know what they're doing, and they expect lower prices. Maybe they know something you don't.

Just such changes in market sentiment are gathered from the field and published twice each month by the Commodity Futures Trading Commission in Washington, DC. The report is called the *Commitments of Traders Report*. It is published every other Monday.

The categories reported on are "commercial" (hedgers), "noncommercial" (large speculators), and "nonreportable positions" (small traders). Shown for each category are the number of long positions, short positions, and the changes since the previous report. All major futures markets are covered.

Information about how to obtain the *Commitments of Traders Report* and other reports and publications of the Commodity Futures Trading Commission can be found in Chapter 17.

Other Technical Tools

Support and resistance levels, price chart analysis, and moving averages are the most common technical phenomena. Technicians employ other means in their effort to forecast prices.

Elliott Wave analysis seems well adapted to longer-term price forecasting. Named after a man who lived in the early 1900s, the method finds a major trend complete when it has formed five waves in the main direction. Reactions along the way comprise three waves in a countertrend direction. Elliott considered the waves as "behavioral tides," found throughout nature.

Investigation has also been made into price *cycles*. Cyclical price activity is most pronounced in the seasonal agricultural commodities, but it is identifiable to some degree in virtually all futures markets.

A very useful Web site for the technical analyst is www.prophet.net. It provides streaming price quotes, historical futures information dating back to 1959, risk/reward analysis, interactive trendlines, customized watch lists, Fibonacci tools, and more. The service is available by subscription; a free 7-day trial is offered.

But there is something else. Go to the prophet.net Web site and click on "quotes." Then click on "futures" to learn the symbols to use. At the bottom of the page, find a column entitled "Analyze." Under that heading, click "Snap Charts." Snap Charts allows you, for no charge, to create a current price chart for any futures contract. You can choose the chart type (bar, line, or candlestick), the total time period to be covered, and the chart's scale (daily, weekly or monthly). Prices are delayed 20 minutes.

For more information on their subscription services, you can also call Prophet Financial Systems, Inc. at 1-800-772-8040.

Caveats

Few traders put all their technical eggs in one basket. Most use more than one indicator. When the indicators disagree, the technical trader stays out of the market. When the indicators concur, he can take a position with a degree of confidence. When there are only shades of difference, the trader must decide which technical indicator he trusts most and give it precedence.

An analogy to a weather forecaster is apt. The forecaster doesn't base his prediction on only one aspect. He looks at temperature, dew point, wind direction and velocity, cloud cover, and relative humidity before deciding whether it's going to rain on your picnic.

The Law of Disappearing Qualifiers also applies to conclusions arrived at through technical analysis. There is as much art as science in identifying support and resistance levels, trends, and price objectives. The technician needs to remind himself from time to time that he is dealing with mathematical probabilities, not certainties.

Not all technical phenomena behave as well as those we have shown in this chapter, which were selected to demonstrate our points. Trendlines occasionally have to be redrawn on the basis of later evidence. Prices sometimes move in fits and starts, apparently trending in one direction for a short time and then suddenly reversing course. Extended upward or downward price trends are, unfortunately, not common occurrences.

Technical analysis works best in routine markets, those that are not subject to unusual stress. The best technical forecasts can be overwhelmed by sudden changes in supply or demand. Discovery of a serious crop disease, drought, a surprise announcement of a huge foreign purchase, or an unexpectedly bullish or bearish government crop report are examples of events that can put technical analysis into abeyance until the news is assimilated and the market affected settles back down again.

Smart Investor Tip

Technical analysis deals with probabilities, not certainties.

Suggested Reading

The Visual Investor: How to Spot Market Trends, John J. Murphy. Wiley, New York, 1996.

Trading Systems and Methods, Third Edition, Perry J. Kaufman. Wiley, New York, 1998.

Candlesticks Explained, Martin J. Pring. McGraw-Hill, New York (CD ROM and workbook), 2002.

Technical Analysis of the Futures Markets, John J. Murphy. New York Institute of Finance, New York, 2003.

Chapter

11

Hedging Revisited

I n Chapter 5 we introduced the rudiments of hedging. We said that the purpose of hedging is to reduce the risk of price changes in a cash commodity, and that a traditional hedge involves a futures position that is roughly equal and opposite to the cash position held by the hedger.

Hedging is not a rote process. Risk exposure must be evaluated; it may turn out to be acceptable. The damage that an adverse move in the cash price would do must be weighed against the probability of its occurrence. The price history of the proposed hedge should be examined. Particularly in financial futures, prospective hedgers should ensure that their intended actions do not violate any regulations.

A hedge is not always benign. In all the examples given up to this point, the hedge was necessary. Prices subsequently moved against the hedger's cash position, causing losses on the cash side and offsetting gains on the futures side. It is possible for prices to move in the other direction, creating losses in the hedger's futures position and triggering margin calls. A call for more money is disquieting, even though the "loss" will be recovered when the cash asset is sold. Unless the hedger has made credit arrangements to cover them, a series of margin calls may present a cash flow problem.

Smart Investor Tip
Hedging is not a rote process.

The hedges we used as examples in Chapter 5 also worked perfectly; that is, the money lost on the cash side and the amount gained on the futures sides were identical. That rarely happens in the real world. There are several reasons that the gains and losses in a hedge may not be equal. Most important is the fact that futures prices and cash prices may not change by the same amount because the two prices are subject to different influences. Cash prices respond to the supply and demand for the actual commodity. Futures prices are influenced strongly by traders' expectations.

Smart Investor Tip
Basis is defined as the difference between the cash price and the futures price of a commodity. It can be either a positive or negative value and is best thought of as the cash price minus the futures price.

What follows is the bond dealer example from Chapter 5, but with a difference. To make it more realistic, we have changed the T-bond futures price in the closing transaction from 104-28 to 104-31:

Short Hedge in T-Bond Futures

Cash Market			*Futures Market*	
Buy cash bonds at	105-07	Now	Sell T-bond futures at	105-17
Sell cash bonds at	104-18	Later	Buy T-bond futures at	104-31
Loss	0-21		Gain	0-18

Net result = loss of 0-03

Now the hedge does not balance. The dealer lost $^{21}\!/_{32}$ on his cash bonds while he held them, but the hedge earned back only $^{18}\!/_{32}$. Three thirty-seconds of the loss taken on the cash side were not offset.

To understand what happened, it is necessary to meet another new concept, that of *basis*. Basis is defined as the difference between the cash price and the futures price of a commodity. Basis can be either a positive or negative value and is best thought of as the cash price minus the futures price. A change in the basis while the hedge is on is one of the reasons why hedges may not work 100 percent.

Let's take a look at the basis in the hedge just given:

Cash Market			*Futures Market*		*Basis*
Buy cash bonds at	105-07	Now	Sell short T-bond futures at	105-17	–0-10
Sell cash bonds at	104-18	Later	Buy T-bond futures at	104-31	–0-13
Loss	0-21		Gain	0-18	–0-03

Net result = loss of 0-03

The basis in the opening transaction was minus 10 (105-07 minus 105-17). In the closing transaction, the basis was minus 13 (104-18 minus 104-31), or $\frac{3}{32}$ less. It is not a coincidence that the basis change and the loss in the hedge are the same amount, $\frac{3}{32}$. The change in the basis is what caused the loss.

Potential losses resulting from basis changes cannot be controlled by the hedger. His hedge will protect him against changes in cash prices, but he is always vulnerable to a change in the basis. In this case, the basis fell; that is, it went from minus 10 to minus 13, which is a decrease. If the basis had increased, the hedger would have had the pleasant experience of earning more from his futures position than he lost on the cash bonds.

Smart Investor Tip

When a hedger is short futures, increases in the basis would create windfall gains. If a hedger is long futures, the situation is reversed: A decrease in basis creates gains.

When a hedger is short futures (as the bond dealer was in this example), *any decrease in the basis will cause losses; increases in the basis would create windfall gains. If a hedger is long futures, the situation is reversed: Increase in basis causes losses, and a decrease in basis creates gains.*

A hedger is not entirely helpless when it comes to dealing with the basis. In some markets, particularly the agricultural markets, basis itself has seasonal tendencies, trending higher during certain times of the year and lower during others. A sophisticated hedger will be aware of the trends in the basis and will try to place his hedge during a period when the basis is most likely to move favorably for him.

Here's another example from Chapter 5 with the outcome changed:

Long Hedge in Corn Futures

Cash Market		Futures Market
Cash corn at $2.85/bushel	Now	Buy corn futures at $2.96/bushel
Buy cash corn at $3.10/bushel	3 months later	Sell corn futures at $3.25/bushel
Loss $.25/bushel		Gain $.29/bushel
	Net result = +$.04	

The corn exporter was long futures. The basis on the opening transaction was $2.85 – $2.96 = –11. The basis in the closing transaction was $3.10 – $3.25 = –15. Recall that when a hedger is long futures, a decrease in the basis creates gains; the basis fell from –11 to –15 while the hedge was in place, providing the hedger with a windfall gain of 4 cents per bushel on his corn sale.

Smart Investor Tip

The main reason why a hedge may not provide 100 percent price protection is that cash prices and futures prices do not always change by equal amounts.

Other Reasons for an Imperfect Hedge

A change in the basis is not the only reason that a hedge could fail to provide 100 percent protection against cash price changes. Futures contracts are not divisible. A cash position of $470,000 in 10-year Treasury notes, for example, cannot be offset exactly, because the 10-year T-note futures contract on the Chicago Board of Trade is based on $100,000 par value in 10-year T-notes. Five T-note futures contracts ($500,000) would be too much hedge; four futures contracts ($400,000) would leave $70,000 worth of cash T-notes exposed.

When faced with this dilemma, bear in mind that any part of an intended futures hedge that does not have an offsetting cash position is a speculation and carries with it speculative risk. The more conservative business decision in this example would be to underhedge the cash position; that is, to protect as much of it as possible without creating any speculative exposure.

Overhedging a cash position in such circumstances requires a favorable price forecast. In the previous example, overhedging would not even be considered if interest rates are expected to move lower, as the "extra" short futures position would be expected to generate market losses. (Remember: Prices of fixed-income financial instruments go up when interest rates go down.) If interest rates are expected to rise while the hedge is on, overhedging could be considered by an experienced trader.

An example will help you understand how an unbalanced hedge works. Assume you are a cattle feeder. It is March, and you have 62 steers out in the feedlot munching corn. They weigh about 800 pounds each now, and you are going to feed them up to about 1000 pounds each. That should take about 7 weeks, at which time you'll market the steers.

The present cash price for fat cattle is 62.50 cents per pound. June cattle futures are trading at 62.90 cents per pound. You want to hedge your cattle. The live cattle futures contract on the Chicago Mercantile Exchange is based on a contract size of 40,000 pounds, or about 40 steers weighing 1000 pounds each. You will have about 62,000 pounds of cattle at market time. Your hedge will have to be unbalanced.

Cattle prices are forecast to ease during the time your hedge will be in place, so you decide to take the speculative risk and overhedge your cash position. You sell short two contracts of June cattle. Your assessment of the market proves to be right; when it comes time to market your cattle, prices have declined a little over 1½ cents. The results of your hedge would look something like this (no change in basis):

Cash Cattle			*Futures*	
	62.50	March	Sold two June cattle at	62.90
Sold 62 head at	60.72	May	Bought two June cattle at	61.12
	−1.78			+1.78

The cash price and the futures price have changed by the same amount, so it appears at first glance that you received an effective price of (60.72 cash price +1.78 futures gain =) 62.50 cents a pound for your cattle. However, that's not so, because the underlying assets were different sizes. There were only 62,000 pounds of cash cattle; there were (40,000 × 2 =) 80,000 pounds of cattle futures.

To calculate the price per pound you received for your cattle, you have to figure out your total receipts and divide that number by 62,000 pounds. You were paid $37,646.40 for your cash steers (60.72 cents per pound × 1000 pounds × 62 head). Your short futures hedge of two contracts returned you 1.78 cents per pound times 80,000 pounds, or $1424.00.

The total amount you received for your cash cattle was therefore ($37,646.40 + $1,424.00 =) $39,070.40. That total divided by 62,000 pounds of live cattle equals 63.02 cents per pound.

Because prices moved in a favorable direction (in this case, down) the unbalanced short hedge increased the effective price you received for your cattle from 62.50 to 63.02. If prices had instead increased, the unbalanced hedge would have reduced your effective price; you would have lost more on the short futures side than you gained on the cash side.

Another possible reason for an imperfect hedge is a difference between the futures and the cash crop. In some commodities, particularly the agricultural ones, the cash commodity being hedged may not be identical to the commodity underlying the futures contract. The coffee futures contract on the New York Board of Trade, for example, is based on arabica coffee. There are many other varieties. A grower or processor who uses New York futures to hedge another kind of coffee may encounter unexpected gains or losses because the price of his coffee and the price of arabica coffee diverged.

Selecting the Delivery Month

In most hedging situations, there will be more than one futures delivery month that could be used for the hedge. The first requirement is that the delivery month be beyond the date when the hedge is to be lifted. Unless you have reason to do so, there's no point in having to close out one expiring futures position and open another to keep your hedge intact.

It is also usually desirable to use the nearest futures contract that meets the first requirement. The closer the futures contract is to maturity, the more responsive it will be to changes in the cash price, and the lower will be the risk of changes in the basis. Nearby futures contracts are also generally more liquid; there is more trading activity in them than in the distant contracts. As a result, your orders to buy or sell will be filled quickly and with minimal impact on the price level.

Experienced hedgers look at other criteria when selecting the futures delivery month they will use. Some delivery months have a history of gaining ground on other delivery months at certain times of the year. One delivery month may offer a better "opening" basis than another, setting the stage for a possible planned basis gain.

Margins in Hedges

The amount and nature of initial and maintenance margins required of a hedger depend on the exchange, the futures commission merchant (FCM), and the customer. An unknown, thinly capitalized hedger could be required by the FCM to post margins greater than exchange minimums, and in cash. An old, well-heeled customer of the FCM may be able to satisfy both original and any maintenance requirements with a letter of credit issued through a local bank.

The point to be made here is that an established futures hedge may make considerable further demands on short-term capital. To take an example, let's assume that you have a short hedge in soybean futures. The original margin is $2500, the maintenance level is $2000, and you are on a cash basis with your FCM. You will be called for additional margin if beans go up more than 10 cents from your entry level, as your equity would drop below $2000. For every dollar that bean prices rise, the additional margin required to maintain your short hedge would be $5000. That's for one contract of 5000 bushels. If your hedge is for 10 contracts, each dollar gain in soybean prices would create a margin call for $50,000. Granted, you get the money back when you sell your beans at the new higher cash price. But in the meantime you have to come up with the necessary short-term financing for the hedge.

Nonregular Hedges

There are bona-fide hedges that do not fit the patterns we have been discussing. We don't want to dwell on these nonstandard hedges, but we think you should at least be introduced to them. They are cross-hedges, ratio hedges, and on-call transactions.

Cross-Hedges

If no futures market exists for a certain commodity, it is sometimes possible to use a related futures market for hedging. These are referred to as cross-hedges and are recognized by the Commodity Futures Trading Commission as legitimate. The key is that the two commodities be economically related, so their prices will tend to move up and down together.

A classic example of a cross-hedge is palm oil/soybean oil. Palm oil is one of the major edible oils in the world; it has no futures market. Soybean oil, the most important edible oil, has a very active futures market. The positive correlation between the price movements in the two markets is well above 90 percent. Soybean oil futures can therefore be used effectively to hedge cash positions in palm oil.

Cross-hedging is common in interest rate futures. Commercial paper and CDs can be hedged with short-term Treasury futures. High-quality corporate bonds can be hedged with T-bond futures. The key, once again, is the basis: the relationship between changes in the cash price and changes in the futures price. If history has shown that the two prices tend to move together, a cross-hedge is feasible.

Ratio Hedges

When you hedge soybean risk in soybean futures, there is little question of how the futures price will respond to a change in the cash price. Cash soybeans and the soybeans underlying the futures contract are identical. Their price volatility is virtually the same. As a consequence, there is no need for the value of the futures contracts used in the hedge to differ from the amount of exposure. Or, to put it another way, a hedge ratio of 1 to 1 is generally effective: $1 worth of futures for every $1 worth of cash exposure.

Smart Investor Tip
If the price of the product hedged and the futures price do not have the same volatility, a ratio hedge may be more efficient.

If the price of the product being hedged and the futures price march to different drummers, the most efficient hedge may be an unbalanced hedge. For example, assume that the price volatility of commercial paper is 1.2 times the price volatility of 2-year T-notes. If 2-year T-note futures are used to cross-hedge a cash position in commercial paper, the best combination may not be 1 to 1; it might be something like 1.2 to 1, or $1,000,000 worth of 2-year T-note futures for each $833,333 worth of commercial paper. Then if the market value of the more volatile commercial paper changes by .60, 2-year T-note futures prices should change by .50, equating the change in the value of the two holdings (.60 × 833,333 = .50 × 1,000,000) and enhancing the probability that losses on the cash side will be recouped by gains in the futures.

On-Call Transactions

Cotton was king in New Orleans at the turn of the twentieth century. A practice developed there that capitalized on the fact that a favorable movement in the basis virtually guarantees profits in a fully hedged cash position.

For example, suppose a cotton dealer buys 1000 bales of combed cotton from a local grower and stores them in his warehouse. The dealer does not have an immediate buyer for the cotton, so at the same time he sells short two contracts of December cotton futures on the New York Cotton Exchange (each futures contract is 500 bales; each bale is 100 pounds).

At this point, his balance sheet might look something like this:

Cash	Futures	Basis
Bought 1,000 bales at 71.27	Sold 2 contracts December cotton at 72.77	Minus 1.50

A week later a buyer phones the cotton dealer. The buyer wants to purchase 1000 bales of cash cotton. During their conversation, the buyer indicates that he believes cotton prices will soften over the next several days. He asks the dealer for his best offer.

The dealer reviews his status. He is "long" the basis (short futures), so every penny that the basis increases will earn him $1000 in revenue (1 cent per bale × 100 pounds × 1000 bales). The dealer would be satisfied with a $1000 gross profit on the transaction. But he doesn't tell the buyer that the price for the cash cotton is 72.27 (1 cent more than the dealer paid). He tells the buyer that if he buys the cotton now, he can pay for it at any time he chooses over the next 10 days at an effective price of December futures minus .50.

The dealer has forced the basis to move in a favorable direction. Whether cash cotton prices go up or down in the interim, the dealer will earn his $1000 profit. He has also given the buyer the opportunity to exercise his market judgment and, if he is correct, to buy the cash cotton at a better price.

To prove it, we'll continue with our example. Suppose the buyer were right on the market forecast; cash cotton fell to 67.44 cents per pound over the next week, and December futures kept exact pace by dropping to 68.94. At that point the buyer elected to pay for the cotton, giving the dealer the agreed cash price of 50 points "off" December futures, or (68.94 − .50 =) 68.44 cents per pound. The dealer closed out his short hedge at that time.

Here's how the dealer fared:

Cash		*Futures*		*Basis*	
Bought 1000 bales at	71.27	Sold 2 contracts December cotton at	72.77	Minus	1.50
Sold 1000 bales at	68.44	Bought 2 contracts December cotton at	68.94	Minus	.50
	−2.83		+3.83		+1.00

The dealer received 68.44 cents per pound from the buyer. He also received 3.83 cents per pound from his profitable short futures position. The effective selling price for his cotton was therefore (68.44 + 3.83 =) 72.27 cents per pound. This is 1 cent per pound more than he paid for the cash cotton, so he has in fact received his desired gross profit of $1000 on the transaction. The buyer is also pleased. By waiting a week or so, he saved almost 3 cents a pound on his purchase of cash cotton.

But note this important point in an on-call purchase:

The buyer is at price risk; the dealer is not.

If cash cotton prices had risen sharply in the interim, the buyer would have had to pay the higher price; the dealer would still make his $1000 profit. Here are the numbers:

Cash		*Futures*		*Basis*	
Bought 1000 bales at	71.27	Sold 2 contracts December cotton at	72.77	Minus	1.50
Sold 1000 bales at	74.36	Bought 2 contracts December cotton at	74.86	Minus	.50
	+3.09		−2.09		+1.00

The dealer received an effective price of (74.36 − 2.09 =) 72.27 cents per pound for his cotton, as before. However, the buyer, because he waited, had to pay 74.36 cents per pound for the cash cotton, which is more than 2 cents a pound higher than the cash price when he first phoned the cotton dealer.

This transaction is referred to as an "on-call" transaction. In this case, the payment awaited the buyer's call. The same general approach can be used for transactions based on a seller's call. On-call transactions are not widely used today, although they may still be found in the cotton market, and to some extent in the futures markets for sugar and U.S. Treasury bonds.

Suggested Reading

The Business of Hedging, John Stephens. Prentice-Hall, New York, 2000.

12

The Financial Futures

Before financial futures were introduced in the 1970s, futures markets dealt with consumable commodities like the grains, meats, and metals. These traditional futures markets are similar in many respects and therefore lend themselves well to a general discussion.

Financial futures markets do not fit the same mold. The assets underlying these new futures are not always tangible. The commodities may not be consumed at all but simply change form or ownership. In some cases, physical delivery is impracticable, so settlement is by cash only.

Financial futures not only differ from the traditional commodities, they differ among themselves. Financial futures fall into three broad categories:

Foreign currency futures

Stock futures

Interest rate futures

Stock futures comprise two different categories: stock indexes, which we discuss in this chapter, and single-stock futures, which have their own Chapter 13.

We present the basic information you need to understand how each of these markets works. As with commodities, detailed information on the individual futures contracts may be found in Chapter 17.

Derivatives

It is the financial futures that have spawned the new trading vehicles known as derivatives. A *derivative* is any asset that derives its value from a different asset. A ticket to the annual Super Bowl football game is a derivative. It derives its value from the worth of the seat in the stadium. Its value changes when scalpers start to bid up the price of the seat.

In financial markets, the most familiar derivatives are options. The value of a stock option is derived from the value of its underlying stock. A futures contract is also a derivative, as its price depends on the price of the underlying commodity.

Even so, the term *derivative* seems today to have a black eye. It has come to refer to a family of synthetic, nonstandard, unregulated financial contracts that carry the potential risk of derailing the world's established financial engines.

Encouraging such beliefs have been several recent incidents: the failure of Britain's Barings Bank in 1995, after bank trader Nick Leeson lost more than a $1 billion of the bank's money and, in this country, in September 1998, when a bevy of marquee Ph.D. economists brought multibillion-dollar Long Term Capital Management to the brink of bankruptcy. As we write this, the suspended chief executive of China Aviation Oil is being questioned about a $550 million loss at his company.

The alleged culprit in all three failures: transactions in derivatives.

The most common of the unregulated derivatives is known as an interest-rate swap. A fiduciary who has a fixed income stream from a U.S. Treasury bond, for example, could enter into an agreement to swap income streams with the holder of a British bond that had a floating yield. The fiduciary would pay (give up) fixed rates and receive floating rates. Neither cash bond position would be disturbed.

Equity swaps are similar to interest-rate swaps. The difference is that one of the two payment flows is linked to the return on an equity index, a group of shares, or even a single stock. For example, a fiduciary could agree to pay a fixed monthly amount to a bank over a certain period of time. In return, the bank would pay the fiduciary the market return on, say, the S&P 500 Index or Microsoft common stock.

Currency swaps are also common. To take an example, let's say that an American company, to get a more favorable interest rate, sells corporate bonds denominated in euros. After the sale is complete, the company immediately converts the entire proceeds to dollars so it can buy supplies and pay its employees. The company makes the semiannual bond interest payments to the bank in dollars, which the bank passes through to bondholders in euros. When the bonds mature, the entire amount is converted from dollars back to euros at a predetermined exchange rate. The bank stands at the crossroads throughout the process, collecting fees for its services.

The American company has, in effect, funded its U.S. operations with euros. The currency swap has allowed the company to take advantage of a favorable capital market outside the United States.

Finally, there is the structured note. On its face, this is a simple fixed-income investment; but buried in the note are other financial instruments—often options—that affect the note's return as the price of the option rises or falls.

There are other possibilities, some of which are so complex that even their designers are uncertain how they will respond to market changes. They're beyond our scope here.

Foreign Currencies

Exchange rates for the major foreign currencies have fluctuated widely in recent years. But this has not always been the case. From 1944 to 1971, member nations to the Bretton Woods agreement—which included most major world trading partners—pegged their currencies to a specified number of U.S. dollars or given amount of gold (at $35 per ounce). Exchange-rate fluctuations during those years rarely exceeded 2 percent.

This stability was threatened by massive U.S. spending in the late 1960s to support the Vietnam War and fuel expansionary fiscal policies at home. By 1971, the number of dollars in circulation was greater than the total U.S. gold reserves, and President Nixon announced that the U.S. dollar would no longer be convertible into gold. The action removed the basis for parity between currencies. Since 1973, European central banks have allowed their currencies to seek their own levels, and the resulting movement in exchanges rates has been dramatic. It was not unusual for a currency's value to vary as much as 20 percent within a year, and a swing of 25 percent has been recorded in a 3-month period. Such volatility added a new dimension of risk to international business.

Using Foreign Currencies

If you are going to buy a product from someone who will accept only a certain foreign currency in payment, you are first going to have to buy that foreign currency. Its exchange rate will have a direct effect on the cost of the product to you.

For example, suppose you ordered a Swiss watch direct from the manufacturer in Zurich. The price is 750 Swiss francs (SF). The following table shows what the watch could cost you in U.S. dollars, depending on the exchange rate for the Swiss franc at the time of your purchase:

Price of Watch	Exchange Rate	Cross-Rate	Cost of Watch in U.S. Dollars
750 SF	.55	1.818	(750 × .55) = $412.50
750 SF	.60	1.666	(750 × .60) = $450.00
750 SF	.65	1.538	(750 × .65) = $487.50
750 SF	.70	1.428	(750 × .70) = $525.00

The "Exchange Rate" column in the table shows the value of one Swiss franc in U.S. currency, which is the way all foreign currency futures prices are expressed. International banks use a cross-rate, which is the amount of the foreign currency you can buy for one U.S. dollar. The cross-rate is the inverse of the futures price.

(We've taken a liberty with the notation, abbreviating 750 Swiss francs as 750 SF instead of SF 750. The notation is uniform throughout the book.)

Example: You buy a small cottage on one-half acre near Acapulco, Mexico. The price is 500,000 pesos. The exchange rate at that time is 8.7 pesos to the dollar, so each peso costs you $0.115, or 11½ cents. Your cost for the cottage, excluding commissions, is $57,500 (500,000 × 0.115).

Six months later, you decide that buying the cottage was a bad idea. You put it on the market for 530,000 pesos, which is 30,000 pesos more than you paid for it. You are pleasantly surprised when it sells right away, and you figure that you have recovered nicely from an errant decision.

When you go to the bank to convert your pesos back into dollars, however, you discover that during the interim the exchange rate for the peso has risen to 9.5. Your proceeds from the conversion of pesos back to dollars are $55,789 (530,000 ÷ 9.5), which is $1700 less than you paid. A change in the exchange rate has turned an apparent profit into a loss.

Example: Your U.S. firm makes a product that sells like potato hotcakes in Germany. You are paid for your product in euros. Before you can put that income on your company books, you have to convert the euros to dollars.

Your projected German sales for the first quarter of next year are 2.5 million euros. That includes a profit of 125,000 euros. The current exchange rate for the euro is 1.17, so your expected first-quarter receipts are (2,500,000 ÷ 1.7 =) $2,136,752, and your expected profit is (125,000 ÷ 1.7 =) $73,529.

But something unexpected happens. The exchange rate for the euro begins to rise. The following table shows how your returns would be affected:

Euros Received	Exchange Rate	Effective Receipts
2.5 million	1.17	2,136,752
2.5 million	1.19	2,100,840
2.5 million	1.21	2,066,116
2.5 million	1.23	2,032,520

If the exchange rate were to rise to 1.21, your total receipts would be $70,636 less than you had anticipated. That was most of your original expected profit, and it would now be completely erased.

Futures Markets

It was against the backdrop of freewheeling exchange rates that trading in foreign currency futures began at the International Monetary Market in Chicago in 1973. Before the introduction of the euro in 2002, futures were traded on a dozen different foreign currencies. Today's active foreign currency future markets comprise only six:

British pound	Mexican peso
Japanese yen	Canadian dollar
Australian dollar	euro

Futures are also traded on a U.S. Dollar Index. The Index is the average value (in dollars) of 6 foreign currencies, weighted by the amount of trade that each nation does with the United States. The relative weightings are euro (58 percent) Japanese yen (14 percent), British pound (12 percent), Canadian dollar (10 percent), Swedish krona (4 percent), and Swiss franc (4 percent).

The Index's relationship with the dollar is inverse; that is, when the value of the U.S. dollar declines, the value of the Index rises.

Like all index futures, the U.S. Dollar Index is broad-based. It is not designed for hedging exchange-rate risk in a single currency. However, it may be used effectively by international firms or investors with exchange-rate risk in several different foreign currencies.

As additional nations adopt the euro as their official currency, the euro itself is becoming a virtual dollar index.

Risk

Not long ago, 200 of the largest nonfinancial companies in Chicago were asked (1) whether the company had foreign exchange risk; (2) if so, whether the risk was being hedged; and (3) if so, how. Three-fourths of the companies with exchange-rate risk indicated that they hedged their exposure. Most of the hedgers were conservative in their approach, aiming to minimize foreign exchange losses or just break even. Companies with large foreign exchange exposure were twice as likely to hedge as smaller companies. Bank forward contracts were the hedging vehicles most commonly used.

Forward contracting in foreign currencies is a natural outgrowth of the relationship between a multinational bank and its commercial customer. The customer depends on the bank for a variety of services and information, including information on exchange rates. It is a logical step from buying foreign currency for delivery today to buying the same foreign currency for delivery at a later time.

As we pointed out in an earlier chapter, the forward contract offers certain relative advantages over a futures contract. The forward contract may be for any amount, of any currency, for delivery at any time. There is no explicit cash margin required, although banks may ask for compensating balances or other collateral. Futures offer other benefits. Banks generally consider $1 million as the basic unit for forward contracting. This may be more money than a small company needs. The value of most individual foreign currency futures contracts falls in the $80,000 to $100,000 range. Another major benefit of the futures contract is its flexibility. A futures position can be reduced or abandoned altogether without incurring additional transaction costs. Finally, futures may offer considerably lower transaction costs, particularly if your business is not located in one of the major financial centers.

Hedging

Foreign currency futures are the financial futures most like the traditional futures markets. Hedging is straightforward; the holder of a foreign currency bank balance would use a short futures hedge to protect against a decline in its value. An international businessman who would suffer losses if the value of a foreign currency were to rise relative to his own would use a long hedge in the foreign currency future.

An example will make this clearer. Let's say that Barbara Bradford, Inc., an American firm, imports designer buttons from Switzerland. The Bradford company buys in large quantities and resells the buttons to U.S. manufacturers of high-fashion clothes for women. The buttons are priced in Swiss francs when they are ordered. Because many of the buttons are specially made, there is often a considerable lapse of time between order and payment. Bradford has noticed that on some delayed orders, a large part of her expected profit has been lost to changes in the exchange rate.

Smart Investor Tip

Settlement of the foreign currency futures contract can be made by either futures market offset or physical delivery of the actual foreign currency.

She has just ordered 125,000 Swiss francs worth of buttons. The exchange rate for the Swiss franc at the time is .70, so she expects the buttons to cost her (125,000 francs × .70 =) $87,500. She has based resale prices to her customers on that cost. To protect herself against an increase in the price of the Swiss franc in the interim, she buys one contract of Swiss franc futures (contract size = 125,000 Swiss francs).

Six weeks later the buttons are received, and Bradford buys 125,000 Swiss francs in the cash market to pay for them. At the same time she sells her futures position. She notes with satisfaction that the hedge did its job; although the price of the Swiss franc has risen to .7324, her effective exchange rate is still .70, and her effective cost for the buttons is $87,500.

The complete hedge transaction:

Long Hedge in Swiss Franc Futures

Cash Exchange Rate			Futures	
	.7000	Now	Buys 1 SF at	.7015
	.7324	6 weeks later	Sells 1 SF at	.7339
Opportunity loss =	.0324		Gain =	.0324

Bradford actually pays 73.24 cents for each cash Swiss franc. But the gain of 3.24 cents from the long futures position fully offsets the added cost on the cash side, reducing her effective price to 70 cents per Swiss franc, which is what she expected to pay.

If she had not taken the hedge, there would have been no offset, and the cash francs would have cost her $91,550 (125,000 × .7324). This would have been $4050 more than she had anticipated; to look at it in a different light, she would have seen her profit in the transaction shrink by $4050.

Short Hedge

The Johnston Company sells personal computers to the British government. It
has just received an order for 200 units to be delivered in London in 6 months.
The British government has agreed to pay a total of 250,000 British pounds
(1250 pounds per unit) on receipt. At the current pound exchange rate of 1.74,
that's equal to $2175 U.S. for each computer, an acceptable price to the John-
ston people.

   The Johnston Company cannot put British pounds on its books. It has to
exchange them for U.S. dollars. This places the company at exchange-rate risk.
If the value of the British pound were to decline before the computers were
shipped and paid for, the effective sales price received by the Johnston Company
would be less.

   The company decides to hedge the exchange-rate risk. It does so by selling
short British pound futures. The amount to be hedged is 250,000 pounds. This
is four times the futures contract size of 62,500 pounds, so four futures contracts
are sold at $1.78. Six months later, when the computers are shipped, the cash
pound has fallen to 1.68; however, as shown in the following table, the Johnston
Company still receives an effective price of $2175 per computer:

Short Hedge in British Pound Futures

Cash Exchange Rate		*Futures*	
$1.74	Now	Sold at	$1.78
1.68	6 months later	Bought at	1.72
Opportunity loss = $ .06		Gain = $ .06	

   Each British pound the Johnston Company receives on delivery of the
computers can be exchanged in the cash market for $1.68. The 6 cents per
pound profit on the short futures position is added to that, making an effective
total of $1.74 that the Johnston Company received for each pound. The price in
U.S. dollars that the company received for each computer is calculated by multiplying $1.74 times 250,000 pounds and dividing the answer by 200. That
equals $2175.

What happens if the value of the British pound goes up? Will the Johnston Company reap a windfall gain? The answer is no. The hedge will block any windfall profits because the loss on the short futures position will offset the potential gain in the cash market, as shown in the following table:

Short Hedge in British Pound Futures

Cash Exchange Rate		*Futures*	
$1.74	Now	Sold at	$1.78
1.82	6 months later	Bought at	1.86
Apparent windfall gain = $ .08		Loss =	$ .08

The value of the British pound has risen by 8 cents. But so has the futures price. When you add up the gain in the pound and the loss on the short futures position, you find that they offset; the Johnston Company still receives $1.74 for each pound and $2175 for each computer, as it had planned.

In this case, if the Johnston Company had not put on the short hedge, it would have had no futures losses. Each pound it received would have bought $1.82 instead of $1.74, and its effective price for each computer would have been $2275 ($1.82 × 250,000 ÷ 200). That's $20,000 in additional profits, or a 4½ percent bonus. Does that mean the hedge was a bad idea? Absolutely not. That's hindsight, which is always 20/20 vision. To complain about a hedge after the fact is tantamount to begrudging your term life insurance last year because you didn't die. The hedge did its job. The cash price of $2175 for each computer was protected.

Smart Investor Tip

Dynamic hedging requires a price forecast, in order that the hedge may be held in abeyance during periods when favorable cash price movement is expected.

Dynamic Hedging

The hedging strategies discussed up to now are static. The hedges are put in place and left there until they are no longer needed. Their goals are to minimize losses or just to break even against exchange-rate movement.

Dynamic hedging is intended to take advantage of a favorable short-term movement in cash prices. The goal is to have the hedge in place only when it is beneficial.

For example, if a short hedger believes that cash prices will firm over the near term, he can close out his short futures position temporarily. When the rally (or threat of rally) subsides, he can reinstate it.

Likewise, if a long hedger expects a decline in cash prices in the next few weeks, he can sell his futures position, putting his long hedge in abeyance until the decline is over.

There is a parallel in boating. Many insurance policies on large private yachts provide for reduced premiums in the off-season, when the boat is out of the water and inactive. But it's not exactly the same. As you may have already concluded, dynamic hedging entails price risk. It leaves a cash position temporarily exposed, and it requires a price forecast. If the forecast is wrong, the tactic will generate losses, not gains.

For an example, let's assume that a corporate financial officer has just bought Treasury bonds that he plans to hold for revenue. He will need the cash in mid-November, and he will sell the bonds then. It is now early July. To protect the cash price of the bonds over the next 5 months, he sells December T-bond futures as a hedge.

If he holds his hedge until November, the results might look something like this:

Short Hedge in T-bond Futures

Cash Market			Futures Market	
Buy cash bonds at	105-07	July 6	Sell T-bond futures at	105-17
Sell cash bonds at	104-18	Nov. 12	Buy T-bond futures at	104-28
Loss	0-21		Gain	0-21

Net gain or loss = 0

But suppose he's more venturesome. By early August, he has come to believe that interest rates are going to rally over the next couple of weeks. If that were to happen, bond prices would rise, and he could save some money if his short position in bond futures were off the table then.

At this point, the corporate financial officer has to decide whether he is a shepherd or a sheep trader; whether he is the business of forecasting interest rates or guarding company funds.

He decides to take the risk. He buys bond futures to close out his short position. His position in cash bonds is now temporarily unprotected.

Let's say that he was correct in his market forecast. In the next 3 weeks, interest rates fall, bond prices rise, and on August 27 he is able to reestablish his short hedge in bond futures at a price of 106-10, which is 25 ticks (25/32) better than the price he received originally. The hedge looks different now:

Short Hedge in T-bond Futures

Cash Market			Futures Market	
Owns cash bonds at	105-07	Aug. 27	Sell T-bond futures at	106-10
Sell cash bonds at	104-18	Nov. 12	Buy T-bond futures at	104-28
Loss	0-21		Gain	1-14

Net gain = 0-25

The financial officer has improved his hedge performance. His hedge will not now just break even; it will provide him with a trading profit.

However, if he had misread the market, and interest rates had instead moved upward while his short hedge was in suspense, he would have had to reinstate his short position at a lower bond price than originally, and he would have sustained an opportunity loss.

The question that remains to be answered is whether dynamic hedging is really speculation—or, more generally, whether it is a speculative to defer any hedge because favorable movement is expected in cash prices. Speculation is usually defined as a futures position that has no cash counterpart. In this case, the situation was reversed. There was no net futures position; the exposure was entirely on the cash side.

Perhaps the question should be asked of a potential hedger who temporized and wound up sustaining a serious loss in his cash position that was entirely avoidable.

Caveat Revisited

We've said it before, and we'll say it again. To keep things simple, we have made a lot of things come out even in the examples above—hedges comprised whole numbers of futures contracts, the basis didn't change, and cash payment dates and futures delivery months coincided. This symmetry is rarely encountered in actual practice.

Stock Indexes

Futures contracts on stock indexes began trading in February 1982 on the Kansas City Board of Trade. The index underlying this ground-breaking new futures contract was the Value Line Composite Index, an unweighted average of the market prices of some 1700 stocks. This was soon followed by futures contracts on the Standard & Poor's (S&P) 500 Stock Index, the New York Stock Exchange Composite Index, and the Major Market Index.

Smart Investor Tip

Because of the virtual impossibility of delivering one share of each of several hundred stocks, settlement of stock index futures is made by cash only.

Before the behavior of these new futures could be observed, economists theorized they would spend most of their time at discounts to their underlying cash indexes. After all, stocks pay dividends; stock index futures do not. Gains in stock transactions may be deferred almost indefinitely; gains in futures must be marked to the market on December 31 each year and income taxes paid on any unrealized gains.

In fact, futures prices have been both above and below the prices of the corresponding cash indexes. The key has not been taxes or dividends but traders' expectations. When traders are bullish on the stock market, they buy stock index futures contracts, and futures move to a premium to the cash index. When traders expect lower stock prices, they sell stock index futures in anticipation, forcing futures to a discount to the cash index.

Over the years, successful new stock index futures contracts have been introduced, and older ones have fallen into disfavor. Today, the most active stock index futures contract in the world is the E-mini S&P 500. Other active U.S. stock index futures contracts include those for the S&P 500, Nikkei 225, NASDAQ 100, and the S&P MidCap.

Each index represents an average value of the stocks that are included in the index and changes every time the price of any one of the stocks changes. The indexes vary in both their composition and method of calculation. A detailed description of each index may be found in the information sheets in Chapter 17.

Using Stock Index Futures

A stock index represents the broad market. Changes in the index reflect price movement in many different stocks. The index can mask the price movement of individual stocks within it. That is, it is possible for a decline in one stock to be offset by a rise in another, and the index not to move at all. Stock index futures are therefore of little value in hedging a small portfolio comprising only a few stocks because there would be no dependable correlation between the movement of the index and the price movement in the stocks. However, stock index futures can act as an effective hedge when used to protect against price changes in a large, diverse portfolio.

Long Hedge

Suppose you were a successful private money manager with 50 percent of your assets invested in the common stocks of moderately sized U.S. companies. You know from experience that your $100 million portfolio tracks very closely with the value of the S&P MidCap 400 Stock Index. It is now February 1. In May you will receive $5 million in cash from a new client, and, in keeping with your asset allocation, you plan to put $2.5 million of it into equities. The problem is, you expect the stock market to rally substantially in the interim and the prices of the issues you intend to buy to be directly affected.

To hedge against this potential opportunity loss, you decide to buy stock index futures. Inasmuch as the value of your portfolio has a high positive correlation with the S&P MidCap Index, you use that futures contract. You choose the June maturity month because it will be more responsive to current economic forces than a more distant futures contract (and will therefore have less risk of basis change) and yet will not expire before you receive the cash.

To calculate how many futures contracts you will need, you first have to determine the value of the futures contract. You do this by multiplying the futures price by $500.

Let's say that June MidCap 400 cash index is at 645.40 and the futures are trading at 648.00. Five hundred dollar times 648.00 equals $324,000. That's the present value of one June MidCap 400 futures contract. You divide $324,000 into $2.5 million, the amount of stock to be hedged, and you get 7.71 futures contracts. Because you can't buy a fraction of a futures contract, you settle for 8 contracts.

Your forecast proves to be correct. In May, when you have the $2.5 million cash in hand, the stock market is in the middle of a rally. The S&P 400 MidCap cash index stands at 666.70, and the June futures are at 669.30. You set your stock-buying program in motion and sell your 8 June S&P MidCap 400 futures contracts.

Long Hedge in S&P MidCap 400 Futures

Cash Index			**Futures**	
S&P MidCap Index at	645.40	March 1	Buy 8 June S&P MidCap at	648.00

S&P MidCap		May	Sell 8 June S&P	
Index at	666.70		MidCap at	669.30
Opportunity loss =	21.20			Gain= 21.30

The cash S&P MidCap 400 Index rose 3.3 percent in the interim. Given that the prices of stocks that you intended to buy moved right along with the cash index, $2.5 million buys 3.3 percent less stock in May than it would have in March. However, the hedge gives all of the lost purchasing power back to you—and then some. That's because your short futures position was slightly greater than your cash position. You were, as they say in Texas, "overhedged."

The bottom line: The hedge saved you $85,200 (21.30 × $500 × 8 contracts).

Short Hedge

Bill Thompson is the financial trustee for a major eastern university. The endowment fund he controls is $26 million, about half of which is currently invested in high-quality common stocks.

Thompson does not believe in finessing the stock market. His goal is to buy and hold top-tier securities for long-term appreciation rather than to make several small trading profits. He is, however, attuned to major market swings, and he has come to the conclusion over the past few weeks that the stock market is due for a sizable correction.

He has several choices: He can sit tight and weather the storm, if any. He could sell a portion of his stocks and put the proceeds temporarily into cash or fixed-income securities. Or he could hedge his holdings with a short position in stock index futures.

Sitting tight does not appeal to him. It leaves him vulnerable to possibly deep interim losses and would look to the world as if he either didn't see the setback coming or didn't know what to do about it. Selling off part of his stock portfolio would be disruptive and create large transaction costs; if he's wrong about the decline, he could be faced with the unsavory situation of having to buy the same stocks back at higher prices.

He knows from his research that the overall value of his stock portfolio tracks very closely with the value of the Standard & Poor's (S&P) 500 Index, so S&P 500 futures would provide an effective hedge. A futures hedge would leave his stock holdings undisturbed. Transaction costs would be limited to nominal futures commissions and the opportunity cost of the margin put up. Further, a sell stop order could be used for the opening transaction, requiring prices to demonstrate a specified degree of weakness before the hedge was triggered.

He decides to hedge. But this still leaves two questions: How many futures contracts will it take and when should the hedge be put on? The first question is easily answered. The contract size for S&P 500 futures is $250 times the index.

With the index at 1400.00, for example, the value of one S&P 500 futures contract is ($250 × 1400.00 =) $350,000. Stocks comprise half of the $26 million portfolio, or $13 million. Thirteen million dollars divided by $350,000 equals about 37; that's the number of S&P 500 futures contracts needed to hedge $13 million worth of stocks.

The second question is not as straightforward, as it requires a market judgment. The stop order to initiate the hedge must be placed far enough away so as not to be triggered by random price movements but no so far that serious losses are sustained before the hedge is activated. Technical analysis can be used to good advantage in selecting the price level at which to place the resting sell stop order.

We'll assume that Thompson places his futures hedge and that his assessment was correct: The broad stock market falls some 11 percent over the next 6 weeks. The results of his hedge would be:

Short Hedge in S&P 500 Futures

Cash Index		Futures	
1400.00	Now	Sold 37 contracts at	1410.00
1246.00	6 weeks later	Current price:	1256.00
Loss = 154.00		Gain =	154.00

His portfolio, which is represented by the cash index, would have sustained short-term losses of about $1.4 million (154.00 × $250 × 37) during the period if it had not been hedged. Because there was no change in the basis in this example, the short position earned back the same amount, so his unrealized losses are, at the moment, zero. If Thompson concluded that the decline had run its course and that the prevailing uptrend was about to take hold again, he would close out his short futures position at this point, returning his stock portfolio to an unhedged status.

However, let's assume that that is not the case. New factors have entered the picture during the 6 weeks, causing our money manager to revise his outlook. He no longer considers the setback as a reaction in a bull market but as the first downward step in a new bear market. The assessment calls for him to sell his common stocks and move the money into the fixed-income sector. However, there's no need for him to "dump" his stock, as the hedge will continue to protect his holdings. He sets an orderly selling program in motion. As his portfolio of stocks is reduced, he gradually closes out his futures positions, leaving the hedge as balanced as he can, until all the stocks are sold and the last short futures position has been covered.

What would have happened if Thompson had misread the market and stock prices had continued to climb after he had placed his short hedge? Like most investment miscalculations, it would have cost him money. However, in this case the losses would be mostly ones of opportunity. He would lose the potential income that the margin money might have earned elsewhere. He would lose the gains from rising stock prices because the loss on the short futures position—as long as he has it—would cancel them out. And he would be out the brokerage commissions.

Portfolio Insurance

You don't hear much mention of portfolio insurance anymore, perhaps because the concept has proven to be so difficult to implement. But it's worth taking a look at.

Portfolio insurance is another name for dynamic asset allocation. It is also known as dynamic hedging, which you met earlier. The idea is straightforward enough. Over the years, stocks have outperformed all other liquid investment media. The goal of dynamic asset allocation is to keep money in stocks as long as stock prices are going up. When stock prices start to decline, some stocks are sold and the money moved into risk-free media. When the decline has ended and the stock market has turned up again, the stocks are repurchased.

For large portfolios, stock index futures simplify the strategy somewhat by making it unnecessary to sell and rebuy actual shares. If strategy calls for reducing equity exposure by 2 percent, for example, the portfolio manager can sell short an amount of stock index futures equal to 2 percent of the portfolio's value. That is equivalent to converting 2 percent of the portfolio to cash. When the decline subsides, the portfolio manager covers his short position in futures. The portfolio remains undisturbed. Transaction costs are also less than those incurred in selling and buying actual stock.

However, if the theory of portfolio insurance is simple, the practice is not. There are many difficult questions to be answered. The portfolio insurer must decide the minimum performance he will accept from his portfolio. He must determine what percentage of his portfolio is to be hedged and how much of a decline he will accept in portfolio value before he starts selling futures.

The strategy described above assumes that stock prices have an upward bias and that declines will be moderate and soon corrected. That may not be the case. If the market is very volatile, the portfolio insurer may be forced to sell index futures at much lower prices than he expected, receiving, as a result, little or no hedge protection.

Effective portfolio insurance requires very frequent futures transactions. The portfolio insurer must decide on the timing of his reaction to a stock market decline; will he react instantaneously, or will he wait an hour? 2 hours? until tomorrow? A lagged response may lower transactions costs in a sideways trending market, but it could prove deadly if the market falls sharply for several days in a row.

A hedge in stock index futures *options* is an alternative. Taken before the fact, it would preclude some of the foregoing problems. We discuss options in Chapter 15.

Interest Rates

On October 12, 1975, the opening bell rang on a new breed of futures. On that date, the Chicago Board of Trade began trading in the first interest rate futures contract—the Ginnie Mae.

Ginnie Mae stands for GNMA, which stands for Government National Mortgage Association, a division of the Department of Housing and Urban Development. The asset underlying this new futures contract was a certificate issued by Ginnie Mae. The certificate represented a pool of $100,000 worth of Federal Housing Administration and Veterans Administration home mortgages. Payment of principal and interest was "passed through" by Ginnie Mae to the bearer of the certificate and was guaranteed by the U.S. government.

The original Ginnie Mae futures contract was settled by the delivery of a receipt signifying ownership of a Ginnie Mae certificate. Later, when the Ginnie Mae futures market was faltering, a cash-settled contract was introduced in an attempt to revive it. It was not successful, and Ginnie Mae futures are no longer traded.

Today's interest rate futures markets can be broken down into short-term and long-term interest rates. The short-term markets comprise 2-year U.S. Treasury note futures, Eurodollar futures, 30-day Federal Funds futures, and 1-month London InterBank Offered Rate (LIBOR) futures. The long-term markets are the 5- and 10-year U.S. Treasury note futures and U.S. Treasury bond futures.

Before we talk about futures, let's take a brief look at the underlying instruments themselves.

Three- and 6-month Treasury bills are the shortest-term Treasury securities. The futures market for T-bills was once very active, but trading volume has fallen to virtually zero in recent years. Next in longevity are Treasury notes, with maturities of 2, 5, and 10 years. Annual yields are stated in the coupons they bear, and payments are made to noteholders every 6 months. Two-year treasury notes are issued monthly; 5- and 10-year Treasury notes are sold quarterly.

Treasury bonds are the longest-term Treasury security, with original maturities extending out to 30 years. U.S. Treasury bonds have historically been the international benchmark for long-term interest rates. Issuance of fixed-principal Treasury bonds was discontinued by the U.S. Treasury in October 2001, and the 10-year T-note has since assumed the mantle of bellwether. There is an active secondary market in the T-bonds outstanding.

A Eurodollar is simply a U.S. dollar on deposit in a bank outside the United States, typically in London, England. The Eurodollar market began in the late 1950s, ostensibly as a way to avoid certain domestic banking regulations, and it has grown dramatically. As mentioned earlier, 3-month Eurodollar futures were the most actively traded futures contract in the world in 2004.

The "instruments" underlying 1-month LIBOR futures and 30-day Fed Funds futures are nominal bank deposits. For 1-month LIBOR, the deposit is 3 million Eurodollars. For 30-day Fed Funds futures, it is 5 million U.S. dollars. These two relatively new futures markets provide vehicles for hedging very short-term interest-rate exposure, filling a niche in the risk spectrum that was vacant before their arrival on the scene.

The Yield Curve

No discussion of fixed-income securities is complete without mention of comparative yields. In the financial markets, *yield* refers to the rate of return on an investment. If you buy a $1000 par value U.S. Treasury bond with an 8 percent coupon, it will pay you $80 per year in interest. That dollar amount is fixed. But the market price of a Treasury bond is not fixed. It changes with market conditions. If you paid only $900 for the bond, your yield would be 8.1 percent ($80 ÷ $900). That is referred to as the bond's current yield.

There is also something called "yield to maturity." This number takes into consideration that you will receive par value ($1000) for the bond when it matures. If you bought the bond for less than par, its yield to maturity would be slightly higher than its current yield, reflecting the extra cash you will get when the bond matures. By the same token, if you bought the bond at a price above par, its yield to maturity would be less than the current yield.

Smart Investor Tip
A yield curve plots yield against time to maturity for an array of like securities.

A shorthand way to express the relationship between the yield to maturity of different securities is to plot them together on a graph. The plots are then connected to form a "curve." To be certain that it is only yields that are compared, it is necessary that the securities plotted be similar in risk, callability, conversion features, and the like. The idea is to measure yield against time to maturity, and nothing else.

Treasuries make an excellent example. Suppose the following (hypothetical) conditions pertain:

U.S. Treasury Notes and Bonds

Maturity Date		Yield to Maturity
September	2001	4.05%
February	2002	5.24%
August	2002	5.57%
November	2002	5.66%
April	2003	5.79%
October	2003	5.90%
October	2004	6.09%
May	2008	6.36%
July	2012	6.68%
March	2014	6.70%
April	2019	6.83%
June	2024	7.01%

A yield curve based on these data is shown in Figure 12.1. As you can see, short-term yields are lower than the yields further out. Yields increase as maturities lengthen, so the curve slopes upward to the right. This is referred to as a "normal" yield curve. Investors receive a greater return to compensate them for tying up their money for a longer time. Banks, which generally borrow short term and lend long term, find this a healthy economic environment.

Smart Investor Tip

Prices of fixed-income securities and interest rates are inversely related. When interest rates go up, their prices go down; when interest rates go down, their prices go up.

When short-term yields are above longer term yields, the yield curve is said to be "inverted." One of the possible causes of an inverted yield curve would be investor expectations that long-term rates are about to fall sharply. Their active buying of long-term paper drives its price up (and yield down).

The entire yield curve structure may also move up or down without changing its shape or angle, reflecting higher or lower interest rates across the board.

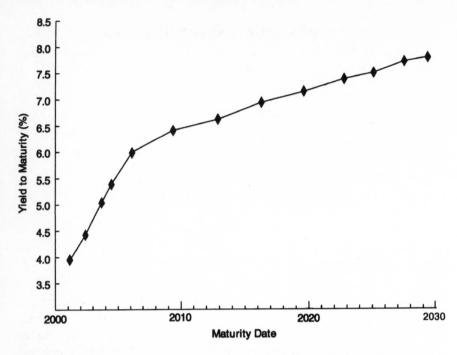

Figure 12.1   A yield curve compares securities that differ only in their time to maturity. This example is for U.S. Treasury securities and is based on the maturities and yields shown in the accompanying table. Yields increase as maturities lengthen, so the curve slopes upward to the right. This is referred to as a "normal" yield curve.

Price Up, Yield Down

Because the returns on T-notes and T-bonds are fixed dollar amounts, the only way an old note or bond can reflect current interest rates is for its market price to change. For example, an 8 percent note with $1000 par value pays $80 per year interest. That's constant. If the current rate for other investments of that same length and degree of risk is 7 percent, investors will buy the 8 percent note for its higher yield, and in so doing drive its market price up to the point ($1143) where its effective yield is 7 percent ($80 ÷ $1143 = .07).

The process works the same way in the other direction. If a note paying $80 a year is considered by the market to be overpriced (yield too low), investors will sell it and buy something else. Their selling pressure drives the price down. This effectively raises the yield because the $80 per year return does not change, as shown in the following:

$1,000 Par Value Bond with 8% Coupon		
Ambient Long-Term Interest Rate (%)	Annual Return on Bond ($)	Market Price of Bond ($)*
6	80	1333
7	80	1143
8	80	1000 (par)
9	80	888
10	80	800

*$80 divided by the interest rate.

Futures Markets

Interest rate futures markets reflect this inverse relationship. Interest rate futures express the values of the underlying instruments, not the interest rates themselves. Falling interest rates mean rising T-note, T-bond, and Eurodollar futures prices. A speculator who is looking for interest rates to go down buys interest rate futures. A speculator who expects interest rates to rise sells interest rate futures.

Price Relationships

Interest rate futures prices may be at a discount or a premium to the prices for cash instruments. These price relationships do not reflect a shortage or surplus of the cash commodity, as in the agricultural futures markets. They reflect the nature of the yield curve for the underlying cash asset. If the yield curve of the underlying cash asset is negative, with yields falling as maturities become more distant, futures prices will be at a premium to cash. If the underlying yield curve is positive (yields rising with increasing maturities), futures will trade at a discount to cash.

Arbitrage between the cash and futures markets keeps these relationships intact. The rationale is the same as that presented earlier for grains; arbitrageurs buy the cheaper asset (cash or futures) and sell the one more dear, forcing the two prices back into line. As with all futures contracts, the difference between cash and futures prices disappears as the futures contract approaches maturity. However, there are other considerations, and their complexity puts them outside the scope of our discussion here.

Hedging

A hedger who wants to protect against a rise in interest rates would take a short position in interest rate futures. For example, suppose a regional telephone company has just won a long-standing dispute with the state utilities commission. As a result, the company has been awarded damages of $5 million in state funds.

The check has just arrived. The telephone company intends to use the funds to buy a small subsidiary, but the purchase will not take place for 9 months. Until then, the comptroller intends to park the money in 2-year T-notes, which are yielding 4 percent annually. To ensure that the cash value of the 2-year T-notes does not decline while he is holding them, he decides to establish a short hedge in T-note futures.

Cash 2-year T-notes are 104-23 and June 2-year T-note futures are trading at 105-00. Because the size of the 2-year T-note futures contract is $200,000, he needs exactly 25 futures contracts for his $5 million cash position to be fully hedged.

Short Hedge in 2-Year T-Note Futures

Cash		*Futures*
T-notes at 104-23	January	Sold 25 at 105-00

On August 1, 9 months later, interest rates have indeed risen, and the market price of fixed-income securities has declined. In preparation for buying the small subsidiary, the comptroller sells the cash T-notes and closes out his short futures position.

Short Hedge in 2-Year T-Note Futures

Cash			*Futures*	
Bought T-notes at	104-23	January	Sold 25 at	105-00
Sold T-notes at	103-13	August	Bought 25 at	103-22
	−1-10			+1-10

The hedge did its job. The 1-10 fall in the cash value of the 2-year T-note was fully offset by the gains in the short futures position, protecting the comptroller's purchasing power. In addition, the comptroller received a 4 percent annual yield on the T-notes while he held them.

Convergence Cost

As we have said before, the difference between cash and futures prices tends to decrease as the futures contract approaches maturity, and the difference shrinks to near zero during the delivery period. This convergence of futures and cash prices can create windfall gains or losses for the hedger, depending on the particular situation.

Smart Investor Tip

If a short hedge is placed in a normal market (where futures prices are higher than cash), the convergence of futures and cash creates gains for the hedger.

If a short hedge is placed in a normal market (where futures prices are higher than cash), the convergence of futures on cash creates gains for the hedger. It doesn't matter whether the (short) futures price goes down or the (long) cash price goes up; both movements create gains. With a long hedge in a normal market, convergence causes losses. These effects are shown graphically in Figure 12.2

The situation is reversed in an inverted market. When futures prices are below cash, convergence of cash and futures prices creates gains for a long hedge and losses for a short hedge (see Figure 12.2).

CONVERGENCE OF CASH AND FUTURES PRICES

	SHORT HEDGE	LONG HEDGE
INVERTED MARKET	Cash (Long) ↓ Loss	Cash (Short) ↓ Gain
	Futures (Short) Loss ↑	Futures (Long) Gain ↑
NORMAL MARKET	Futures (Short) ↓ Gain	Futures (Long) ↓ Loss
	Cash (Long) Gain ↑	Cash (Short) Loss ↑

Figure 12.2 Cash and futures prices converge as futures approach maturity and are virtually equal during the delivery period. This convergence changes the basis, creating gains or losses for the hedger, depending on the situation. Long hedgers sustain convergence losses in normal markets and convergence gains in inverted markets. The reverse is true for short hedges. The effect is so strong, in fact, that short hedges may be inadvisable in a steeply inverted market. The diagram here depicts these effects graphically.

Another Example

The financial officer of a small midwestern college receives a bequest from the estate of an alumnus who has recently died. The gift is in the form of securities, specifically $1 million par value of U.S. Treasury bonds. The financial officer's long-range outlook for interest rates is higher, and he'd rather have the money in other investment media; however, the alumnus has specified in his will that the bonds are not to be sold for 1 year after his death. To protect the market value of the bonds during that time, the financial officer hedges by selling 10 T-bond futures contracts on the Chicago Board of Trade, selecting a maturity month that is beyond the 1-year waiting period.

The financial officer's forecast turns out to be correct. One year later, long-term rates have risen $1\frac{1}{2}$ percentage points, and the prices of cash T-bonds have fallen from near 100 down into the mid-80s.

The results of the hedge (no basis change) are:

Short Hedge in Treasury Bond Futures

Cash Bonds			Futures	
Own	99-22	Now	Sold 10 contracts at	98-22
Sold	84-29	1 year later	Bought 10 contracts at	83-29
	−14-25			+14-25

The $14^{25}\!/_{32}$ fall in the price of cash bonds translates to a loss of $147,800 for the $1 million portfolio. If the financial officer had not hedged the cash T-bonds, they would have lost nearly 15 percent of their value in 1 year.

Is this example realistic? It would not have been 30 years ago, when bond prices moved like turtles. It is now. In 1994, for example, Treasury bond prices tumbled 16 points. The following year they regained all the lost ground, creating a swing of $102^{4}\!/_{32}$ in a 24-month period. More recently, T-bond futures prices climbed 27 points without interruption from mid-1997 to mid-1998. They repeated the performance 4 years later, gaining 26 points from early 2002 to mid-2003.

Suggested Reading

Asset Allocation: Balancing Financial Risk, Roger C. Gibson. New York Institute of Finance, New York, 2000.

The Bond Bible, Marilyn Cohen. Prentice Hall, New York, 2000.

Inside the Financial Futures Markets, Mark J. Powers and Mark G. Castelino. Wiley, New York, 2002.

Currency Trading: How to Access and Trade the World's Biggest Market, Philip Gotthelf. Wiley, Hoboken, 2003.

Single-Stock Futures

Futures contracts in single stocks are the newest kid on the block.

The "commodity" underlying the futures contract is the common stock of a single major corporation. Single-stock futures behave characteristically. Futures prices take their cue from the cash price of the stock, but expectations can play a significant role. Arbitrageurs ensure that the futures price and the cash price of the underlying stock converge as the futures contract approaches maturity, thus enabling effective hedging. There are reduced commissions and margins on spreads.

As in other futures markets, successful futures trading requires an active cash market. There are today probably 1000 major U.S. corporations whose stock is liquid enough to potentially support a stock futures contract.

As in other futures markets, the underlying stock is subject to surprise news that can send prices reeling or soaring—the announcement of a Securities and Exchange Commission (SEC) investigation into the company's accounting practices, government disapproval of a company's potential new product, surprise news that the company is merging with another, or the company's announcement of unexpectedly good or bad earnings.

The main differences between single-stock futures and other futures markets are: (1) single-stock futures contracts are traded only electronically and (2) the minimum margin for a stock-index futures trade is fixed by U.S. government regulation at 20 percent.

History

Futures contracts on single common stocks have been traded off and on over the years, but the official architect of modern single-stock futures is generally considered to be the London International Financial Futures and Options Exchange (LIFFE), which began trading Universal Stock Futures on January 29, 2001. It is likely that single-stock futures would have been introduced earlier in the United States, but a turf war between the SEC and the Commodity Futures Trading Commission (CFTC) in the 1970s resulted in a government ban on single-stock futures that was not lifted until the year 2000.

Today, single-stock futures are traded on several exchanges around the world. The lone U.S.-based exchange for single-stock futures is OneChicago, a joint venture among CME, CBOT, and the Chicago Board Options Exhange. (NASDAQ-LIFFE, another new U.S. exchange for single-stock futures, suspended trading on December 17, 2004.) OneChicago trades futures contracts on the common stocks of 140 or so major U.S. corporations. The current names of the underlying stocks are listed in Appendix E. Also traded are futures on 15 separate Dow Jones Microsector Indexes, each of which comprises five stocks within an industry sector, and an exchange-traded fund (ETF) in diamonds.

Single-stock futures are also traded on LIFFE CONNECT, the electronic trading platform of Euronext.liffe that has been adopted by the CBOT and some other North American futures exchanges. LIFFE CONNECT trades futures contracts in some 145 international stocks, including major U.S. corporations. The underlying stocks are listed in Appendix F.

The most recent foreign arrival on our shores is Eurex U.S., a Chicago-based branch of the joint Swiss-German electronic derivatives exhange. Eurex U.S. presently trades only interest-rate and Russell Stock Index futures, but single-stock futures may be on the drawing board.

The Futures Contract

The contract size for single-stock futures contracts is 100 shares of common stock. The minimum price fluctuation for the futures contract is $0.01, which translates to a $1.00 change in the value of the contract ($.01 × 100). There are no daily limits on futures price movement.

Maturity months for futures contracts fall in the typical quarterly cycle for financial futures: March, June, September, and December. The four nearest months are listed for trading. Expiration day is the third Friday of the contract month. Settlement is by physical delivery of shares of stock, except for the Microsector Index futures on OneChicago, which are cash settled.

Initial and maintenance margin requirements for single-stock futures traded in the United States are 20 percent of the cash value of the contract.

Stock versus Futures

If you are bullish on the prospects of say, IBM, and want to effectively own the stock, you could buy the shares outright, or you could take a long position in IBM futures. (You could also buy an IBM call option, but we talk about that elsewhere.)

Let's take a look at the differences between owning the stock and owning a long futures position in the same stock. The first difference is the stock dividend. The owner of the stock gets any dividend that the stock pays; the owner of a futures position in the stock does not.

In stocks, the "uptick" rule applies. A short sale may be made only on an uptick in the price of the stock. If a stock price presses downward relentlessly, the short sale has to be put on hold. Selling short a futures contract in the stock has no such requirement.

Stock short sellers must borrow the actual shares to sell; sellers of stock futures do not. A stock position can be held indefinitely; all futures contracts eventually expire.

The holder of a stock futures position has no stock voting rights.

Finally, you get more bang for your buck in futures. The reason is capital leverage, which we have talked about before. The minimum margin for a stock purchase is 50 percent; the minimum margin for a stock futures purchase is 20 percent. With the same amount of margin money, a futures trader can effectively "own" 2½ times as much stock. Price movement in the underlying stock—up or down—is magnified 2½ times in the stock futures price.

To take an example, suppose that IBM stock and the nearby IBM futures are both trading at 80. You want to own 100 shares. You could buy IBM stock outright (50 percent margin), or you could buy one futures contract (20 percent margin).

If the price of IBM stock were to rise from $80 to, say, $84 a share, here's how the two possible investments would compare:

	Old Price	New Price	Percentage Change in Price	Change in Value	Equity	Percentage Change in Equity
IBM	80	84	+ 5.00%	+ $400	$4000	+10%
Futures	80	84	+ 5.00%	+ $400	$1600	+25%

The $4 rise in the price of the underlying stock created a gain of 10 percent in the equity of the margin stock trader. Thanks to capital leverage, the same $4 rise created a gain of 25 percent in the futures trader's equity.

The comparison is even more dramatic if you pay in full when you buy the stock:

	Old Price	New Price	Percentage Change in Price	Change in Value	Equity	Percentage Change in Equity
IBM	80	84	+ 5.00%	+ $400	$8000	+ 5%
Futures	80	84	+ 5.00%	+ $400	$1600	+ 25%

In this example, the percent gain in equity in the stock futures position was five times greater than the gain in equity in the cash stock position.

As we pointed out in Chapter 6, however, capital leverage cuts both ways. In these examples, if the price of IBM stock had gone down, losses would have been equally magnified.

The Speculator

The simplest use of a stock futures contract is for speculation; that is, to place a leveraged bet that the underlying stock will make a meaningful price move up or down.

Spread positions are also practicable, as the stocks of most industry groups tend to move together. If, for example, you believed that Morgan Stanley was to be the beneficiary of good news, news that would not affect other stocks in the investment services group, you could set up a spread to take advantage of the situation.

The spread would, of course, comprise a long position in Morgan Stanley futures and an equal short position in, say, Bear Sterns futures. As you remember from Chapter 4, regardless of the absolute change in the two stock prices, you will earn a profit in your spread position as long as the price of Morgan Stanley stock goes up more or down less than the price of Bear Sterns stock.

The Short Hedge

Using a short hedge in futures to protect a long position in a stock is a concept that we have met before, in earlier chapters. Because the futures price follows the stock price closely, losses in the stock are offset by gains in the short futures position.

Let's take an example. You own 1000 shares of Bristol Myers (BMY), and you have reason to believe that the price of the stock is in for a near-term setback.

You don't want to sell the stock itself. That would create roundtrip transaction costs and disturb your portfolio. You believe that Bristol Myers is a good long-term holding, but you'd just as soon avoid any possible losses in the next several weeks. You decide to sell futures as a hedge.

It is July. Bristol Myers stock is selling for $25.50, and the nearby December futures contract in Bristol Myers on OneChicago is selling for $25.70. (That .20 difference between the cash price and the futures price is called the *basis*. See Chapter 11.) You figure that any shakeout will be over in a couple of months, so you use September BMY futures for your hedge. (The kinds of buy and sell orders available are discussed in Chapter 7.)

Here are the numbers:

Short Hedge in Single-Stock Futures

Cash			Futures	
BMY stock	25.50	July 6	Sell 10 Sept. BMY futures	25.70
BMY stock	23.50	Sept. 3	Buy 10 Sept. BMY futures at	23.50
Paper loss =	(2.00)		Gain =	2.20

Net gain = .20

BMY stock went down as you anticipated. But the short hedge did its job—and then some. Although BMY stock lost $2.00, your futures position gained $2.20. In addition to complete hedge protection, you received a 20-cent profit on the transaction. The reason: You captured the favorable change in the basis (from −20 to 0) as the stock and futures prices converged. Without the hedge, you would have been out the full $2.00 per share. In addition, you would have lost the opportunity for the 20-cent trading profit.

What would have happened if your assessment of BMY stock had been wrong, and BMY had rallied after you put on your short hedge? Let's see:

Short Hedge in Single-Stock Futures

Cash			Futures	
BMY stock	25.50	July 6	Sell 10 Sept. BMY futures	25.70
BMY stock	26.80	July 27	Buy 10 Sept. BMY futures	27.00
Gain =	1.30		Loss =	(1.30)

Net gain/loss = 0

In this case, the short hedge worked against you. It protected you from losses if BMY stock had gone down, but it also cancelled the gains when the stock price unexpectly went up.

At this point, you would want to revaluate your outlook for BMY. If you believe a loss is still in the cards, you could leave your hedge in place. If you now think that BMY's prospects have improved, you could lift your hedge by buying 10 September BMY futures.

Your cost for the protection of the hedge? Your commissions and the opportunity cost of the margin you put up. The $1.30 gain in the stock that you missed out on is not part of the cost of the hedge. That's the cost of misjudging BMY's near-term outlook.

Long Hedge

A long hedge in single-stock futures allows you to set the purchase price of a stock now, even though you won't actually buy the stock for several days or weeks.

Let's say that you won't have the funds until a CD matures next month, but you believe that the market will rally while you're waiting, and you want to effectively buy the stock now. We'll stay with BMY:

Long Hedge in Single-Stock Futures

Cash				*Futures*	
BMY stock	25.50	July 1		Buy 10 Sept. BMY futures	25.70
BMY stock	27.80	Aug. 25		Sell 10 Sept. BMY futures	28.00
Opportunity loss =	(2.30)				Gain = 2.30

Net gain/loss = 0

The stock went up while you were waiting, as you expected, but the gains in the long futures position offset your opportunity loss in the stock. You can buy the stock now at an effective price of 25.50, the price when you initiated the long hedge.

What would happen if BMY stock went down while your long hedge was in place? Let's see:

Long Hedge in Single-Stock Futures

Cash		*Futures*	
BMY stock 25.50	July 1	Buy 10 Sept. BMY futures	25.70
BMY stock 22.80	Aug. 25	Sell 10 Sept. BMY futures	22.80
Opportunity gain = 2.70		Loss = (2.70)	

Net gain/loss = 0

On August 25, you would still buy BMY stock at 25.50, which is the price you originally sought to lock with your long hedge. The windfall gain from the unexpected decline in BMY stock while you were waiting is cancelled out by the loss in your long futures position.

These two examples demonstrate a rule that applies to all hedges:

A futures position taken to hedge against adverse movement in the cash price will generally negate any favorable movement in the cash price.

Arbitrage

Arbitrageurs (arbs) make sure that the cash price and the futures price of a stock don't wander too far apart. Their actions ensure that a stock's cash price and futures prices converge as delivery approaches. They accomplish this feat by being always ready to sell the one (stock or future) that is too dear and buy the other against it. This action puts downward price pressure on the former and upward price pressure on the latter, forcing the two prices back together.

Single-stock futures markets lend themselves well to arbitrage. For example, if futures are too high relative to the stock price, an arb would sell the futures and buy the stock. When the futures mature, he would deliver the stock against his short future position, closing it out.

How high is "too high"? The price difference must be enough to cover all of the arb's transaction costs—including the cost of carrying the stock for the interim—and also provide an increment of profit.

Conversely, if the stock price is too far above its futures price—less likely, but possible in the short term—the arb would short the stock and buy the futures. When the futures mature, he would accept delivery of the underlying stock. He would then turn around and pass that stock along to his broker to close out his short stock position.

The prerequisites for successful arbitrage are an electronic link to the markets, up-to-the-second price data for both stock and futures, low commissions, and, ideally, some sort of computer software designed to recognize and act on fleeting arbitrage opportunities.

Other Employment

Single-stock futures can also be used as surrogates for the actual stock in writing (selling) covered call options. The sale of the covered call is made against a long single-stock futures position instead of shares of the actual stock. Because the futures position is cheaper to carry than the actual stock, the potential return on the trade is improved.

Online Classes

Lind-Waldock (www.single-stock-futures.com) offers a free, 13-chapter online course devoted to single-stock futures. The course defines single-stock futures, outlines their relative benefits, explains their pricing, and describes how they may be used in several different strategies for speculation or hedging.

Also available online at the same Web site is an informative, 10-page, color brochure on single-stock futures published by OneChicago.

Suggested Reading

Single Stock Futures: An Investors Guide, Kennedy E. Mitchell. Wiley, Hoboken, NJ, 2003.

14

Money Management for Speculators

I t's difficult to say anything provocative about money management. Most advice sounds like little more than common sense. And yet it is not common. Unsuccessful futures trading can almost always be traced back to bad money management. Anyone can be wrong on the markets. To allow a mistaken futures position to wipe out your trading capital is another matter. The philosophy is summed up in an adage that's been around for so long that it can be easily overlooked:

Cut your losses short, and let your profits run.

We once knew a speculator who would close out a new position immediately if it ended the day with a loss. He might try again tomorrow, but he would not keep any new position overnight unless it settled that first day with an unrealized profit. This may be a bit extreme, but it epitomizes the philosophy.

Smart Investor Tip

Unsuccessful futures trading can almost always be traced back to bad money management.

The difficulty with closing out a losing position is that you have to admit to yourself (and to your broker) that you were wrong about the market. The larger the loss, the more egg on your face. You also convert a paper loss into a re-alized loss. Money that was only in jeopardy before is now irrevocably gone. You can no longer nurture the vain hope that the market will turn around tomorrow and bail you out.

Studies of actual trading performance conducted by the U.S. Department of Agriculture concluded that staying too long with a losing position was one of the major reasons that speculators in the study lost money. Willingness to close out a losing position early was identified as the mark of a successful futures trader.

Setting Maximum Risk

It seems out of keeping with the computer age, but simply deciding beforehand how much loss you are willing to accept in a trade will substantially increase your chances for success. The maximum acceptable loss can be expressed as an amount of money—say, $500—or as a percentage of original margin. If your unrealized loss reaches that predetermined level, you close out the position.

Using Stop Orders

The stop order is tailor-made for cutting losses short. It rests at some predeter-mined point above or below the current price level, waiting to close out the of-fending position with no further action or decision on your part. You could be on the golf course or vacationing in Europe at the time.

Smart Investor Tip

Snuffing out small losses while they are still small is the single most important precept of good futures market money management.

How do you select the price level at which to place the stop order? You can set a maximum acceptable loss, as we discussed just now. Or you could put tech-nical analysis to work for you. For example, let's say that cotton prices have staged a sustained advance over the past 8 months. You now believe that cotton has topped out and is on the threshold of a decline. You are not in the market.

The contract high in December cotton, which was set 3 weeks ago, is 68.70 cents per pound. Since then, prices have backed off a penny or so. You sell short one contract of December cotton at 67.57 and at the same time place a buy stop just above the old contract high at 68.71. If cotton prices rally to new con-tract highs, your buy stop will be activated, and you will be out of the market with a loss of about $600 plus commissions. If cotton prices fail to make new highs and the decline you anticipated begins, you will be well positioned.

Another example: You have been long one contract of December gold futures for 4 weeks and have a $2000 profit. To protect it, you intend to close out your long position if gold prices show evidence of weakening. December gold is trading at $320.50 an ounce. You decide, on the basis of technical analysis, that there is good potential support in December gold at $314.00; that if prices break below that level, the market could go much lower. You place a sell stop order at 313.90, which is one "tick" below $314.00.

If weakness sets in and your stop order is hit, it becomes a market order, and your long position is sold out immediately. If gold continues to rally and never touches 313.90, your stop order will never be activated; you would continue to accrue profits. As gold prices climb, you would move your stop order up, each time using technical analysis to help you determine the price level at which to place the stop.

As you may have noticed, the stop order—in addition to cutting losses short—also allows profits to run. Profits are not taken unless the price level stated in the stop order is reached. As long as the market is moving in a favorable direction, the futures position is left open.

Smart Investor Tip

The stop order—in addition to cutting losses short—also allows profits to run.

A good rule is that a stop-loss order (which is what we have been discussing here) is never moved in the direction of greater losses. In other words:

A sell stop-loss is never lowered; a buy stop-loss is never raised.

Raising a buy stop or lowering a sell stop is wrong on two counts. First, it demonstrates reluctance to take the loss, which is a dangerous mind-set. It also cancels what should have been a good argument for placing the stop at its original level.

Snuffing out small losses while they are still small is the single most important precept of good futures market money management. There is no recovery if you hang on stubbornly to a losing position until it has consumed most of the money you have set aside for trading, as you will have no capital left to try again. On the other hand, a series of small losses can be recouped with one good gain.

This is not to say that such stop orders always work without a hitch. Markets can be perverse. Prices have been known to back down, touch off waiting sell stops, and immediately take off on an extended rally. As we have said before, technical analysis deals with probabilities, not certainties.

Other Money Management Guidelines

Successful futures speculators generally adhere to certain other principles:

1. Diversification. If you have a large equity in the futures markets, it is wise not to place it all in one or two commodities. Unlike the stock market, the prices of most commodities move independently. It is possible for the precious metals to be rallying, the grains to be moving sideways, and the petroleum complex to be in a downtrend—all at the same time. Professional money managers who control large trading accounts will have positions in as many as 10 different futures markets, to take advantage of the fact that a setback in one may be offset by gains in another.

2. Have a Plan. When you take a futures position, consider where you are going with it. Decide how much loss you are willing to take and how much profit you expect to gain. Compare the two. Is the possible profit worth the possible loss? Some traders make a written plan, listing all the factors that bear on a particular trade. Futures positions taken on impulse have a low probability of success.

Even experienced traders can fall into the trap of acting without adequate forethought. A professional floor trader on the Chicago Board of Trade once told this true story to us. He had had a very successful day in the soybean oil pit, where he spends most of his time. He had to pass the silver pit on the way back to his office; it was still active, as it closed later than bean oil. He stopped to say something to a fellow trader there. Before long he was caught up in the buying and selling, and in just a few minutes in that unfamiliar market he lost most of what he had gained that day.

Smart Investor Tip

If the loss of the money you are using to trade would have a significant effect on your lifestyle, the money does not belong in the futures markets.

---

3. Keep Your Own Counsel. Don't underestimate yourself. If you have done your homework and made your trading decision, don't let yourself be swayed by random remarks or rumors. There is never any shortage of "expert" opinion on any topic. If conditions really change, of course you'll have to change with them. But be slow to discard the analysis you did.

4. Be Open to Divorce. Psychologists have established that most of us are vulnerable to what they call the "endowment effect." That is, people prefer the status quo even when faced with good arguments for changing it. There's not much you can do about it, except to be aware of the phenomenon when you are deciding whether to divorce yourself from a losing futures position.

5. How Much Money? Trading capital should be above and beyond the funds set aside for college, medical emergencies, and retirement. A good rule is: If the loss of the money you are using to trade would have a significant effect on your lifestyle, the money does not belong in the futures markets.

6. Try to Keep Cool. An objective, unemotional approach to the futures markets is easy to maintain—until you take a position. The stakes change when real money is involved. A loss taken on paper is philosophical. A loss taken in your bank account represents a vacation, or a new car, or a paint job for the house that you won't have.

Behavioral economists tell us that people seek to avoid loss more than they seek to make gain. A speculative futures position is a unique stress generator. It makes little difference how you're doing. If you have gains, you are concerned that you will lose them; if you have losses, you are concerned that you will have to take them. The resulting psychological pressure can lead you to cut your profits short and let your losses run, which is the exact opposite of the successful strategy discussed before.

One of the benefits of technical analysis, and one that we haven't mentioned specifically before, is that it provides an objective basis for trading decisions. It supplies a mathematical rationale for picking price objectives. It enables a trader to assign values to market strength or weakness and gives him tangible reasons for selecting one point over another to enter or leave the market. It helps maintain an objective approach.

7. Never Add to a Losing Position. The fact that the strategy has the name of "averaging down" gives it no credence. You should be closing out the offending position, not increasing it.

Profitable positions may be added to, but care must be taken not to build a top-heavy structure that will collapse at the first small decline. As an example, suppose you bought one contract of June T-bond futures at 96-10. June bonds immediately rose to 97-00. Pleased with your profits, you bought two more contracts at 97-05. The rally continued, and you jubilantly bought four more contracts at 98-12, which is where June bonds are trading now.

The following is a summary of your transactions:

Purchase	Total Number of Contracts	Average Price
Bought 1 at 96-10	1	96-10
Bought 2 at 97-05	3	96-28
Bought 4 at 98-12	7	98-00

Because you bought a larger number of contracts at each higher price, the average price of all contracts increased sharply. The average price is now only 12 ticks below the current price; any setback of more than $^{12}\!/_{32}$ would place your entire position in a loss. You would have called the market right but self-destructed in your trading strategy.

A more prudent way to add to a profitable futures position is to make each successive addition the same or smaller size than the original position. Then the average price will rise more slowly, and you will never find yourself in the situation where a small decline would cancel all your trading profits.

Professional Money Management

People who manage money for others in the futures markets fall into two categories: commodity trading advisers and commodity pool operators.

Commodity Trading Adviser

A commodity trading adviser (CTA) is defined as anyone who receives pay to counsel others on the advisability of buying and selling futures or futures options contracts. The advice can be verbal or written and includes electronic delivery.

CTAs also manage money directly, utilizing the client's power of attorney to order trades for the client's account. In this case, the CTA is required to provide the client, and the client is required to acknowledge in writing, a risk disclosure document. It spells out the financial pitfalls inherent in futures trading; discloses the business backgrounds of the CTA and his principals for the preceding 5 years; describes the trading program the CTA uses; tells how the CTA is to be paid for his services; and presents the CTA's actual trading performance for the past 5 years.

Unless he is also a futures commission merchant, the CTA cannot accept funds directly from a client. The funds must instead be sent to the futures commission merchant through whom the CTA trades and where the client's account is maintained.

CTAs who manage money directly may charge two kinds of fees. Almost all charge an incentive fee, which is based on performance and typically runs 10 percent to 25 percent of profits above the previous high "watermark." Some CTAs also charge a management fee, which is paid whether or not the account earns a profit. This is generally a fraction of a percentage per month of the funds under management. Most CTAs require a substantial amount of money to open a managed account. Successful and well-known CTAs may have minimum account sizes of $500,000 or more. The client is responsible for all losses incurred by the CTA in trading the client's account.

CTAs must be registered through the National Futures Association, a self-regulatory organization that began operation in 1982. Registration does not constitute a recommendation of the CTA but signifies only that he has met the Commodity Futures Trading Commission's general requirements concerning experience, education, business affiliations, and financial status.

Commodity Pool Operator

The commodity pool is the "mutual fund" of the futures markets. Virtually all commodity pools in the United States are organized as limited partnerships, with the commodity pool operator (CPO) acting as the general partner. The public participant in a commodity pool is a limited partner, and as such his financial risk in the enterprise is expressly limited to the capital he initially puts up. The trading adviser for a commodity pool—the one who makes the day-to-day buy and sell decisions based on market knowledge and experience—is usually a third party chosen by the general partner.

CPOs are required to deliver to each prospective limited partner and receive written acknowledgment of a comprehensive risk disclosure document. It must fully identify the pool; present the business background of the CPO and each of his principals for the past 5 years; name the trading adviser to the pool; disclose any actual or implied conflicts of interest; explain how profits are to be distributed; and show the pool's actual trading performance for its entire history or the preceding 3 years, whichever is less.

The amount of money needed to participate in a commodity pool varies from pool to pool, but it is generally much less than the minimum amounts required by CTAs. Many commodity pools are sold in units of $1000, with a minimum purchase of as few as two units.

Some commodity pools are huge, controlling millions of dollars in assets. Like any other big business, they have administrative, legal, and accounting expenses, and many pools have front-end sales charges. The risk disclosure document provided by the CPO to prospective participants is required to reveal these expenses on its front page and to state how they are to be defrayed.

A person considering joining a commodity pool should be aware of the trading programs used and the trading adviser's track record in the markets. The record should comprise real-time trading, not a hypothetical computer simulation. The performance of commodity pools varies widely. In a recent year in which the best-performing fund gained 90 percent, the worst lost more than 50 percent and was closed out. The average annual return of commodity funds over the years is probably close to 10 percent, but that doesn't mean much if you happen to be riding a tiger.

Inquiry should be made into the procedure for getting out of the pool. Many pools allow the participants to close out their accounts only on certain predetermined dates; for example, on the last day of each calendar quarter. A prospective participant should also learn the pool's policy for distributing any gains.

The principal advantages of a commodity pool are (1) limited risk and (2) the ability to achieve wide diversification and professional money management for as little as $2000 in equity.

Proprietary Trading Systems

You won't be around the futures markets long before you start to receive unsolicited mail selling books, charting services, market letters, and the like. The highest-priced items offered will be trading methods, which can have price tags of $2500 or more.

The trading method will usually have been designed and tested by a private individual, who is now offering it for sale. It is invariably based on technical analysis and may be worked by hand or by computer. Presented in the promotional copy will be a profit/loss record for the advertised method that is very successful.

The first question to ask is whether the trading performance shown in the brochure is real or theoretical. There's a vast difference between trading profits in the real world and a fictitious track record generated by simulated trades using past data.

The simulation process goes something like this: First, some trading rules are devised. They can comprise a few simple criteria or several pages of mathematical formulas. The trading rules are translated into a computer program. This program is fed into a computer along with a bank of historical data containing daily high, low, and closing prices for several futures markets. The computer simulates trading the rules over an extended period in the past. After each run, the results are examined, and the computer program is fine-tuned to optimize the gains and losses. The fine tuning often includes the addition of criteria for increasing the size of winning positions, as that has a dramatic effect on overall profits.

Smart Investor Tip

There's a vast difference between trading profits in the real world and a fictitious track record generated by simulated trades using past data.

The final program comprises a full-blown trading method that has worked extremely well in past markets. But that's not the question. No one can trade yesterday's markets. The question is, How well will the trading method work on tomorrow's markets? To protect prospective buyers of proprietary trading methods, advertisers are required by law to include in their promotional copy statements to the effect that:

- ✔ Unlike an actual performance record, simulated results do not represent actual trading.
- ✔ Because trades shown have not actually been executed, results may under- or overcompensate for certain market factors, for example, lack of liquidity.
- ✔ Simulated trading programs in general are designed with the benefit of hindsight.
- ✔ No representation is being made that any account will or is likely to achieve profits or losses similar to those shown here.

Enough said.

Suggested Reading

The Psychology of Speculation: The Human Element in Stock Market Transactions, Henry Harper. Trader Publishing, New York Institute of Finance, New York, 1926.

The Disciplined Trader: Developing Winning Attitudes, Mark Douglas. New York Institute of Finance, New York, 1990.

The Mathematics of Money Management, Ralph Vince. Wiley, New York, 1993.

Futures Options

You have just been transferred to Washington, DC. You come ahead to house hunt while your wife and children stay with her mother in San Francisco. You find the ideal house. It has just been completed and is standing empty. The price is $525,000. Concerned that the house may be sold to someone else before your wife can see it, you offer the builder $1000 for the exclusive privilege of buying the house for $525,000 at any time during the next 10 days. The builder agrees.

You have bought an option on the house. During the next 10 days, you may exercise the option and buy the house for the agreed price of $525,000. If you do not exercise the option, it will expire at the end of that time and the builder will keep your $1000.

For many years there was an over-the-counter market in options on common stock in the United States. If you're old enough, you may remember seeing the dealer's advertisements in the newspapers. The stocks on which the options were offered were usually "blue chips" like IBM, General Motors, and AT&T. The owner of the stock arranged with a private dealer to sell an option on it at an agreed price. The dealer advertised for option buyers and earned a commission on each option he sold.

Those old over-the-counter stock options were not transferable. Unless a special arrangement could be made with a dealer to take it back and resell it, there were only two courses of action open to the option buyer. If the stock price changed enough to make the option worth exercising, he could do so and acquire the stock. If not, he simply abandoned the option when it expired.

An over-the-counter market in options on futures contracts had a short, scandal-plagued life in the early 1970s. Unscrupulous dealers, promising huge possible rewards with low risk, took in millions of dollars in premiums. But they did not hold the underlying futures contracts. They held only the hope that the options they sold would never become profitable to the buyers. The game ended when a sufficient number of option buyers with winning positions went looking for their rewards and found not cashiers' checks but disconnected telephones and no forwarding addresses.

Since 1982, futures options have been traded on futures exchanges, where their financial integrity is warranted by the exchange and an option clearinghouse. The assets underlying these options are futures contracts traded on that same exchange. Exercise of the option results in the transfer of a futures position from the option seller to the option buyer at the striking price.

Exchange-traded options, in addition to enhancing investor confidence, added an important third possible course of action for option buyers and sellers. No longer were their choices limited to exercising the option or letting it expire. Like a futures contract, an exchange-traded option position can be offset with an opposing market transaction, and the option buyer or seller is then out of the market. This innovation opened the door to a dramatic increase in futures option activity.

Nuts and Bolts

The option you bought on the house in the preceding example is referred to as a *call*. A call confers the right to *buy* an asset within a certain period of time at an agreed price. (It gives you the privilege of calling the asset to you.) The $525,000 was the option's *exercise price* or *striking price*. The day the option ran out is called its *expiration date*. The $1000 you gave the builder is referred to as a *premium*.

There are also options that entitle you to sell something to someone else. These are known as *puts*. (They give you the right to put it to the other person.) The definitions of exercise price, expiration date, and premium are the same.

A futures option takes its name from the futures contract underlying it. For example, a call option on December T-bond futures with a striking price of 90-00 would be referred to as:

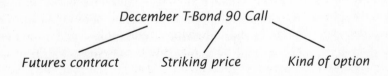

December T-Bond 90 Call

Futures contract   *Striking price*   *Kind of option*

The name of the futures contract is first. This is followed by the striking price, which is chosen by the exchange and is always a round number (no fractions); and, last, the kind of option (put or call).

If you buy a December T-bond 90 call and exercise it, you will receive from the option seller a long position in December T-bond futures at a price of 90-00.

A put option on April lean hog futures with a striking price of 62.00 cents per pound would be referred to as:

April hogs 62 put

If you bought this option and exercised it, you would receive a short position in April lean hog futures at a price of 62.00 cents per pound.

Actual Prices

We can learn a great deal by examining a typical newspaper price table for a day's trading in futures options. The following is for options on light sweet crude oil futures:

Light Sweet Crude Oil (NYM); 1000 Barrels; Dollars per Barrel						
Strike Price	Calls			Puts		
	June	July	August	June	July	August
3800	2.18	2.41	2.46	0.01	0.04	0.11
3850	1.68	1.89	2.02	0.01	0.08	0.18
3900	1.18	1.41	1.60	0.01	0.11	0.25
3950	0.65	1.01	1.35	0.04	0.22	0.41
4000	0.24	0.66	0.91	0.06	0.36	0.56
4050	0.03	0.23	0.43	0.80	0.93	1.08

Est. vol. 195,672; Wed vol. 97,223 calls, 96,449 puts.
Open interest Wed. 383,542 calls, 341,485 puts.

The line of bold type across the top of the table identifies the market. The letters "NYM" stand for New York Mercantile Exchange, where both light sweet crude oil futures and options on light sweet crude oil futures are traded. One thousand barrels is the size of the underlying futures contract. The premium for the option is—like the price of the underlying futures contract—expressed in dollars per barrel. Volume and option interest data are shown at the bottom of the table.

The far left column shows the striking prices that are currently available for trading, with the dollar sign and decimal point missing; a striking price of 3800, for example, means $38.00 per barrel. These striking prices are selected by the exchange, and new strikes will be added when necessary to keep up with the market. For example, if light sweet crude oil futures prices began to trade in the $41–$42 per barrel range, the exchange would add options with strikes of 4100 and 4150.

The next six columns show call and put settlement prices (premiums) for the various maturity months. Call prices are shown for maturities of June, July, and August. Put prices are shown for the same 3 months. Theses maturities coincide with the maturity months of their underlying futures contracts.

In many published price tables, only the three nearest option maturities are shown. When the nearest option expires, a new one is added. In mid-May, for example, when the June crude oil options mature and are taken off the board, the newspaper will add the daily prices for September puts and calls. Options with other maturities, not shown in the newspaper, may also be traded by the exchange. Crude oil futures options, for example, are traded out to 30 months ahead.

To translate the light sweet crude oil futures option premiums into dollars and cents, you have to do some arithmetic. The premium is expressed, as we said before, in dollars per barrel. The premium of 1.41 for the July 3900 call, for example, means $1.41 per barrel. This number multiplied by the contract size of 1000 barrels equals $1410. That's what it would cost you (plus commissions, of course) to buy the July light sweet crude oil 3900 call. That's the amount that would be deposited into your account if you sold short a July light sweet crude oil 3900 call.

In most futures options, the premiums are expressed in the same terms as the underlying futures markets. Premiums for sugar options are in cents per pound for 112,000 pounds; so are sugar futures. Gold option premiums and gold futures prices are both expressed in dollars per troy ounce. Options on grain futures are all based on 5000 bushels, and their premiums have fractions just like grain futures prices ($23\frac{3}{4}$, for example).

There are some exceptions. For example, futures price for T-bonds change in increments of 32nds; premiums for T-bond options change in increments of 64ths. Grain futures prices change by $\frac{1}{4}$ cent; options on them have a minimum "tick" of $\frac{1}{8}$ cent. Option premiums for the soybean complex (beans, meal, and oil) also change exactly half as fast as the prices for their underlying futures.

More Nuts and Bolts

You met some of the special terms that surround options before. We'll go over them again, and then there are a few others you should know:

✔ *Premium.* The market price of an option, paid by the option buyer and received by the option seller.

✔ *Expiration date.* The day on which an option expires. After that date the option is worthless and must be abandoned.

✔ *Exercise (striking) price.* The price at which the futures contract changes hands if the option is exercised.

Smart Investor Tip

The *premium* is the market price of an option, paid by the option buyer and received by the option seller.

Because it confers the right to obtain a long position, the value of a call option increases when the price of the underlying futures contract increases. When the call becomes profitable to exercise—that is, when it is more advantageous to exercise the call option and close out the resulting futures position than to buy the futures outright—the option is said to be *in the money*. A call is in the money, therefore, whenever the underlying futures price is above the option's strike price.

Suppose you held a December gold 325 call and December gold futures were trading at 332.70. If you exercised the call, you could acquire a long position in December gold futures at an effective price of $325 per ounce and immediately resell it at $332.70 per ounce in the open market. The relative advantage of the call would be ($332.70 – $325.00 =) $7.70 per ounce, and the call would be described as $7.70 in the money.

Smart Investor Tip

The *exercise* or *striking price* of an option is the price at which the futures contract changes hands if the option is exercised.

If the price of December gold should fall to 320.00, the call option in the previous example would be referred to as *out of the money*. It would be $5.00 per ounce cheaper to buy the futures contract directly on the exchange (320.00) than to obtain it by exercising the option (325.00).

On the rare occasions when the option's striking price and the price of the underlying futures are the same, the option is said to be *at the money*.

The mechanics of a put are just the opposite. The owner of a put has the right to sell the underlying futures contract at the striking price. Short positions gain in value when prices decline; so, therefore, does a put. A put is in the money when the underlying futures price is *below* the put's striking price because it is then more advantageous to acquire the short position via exercise than through an open futures market sale.

Suppose you owned a December T-bond 104 put and December T-bond futures were currently trading at 103-22. You could sell the futures short at 103-22 on the CBOT. But you could in effect sell December T-bond futures short at 104-00—$^{10}/_{32}$ higher—by exercising the put, so the put is in the money. If December T-bonds were to rally up to 104-12, however, it would cost you $^{12}/_{32}$ more to exercise the put than to sell short outright; the put would now be out of the money.

Option Value

Like futures prices, option prices (premiums) are established by open bids and offers on the trading floor of the exchange. If you dissect the premium, however, you find that it is not homogeneous. An option premium comprises two different kinds of value. One is *intrinsic value*; the other is *time value*.

Intrinsic value is bedrock. It is the difference between the option's striking price and the underlying futures price. It changes when the futures price changes. An option that is in the money will always have intrinsic value.

Time value is what a trader is willing to pay for the time the option has left before it expires. Time value is fleeting, ephemeral. It fades away as the days pass.

To take an example, suppose that the following conditions pertained:

Underlying futures price:	$20.00
Call option striking price:	$18.00
Call option premium:	$ 2.75

The intrinsic value of the call option is $2.00 (futures minus strike) If we take that $2.00 out of the premium, there is $0.75 left. That's time value.

Time value does not necessarily change when the underlying futures price changes. Time value reacts to the ticking of the clock. As an option approaches expiration, its time value gradually diminishes.

It follows, therefore, that the more days an option has until it matures, the greater should be its time value. We can verify this conclusion by using an excerpt from the newspaper price table presented before.

Look at the striking price of 3900. For both calls and puts, the premiums increase as the options move down the calendar. To prove that increasing time values are primarily responsible, we'll separate them out:

Crude Oil Options					
Option	Premium	Maturity	Futures Price	Intrinsic Value	Time Value
3900 calls	1.18	June	20.00	1.00	0.18
	1.41	July	20.02	1.02	0.39
	1.60	August	20.01	1.01	0.59
3900 puts	0.01	June	20.00	0.00	0.01
	0.11	July	20.02	0.00	0.11
	0.25	August	20.01	0.00	0.25

This table shows a snapshot of actual premiums for June, July, and August calls and puts on crude oil futures. The striking price for each option is $39.00 per barrel. The second and third columns show the premium for each option and its underlying futures price. The fourth column shows each option's intrinsic value (futures price minus striking price); the last column shows each option's time value (premium minus intrinsic value).

From the table, it is apparent that buyers are willing to pay more for options with longer maturities because they provide more time for the buyers' hopes to be realized. Sellers demand more for options with longer maturities because they are at risk of exercise for a greater period.

Smart Investor Tip

Buyers are willing to pay more for options with longer maturities because they provide more time for their hopes to be realized. Sellers demand more for options with longer maturities because they are at risk of exercise for a greater period.

The preceding breakdown contains other lessons. All the puts shown are out of the money, as their exercise price of 3900 is well below their underlying futures prices. Their intrinsic value is therefore zero. When an option has zero intrinsic value, its premium comprises entirely time value. And this means that if nothing else changes, the premium will drop to virtually nothing just before the option expires. That's why you sometimes hear an option referred to as a "wasting asset." The June 3900 crude oil put provides an example. This out-of-the-money option is very near expiration, and its (entirely time value) premium is only ($.01 × 1000 barrels =) $10.

Other Influences

We've seen how the time left to maturity affects an option's premium. There are two other major influences on the prices that buyers and sellers are willing to accept: the option's striking price and the volatility of the underlying futures price.

The first is self-evident. If an in-the-money 50 call has a premium of $3, the same call with striking price of 45 is going to be worth $5 more, as it has an additional $5 of intrinsic value.

This effect can be readily seen in the newspaper price table for light sweet crude oil futures options on page 143. The expiring June 3800 call would cost you 1.00 more than the June 3900 call, and that is exactly equal to the difference in their striking prices.

The effect of volatility is not as concrete but is very important. Buyers of options do so in the hope that the underlying futures price will move favorably and the option will increase in value. If the underlying futures price doesn't move, but instead trades quietly in a narrow range, buyers' hopes are dashed. Buyers are therefore willing to pay more for options on high-flying futures, and option sellers likewise insist on receiving more for them.

An extraordinary example of the effect of volatility on option premiums can be drawn from the soybean futures market in early 1988. In April, soybeans traded quietly. Then the specter of drought appeared, and the market erupted. Soybean options should therefore have had much more time value in June than they did in May, before the drought materialized. Here is the actual comparison:

Soybean Call Options					
Date	Option	Underlying Futures Price	Option Premium	Intrinsic Value	Time Value
May 5	August 675	7.08	40	33	7
June 21	September 1025	10.36	95	11	84

From May 5 to June 21, the time value of a slightly in-the-money soybean call option with 3 months to expiration increased from 7 cents to 84 cents, or 12 times over. The only factor that is significantly different between the two options is the volatility of the underlying futures contract at the time. In May volatility was normal. Six weeks later, soybean futures had soared to record highs and were swinging wildly between expanded daily price limits.

Strategies

Buying Calls

The simplest, most direct use for an option is as a straight bet on the direction of prices over the next several days or weeks. If you believe conditions are right for soybean prices to take off, you could buy a call option on a soybean futures contract. If bean prices escalate, so will the value of your option, which can then be sold at a profit.

Smart Investor Tip

The option buyer's risk is limited to the price he paid for the option. No matter how far prices go against him, the option buyer will never receive a margin call. The worst that can happen is that the option expires worthless, and the entire premium is lost.

Why would a speculator choose an option over an outright long futures position in this situation? The most important reason is *limited risk*.

The option buyer's risk is limited to the price he paid for the option. No matter how far prices go against him, the option buyer will never receive a margin call. The worst that can happen is that the option expires worthless and the entire premium is lost.

Known, limited risk makes a futures option a more conservative investment than an outright long or short futures position. The differences can be readily seen if the two are compared in three different scenarios:

Gold: Long Call Option versus Long Futures Position

DECEMBER GOLD FUTURES PRICE = 380.00
DECEMBER GOLD 380 CALL PREMIUM = 9.00

	Gold Futures		*Gold 380 Call Option*	
1. Gold futures advance	Buy at	380.00	Buy at	9.00
to 404.00	Sell at	404.00	Sell at	31.00
		+24.00		+22.00

When futures prices advanced, gains in the call option virtually kept pace with gains in the futures. The difference in profits was $2.00 per ounce. The reason? The option lost some time value while all this was going on.

The unique advantage of the call option shows in outcome No. 2, below, where gold prices fell sharply. A long position in futures would have lost 32.00, or $3200. The loss in the option was limited to $900, the premium that the option buyer paid:

	Gold Futures		**Gold 380 Call Option**	
2. Gold futures decline	Buy at	380.00	Buy at	9.00
to 348.00	Sell at	348.00	Expires worthless	
		−32.00		−9.00

Result No. 1, above, can be viewed in another light. The margin for the futures position in gold would be in the neighborhood of $3000; the rate of return on investment in the futures position is therefore $2400 ÷ $3000 = 80 percent. The premium for the option is $900 ($9.00 per ounce × 100 ounces). The rate of return on the call option is $2200 ÷ $900 = 244 percent.

Before you rush to the phone (or computer) to start taking advantage of such dramatic profit possibilities, let's add another possible outcome:

	Gold Futures		**Gold 380 Call Option**	
3. Gold futures stay	Buy at	380.00	Buy at	9.00
to 380.00	Sell at	380.00	Expires worthless	
		0.00		−9.00

Gold prices don't have to collapse for you to lose your $900 premium. All they have to do is nothing. And if the prospect of limited risk should cause you to become overconfident and buy, say, four of these options, you would have created a situation with more inherent risk than a long futures position. You could lose your entire $3600 without futures prices ever going down one tick.

Smart Investor Tip
Futures prices don't have to change for you to lose your entire premium for an out-of-the-money option. All they have to do is nothing.

In versus Out of the Money

The option bought in the last example was at the money. Its intrinsic value was (380.00 − 380.00 =) zero. The premium of 9.00 was therefore all time value, which characteristically wasted away as the option approached expiration. It's also possible, of course, to buy options that are well into or out of the money, and each strategy has its own goals and purpose.

The greatest *potential* rates of return are found in out-of-the-money options. A speculator who is convinced that futures prices are on the threshold of a powerful rally would look for likely purchase candidates among calls that currently have no intrinsic value, as they will usually provide the highest percentage return on investment if prices advance.

Example: It is early July. You have been tracking cocoa futures for some time, and your technical indicators tell you that a rally is imminent. There are options on cocoa futures, and you decide that you'd be more comfortable with their known, predetermined risk. Nearby September cocoa is trading at $1350 per ton.

The question now is, Which call option do you buy? The following table shows what's available:

Cocoa (NYBT); 10 Metric Tons; Dollars per Ton						
Strike	Calls			Puts		
Price	September	October	December	September	October	December
1250	111	148	159	1	3	14
1300	64	114	120	4	9	25
1350	27	69	88	17	24	43
1400	9	47	67	48	52	73
1450	3	29	46	83	94	103
1500	1	17	36	111	125	141

The first step is to choose an expiration month. The October calls give you a lot of time, but they're relatively expensive; the premium for the at-the-money 1350 is almost $700. The Septembers require a much smaller cash outlay, and they still have 4 weeks before they expire. You decide that's adequate time for the rally to materialize.

The next step is to choose a striking price. (For purposes of discussion, we'll say that your target for September cocoa prices is 1400.)

The 1400, 1450, and 1500 are currently well out of the money. If September cocoa futures do not go above 1500, these three options would expire worthless, and your entire investment would be lost.

As the table shows, the 1350 has the best potential return, but it too is out of the money. Its premium is 100 percent time value. If September cocoa futures stay at or below 1350 until the option expires, your entire investment would be lost here too.

At the other end of the spectrum are the 1250 and 1300. They are in the money, so virtually every point gained in September cocoa futures would also be gained in the call premium. If the underlying futures price does not change, the options will still be worth their intrinsic values at expiration. For example, if Sep-

September Call	Present Premium ($)	Premium If Futures Go to 1400 ($)	Gain (Loss) ($)	Result as % of Premium Paid
1250	111	150	390	35
1300	64	100	360	56
1350	27	50	230	85
1400	9	0	(90)	−100
1450	3	0	(30)	−100
1500	1	0	(10)	−100

tember cocoa futures are still at 1350 then, you could in the case of the 1300 retrieve $500 of your original $640 premium by selling the option for its intrinsic value. You would then be out only the lost time value of $140—plus commissions, of course.

There are other possible outcomes. If cocoa futures were suddenly to collapse to 1250 during the next month, all the options on the list would expire worthless. An unexpected rocket to $1500 per ton would cause the 1450 option—which you could have bought for $30—to be worth at least $500, a gain of 1666 percent.

The option you choose for your speculation reflects your market expectations. If you are convinced that the forthcoming rally will be powerful, you might choose an out-of-the-money call. If you believe a more modest rally is due, you might opt for a call that is currently at or in the money. The option you choose also reflects your personal tolerance for risk. The deep-out-of-the-money calls are not for you if the thought of owning them makes you uneasy.

Reason has to enter into the selection process as well. The possible results shown above for the 1300 call, for example, would require a 7.4 percent increase in cocoa futures prices in the space of about 4 weeks. If you look at a price chart, you'll see that moves of that magnitude are not extraordinary.

Example: It's mid-December. Last summer, a drought in the United States sent soybean prices to new 5-year highs. Since then, prices have come down, and you believe that the rally was badly overdone and that further declines are in store. Recent reports peg drought damage as less than originally thought. Weather in the soybean-growing areas in Brazil is excellent, and a bumper crop is expected there. Furthermore, prices have not yet reached your downside technical chart objective.

Selling soybean futures short entails more risk than you want to take, as there is still quite a bit of volatility in the market. If you're wrong and prices rally, losses could accrue quickly. You decide to buy put options instead. The following options are available:

Soybeans (CBOT); 5,000 Bushels; Cents per Bushel						
Strike	Calls			Puts		
Price	January	March	May	January	March	May
625	53¼	71	86	⅛	7¾	18
650	28	52	68½	1	14	26¾
675	7¾	39	56	1¾	24	38
700	1¼	28	47	4	38	51
725	¼	19¾	38	7¾	55	67
750	⅛	14	32	14	73	83½

March looks like the optimum expiration month. The January options are too close, and the May options are pricey; the slightly-in-the-money May 700 put has a time value of $2050. March soybean futures are currently trading at $6.90 a bushel, but you believe they could drop as low as $6.30 in the next several weeks. On that basis, let's look at a table of possible results:

Put	Present Premium ($)	Premium If Futures Fall to 6.30 ($)	Gain (Loss) ($)	Result as % of Premium Paid
March 625	387.50	0	(387.50)	−100
March 650	700	1000	300	+43
March 675	1200	2250	1050	+87
March 700	1900	3500	1600	+89
March 725	2750	4750	2000	+73
March 750	3650	6000	2350	+64

Given the foregoing scenario, the March 625 put would be out of the money at expiration and would die worthless. The rest of the puts would be in the money at expiration. The one with the best potential return is the March 700.

These conclusions assume, of course, that March soybean futures decline to 6.30 by option expiration. The March 650 and the March 675 puts would also expire worthless and their entire premiums would be lost if the underlying futures price did not move below their exercise prices by the time they expire.

Notice the effect of the relatively high price volatility left over from the drought scare. Because premiums are still carrying a lot of time value, possible percentage gains are relatively modest across the board. This kind of analysis also tells you something else that's worth knowing: that the relatively low-risk, in-the-money March 700 has the highest return if the decline you expect materializes.

Expected Return

Suppose you were offered a local lottery ticket. You have two choices. One is a chance to win $10,000, the other a chance to win $5000. Each ticket costs $5.00. The ticket seller says to you, "Which one do you want?"

You really don't have enough information to answer that question intelligently. You need to know how many tickets are going to be sold in each category, because that has a direct bearing on your chance of winning.

The same reasoning can be used in evaluating any potential investment. The *expected return* of an investment is its projected return adjusted for the probability that the result will occur. A 20 percent probability that you will make a $5000 profit has an expected return of $1000 (.20 × $5000 = $1000). A 5 percent chance at $10,000 has an expected return of only $500 (.05 × $10,000 = $500). The increase in the prize is more than offset by the decrease in the probability of winning.

Strictly speaking, the expected return is the result you would achieve in the long run, if you made the same investment many times. Selecting the alternative with the best expected return does not guarantee that you will win this time, but it does put the odds on your side.

In the preceding two examples, we chose the option expiration month by the seat of our pants. We also selected the target futures price arbitrarily. We made no allowance for the likelihood that our target futures price would be attained. We also did not consider the many other possible combinations of exercise price, expiration month, and futures price; for example, what return we expect if we bought the May 675 put and soybean futures prices fell to $6.20.

We omitted detailed discussions of these considerations in the interest of simplicity. They would be instrumental in any actual options trading program.

Selling Options

There are two strategies for the selling of a call option, and they are different.

If you own the underlying stock futures, the sale of a call option on it is considered a relatively prudent course of action. If the option is exercised, you already possess the futures position to deliver to the option buyer.

If you do not already own the underlying stock, the sold option is considered to be "uncovered" or "naked," and the transaction is deemed very risky. If the option is exercised, you have to get the long futures position then, at whatever the price.

Smart Investor Tip

Uncovered short sales of options require margin, can create margin calls, and expose the seller to virtually unlimited market risk.

Unlike the purchase of an option, there is technically no limit on how much you can lose when you sell an uncovered option.

As an example, suppose you read that Russia is planning to sell gold from its state coffers to raise cash. They've done it before, so you know that they sell the metal on the open market, and that the sale causes gold prices to ease.

It is April and gold futures are trading at $380 an ounce. Seeking income, you sell one uncovered December gold 400 call for a premium of 4.20. You receive $420.

Russia then announces that the gold sale will be temporarily delayed; gold prices start to inch upward. You decide to stick with your short option position. Three weeks later, December gold futures have rallied to $402 an ounce, and the call you sold has moved into the money and is exercised. But you don't have a long December gold futures position to deliver, so you have to get one.

You pay the current market price of $402 an ounce for your December gold futures and deliver them to the option buyer. He pays you $380 an ounce, the option's striking price. The difference is $22.00 an ounce, or $2200. From that you deduct the $420 you received when you sold the call 3 weeks ago, leaving you with a net loss of $1780.

In the ensuing weeks, the Russian gold sale is cancelled and gold futures prices creep above $420 an ounce. If you had doggedly held onto your short gold call, your market loss would now be more than $4000.

Another Point of View

The foregoing example presents the conventional wisdom about uncovered option transactions. Not everyone agrees. John Summa and Jonathan Ludlow, in their book *Options on Futures: New Trading Strategies*, aver that the market risk in an uncovered option—if properly money managed—is about the same as that of a short futures position.

Another significant fact for potential sellers of uncovered options: According to a recent 3-year study conducted by the Chicago Mercantile Exchange, 75 percent of all futures options that are held to maturity expire worthless.

An easy-to-read, self-study primer on the overall subject of options is *Profit with Options: Essential Methods for Trading Success.*

Both of the previously mentioned books are referenced at the end of this chapter.

Covered Sale

If you own the underlying futures position—for example, if you sell a silver call short and have a long position in silver futures—the sale is considered to be "covered." You need to margin the futures position, of course, but you do not need to post margin on the short call because you already have the asset (the long futures position) to deliver to the call buyer if the call is exercised. This is considered a more conservative option strategy and amenable to use by nonprofessional traders.

Suppose you bought one contract of July silver a month ago for $4.00 an ounce, and it is now trading at $4.45 an ounce. You have a profit of 45 cents an ounce. The contract size is 5000 ounces, so your profit translates to $2250. It appears that silver prices will stabilize at current levels for the next month or so. You consider selling a covered call in the hope that you can pick up the premium while you are waiting for the advance to resume.

Available silver options and their premiums are:

Silver (COMEX); 5000 Troy Ounces; Cents per Troy Ounce						
Strike	Calls			Puts		
Price	July	September	December	July	September	December
400	45.5	59.5	79.5	2.8	11.5	17.0
425	21.0	41.0	64.0	7.5	17.5	23.0
450	11.0	29.0	48.5	12.5	19.5	27.0
475	5.8	19.5	46.5	30.5	35.0	38.0
500	3.4	14.0	30.5	55.5	58.5	61.5

The July calls with striking prices of 400 and 425 are in the money. If you sell one of them, you will receive a big premium, but you also run the risk that the call will be exercised and your long position in silver futures will be called away. The July calls with striking prices of 475 and 500 are far out of the money, so there's not much chance they will ever be exercised; but they don't earn you much either. For the 475, for example, you would receive 5.8 cents times 5000 ounces, or $290.

The September calls are richer, but you believe the silver rally will resume before September, and you don't want to be exposed to possible exercise for that long.

The July 450 looks like the best compromise. You would get $550 for it ($.11 × 5000 ounces). If silver prices were to edge higher and the call were exercised, you would receive $4.50 an ounce—the striking price—for your long position in silver futures. But you would also keep the premium, which would make the effective selling price for your long position in silver futures $4.66 an ounce ($4.50 + .11). That's acceptable to you.

If you sell the 450 and it expires unexercised, you would retain the premium of $550 and still have your long futures position. That's the outcome you are hoping for.

Single Strategy

The acquisition of a futures position and the simultaneous sale of a covered call option can be treated as a trading strategy in itself. The goal is to earn most or all of the option premium. The futures position is taken to preclude the risk of being short an uncovered option. An example is given in the following:

Long Silver Futures/Short Silver Call

Futures			*Option*	
Buy September silver at	$4.45	July 2	Sell September silver 450 call for	29.0 cents
Sell September silver at	4.45	August 3	Buy September silver 450 call for	4.5
	$ 0			+24.5 cents

The call option you sold was slightly out of the money. The premium is therefore all time value. If the futures price stays flat, as it did in this case, the time value wastes away as the option approaches expiration. Your gain of 24.5 cents per ounce equates to $1225 before transaction costs.

If silver prices decline, your long futures position would begin to generate losses, and you would have a decision to make. You received a premium of 29 cents per ounce for the call when you sold it, or $1450. That provides a cushion. If you close out both positions when the loss on the futures and the premium for the option (which you will have to buy back) total $1450, you will come out close to even. Below that level, losses continue to deepen and would theoretically be limited only by a silver futures price of zero.

If silver futures advance, your long position will start to earn profits. The call premium will also go up, but it will normally increase at a slower rate because

(1) time value is eroding all the while and (2) for reasons we'll explain later, the option and futures prices don't move in lockstep at this level. At futures prices above $4.50, the call will be in the money and subject to exercise. Here's a snapshot of the situation:

Long Silver Futures/Short Silver Call

Futures			Option	
Buy September silver at	$4.45	July 2	Sell September silver 450 call for	29.0 cents
September silver at	4.90	July 21	September silver 450 call at	44.0
	+$ .45			−15.0 cents

Both positions could be closed out at this point for a gain of 30 cents an ounce. The option is well into the money now, so any further gains in futures will be fully offset by losses on the call. There is still 4 cents of time value left in the call premium; you could hang onto the covered sale in an effort to collect this, but it may not be worth it.

Exercise creates a different outcome:

Long Silver Futures/Short Silver Call

Futures			Option	
Buy September silver at	$4.45	July 2	Sell September silver 450 call for	29.0 cents
Sold September silver for	4.50	July 22	Call is exercised	
	+$ .05			+29.0 cents

In this event, your gain is 34 cents. You don't have to wait to pick up the last 4 cents of time value. The entire premium is yours immediately upon exercise.

As the preceding scenarios demonstrate, the sale of a covered call is not a neutral strategy. Gains are best when futures prices stay flat or advance. A decline in futures prices begins to eat into potential profits and could lead to involuntary closing of the two positions, or worse. The sale of a covered put against a short futures position would similarly fare better in a moderately bearish environment.

The examples here have been kept simple. There are many other considerations. Although we have omitted commissions to keep matters uncomplicated, they are not negligible, particularly for the option transactions. Proper selection of which option to sell should include a comparison of the expected returns for each striking price and maturity month. All of the examples assume that there will be no trading halts or limit moves that would prevent a trader from executing the transactions.

Environment

The preceding examples demonstrate the environment option traders seek. If buyers want options on high-flying futures, sellers of options want the underlying futures market to go to sleep. Most sellers of options do so for only one reason: to earn the premium. Risk is least if the option is simply out of the money when it expires.

For a full description of the profits and pitfalls in the sale of covered and uncovered options, the book by Lawrence G. McMillan, listed at the end of this chapter, is especially readable.

Option Spreads

So far we have talked only about net positions in options; that is, the buying or selling of calls or puts. It is also possible to establish spread positions with options. A call spread comprises a long position in one call option and a short position in a different call option. A put spread comprises a long position in one put option and a short position in a different put option. In each spread, the commodity underlying the options is the same.

> *Option spreads cost less than a net position because of the premium received for the option sold. In return, the spreader accepts a cap on the maximum profit he can earn.*

The number of possible spreading strategies with options is legion. Some are very complex. They have names like "strangle," "condor," and "butterfly." The two most popular spreads (and, not coincidentally, the two that are perhaps easiest to understand) are (1) a bullish spread constructed of two calls and (2) a bearish spread constructed of two puts. These are the only spreads we will discuss.

Bullish Call Spread

As you might surmise, a bullish call spread is established when the underlying futures price is expected to advance. The call with the lower striking price (higher premium) is bought, and the call with the higher striking price (lower premium) is sold. The two opening transactions therefore create a debit, requiring that some cash be put up; that cash is the spreader's maximum market risk.

Smart Investor Tip

In a bullish call spread, the spreader's risk is limited to the cash put up on the opening transaction.

The process is easier to see in an actual example. Let's say that you are mildly bullish on sugar. The time is early May, and the nearby July sugar No. 11 is trading around 8 cents a pound. The following options are available:

Sugar No. 11 (NYBT); 112,000 Pounds; Cents per Pound

Strike Price	Calls			Puts		
	July	October	December	July	October	December
7.50	0.84	1.17	—	0.06	0.21	—
8.00	0.51	0.86	1.07	0.18	0.40	0.48
8.50	0.26	0.61	—	0.47	0.64	—
9.00	0.14	0.45	0.66	0.82	0.99	1.07
9.50	0.08	0.32	—	1.27	1.36	—
10.00	0.05	0.25	0.39	1.76	1.79	1.80

You put on a bullish call spread by buying one July sugar 8.00 call and simultaneously selling one July sugar 8.50 call. You pay a premium of .51 (cents per pound) for the July 8.00 call and receive a premium of .26 for the July 8.50 call. Your opening debit is therefore (.51 – .26 =) .25 cents a pound. If you multiply $.0025 times the contract size of 112,000 pounds, you get $280. That is the amount of cash you have to come up with to put on the spread (we're ignoring commissions), and that is also the most you can lose.

Your maximum gain in the spread is the difference in the two striking prices, which is .50 cents per pound; .50 times the contract size of 112,000 pounds equals $560. However, you would have to deduct the $280 cash you originally put up, so the most you can net out is $280.

To get a clearer picture of how it works, let's track this spread through three possible outcomes at option expiration: maximum gain, maximum loss, and somewhere in between.

If sugar futures advance, you start to earn profits. That's why this is called a bullish spread. If sugar prices go to 9.00, as in this first outcome, you would earn the most you can from the spread: .25 cents per pound, or $280. No matter how high sugar futures climb, you will never earn more than $280 because the two premiums will go up together, and what you gain on the long position in the July 8.00 you will lose on the short position in the July 8.50. Following is the first scenario.

Bullish Call Spread

BOUGHT JULY SUGAR 8.00 CALL AT .51
SOLD JULY SUGAR 8.50 CALL AT .26

	July 8.00 Call		*July 8.50 Call*	
July sugar trading at 8.00	Bought at	.51	Sold at	.26
Outcome No. 1 July sugar climbs to 9.00	Sold at	1.00 +.49	Bought at	.50 −.24
	Net gain = .25			

Now let's look at what happens if prices fall:

	July 8.00 Call		*July 8.50 Call*	
July sugar trading at 8.00	Bought at	.51	Sold at	.26
Outcome No. 2 July sugar falls to 7.90	Expires worthless	−.51	Expires worthless	+.26
	Net loss = .25			

In this case, both options are out of the money and expire worthless. You are left with the debit in your opening transaction. No matter how far sugar prices go down, that is the most you can lose, because the two options will still expire unexercised.

If the sugar market stays relatively flat, as in outcome number 3, results from the spread will be somewhere between the maximum gain and maximum loss:

	July 8.00 Call		*July 8.50 Call*	
July sugar trading at 8.00	Bought at .51		Sold at	.26
Outcome No. 3 July sugar is at 8.17	Sold at	.17 −.34	Expires worthless	+.26
	Net loss = .08			

In this outcome, the 8.50 call is out of the money and expires worthless. The 8.00 call has a bit of intrinsic value left, so part of its original cost can be recovered by selling it. The resulting loss in the spread is .08 cents per pound, or $89.60 ($.0008 × 112,000).

You can glean from the above examples that the break-even point for the spread must be somewhere above 8.17. In fact, it is 8.25, at which point the spreader would just get back the $280 cash he put up when he established the spread:

	July 8.00 Call	*July 8.50 Call*	
July sugar trading at 8.00	Bought at .51	Sold at	.26

Outcome No. 4

July sugar is at 8.25	Sold at	.25	Expires worthless	
		−.26		+.26

$$\text{Net loss} = 0$$

You can also see that the two striking prices define the playing field. The bullish call spread gains the maximum if futures are anywhere above the higher striking price at option expiration; it loses the maximum if futures prices are anywhere below the lower striking price at option expiration.

There's one other possible outcome: If the call you sold goes into the money, it could be exercised by someone who wants to own a long futures position in July sugar. That would put an end to the spread and generate some unwanted commissions, but it would not force you into the sugar futures market. You could obtain the long futures position you need by exercising the call you bought.

Bearish Put Spread

It's mid-April. You've been following the cattle market closely, and you expect futures prices to drift lower over the next several weeks. Right now June cattle futures are trading around 71.00 cents per pound. You'd like to take a bearish position but don't want the risk of being outright short. You look into the possibility of a bearish put spread in cattle options.

The following table shows the cattle options available:

Cattle (CME); 40,000 Pounds; Cents per Pound						
Strike	Calls			Puts		
Price	June	August	October	June	August	October
68	3.80	2.10	2.45	0.20	1.85	2.65
70	2.12	1.20	1.65	0.52	2.92	3.80
72	0.85	0.60	1.05	1.25	4.35	5.15
74	0.25	0.32	0.62	2.65	6.00	—
76	0.05	0.15	0.37	4.45	—	—

You put on a bearish put spread by selling the June cattle 70 put and buying the June cattle 72 put. You pay 1.25 (cents per pound) for the June 72 and receive .52 for the June 70, creating an opening debit of .73 (1.25 − .52). That translates to $292 ($.0073 × 40,000 pounds); that's what it costs you to put on the spread, and that is the most you can lose in it.

The most you can make in the spread is the difference between the two striking prices (2.00 cents). If you subtract from that what the spread cost you (.73), you get 1.27 cents per pound as the maximum possible gain. That's $508 ($.0127 × 40,000 pounds).

Notice that the balance between risk and reward is better in this spread than it was in the sugar spread. In sugar, we risked $280 to make $280. In the cattle spread we are risking $292 to make $508.

To get a better idea of how a bearish put spread works, let's once again look at each outcome:

Bearish Put Spread

BOUGHT JUNE CATTLE 72 PUT FOR 1.25
SOLD JUNE CATTLE 70 PUT FOR .52

	June 72 Put		*June 70 Put*	
June cattle trading at 71.00	Bought at	1.25	Sold at	.52
Outcome No. 1				
June cattle falls to 69.00	Sold at	3.00	Bought at	1.00
		+1.75		−.48

Net gain = 1.27

The bearish put spread delivers its maximum gain, as you might expect, when the underlying futures prices decline. No matter how far down cattle prices go, the gain in the spread will never exceed 1.27 cents per pound, however, because the growing pluses on the June 72 side will be offset by the growing minuses on the June 70 side.

If cattle prices advance after the bearish put spread is established, losses start to accrue; the loss reaches its maximum when June cattle prices surpass 72, the higher striking price, as shown in the following:

Bearish Put Spread

BOUGHT JUNE CATTLE 72 PUT FOR 1.25
SOLD JUNE CATTLE 70 PUT FOR .52

	June 72 Put		*June 70 Put*	
June cattle trading at 71.00	Bought at	1.25	Sold at	.52

Outcome No. 2

June cattle rallies to 73.00	Expires worthless	Expires worthless
	−1.25	+.52

Net loss = .73

The loss remains at .73 cents per pound ($292.00) no matter how far cattle futures go up because at any level above 72.00, both options will still expire worthless, and the spreader will be left with his original debit.

A June cattle price somewhere between the two striking prices at option expiration will return a modest degree of loss or gain. The break-even point here is a June cattle futures price of 71.27 cents per pound, as shown next.

Bearish Put Spread

BOUGHT JUNE CATTLE 72 PUT FOR 1.25

SOLD JUNE CATTLE 70 PUT FOR .52

	June 72 Put		*June 70 Put*	
June cattle trading at 71.00	Bought at	1.25	Sold at	.52
Outcome No. 3				
June cattle is at 71.27	Sold at	.73	Expires worthless	
		−.52		+.52

Net gain or loss = 0

The June 72 put is in the money by .73 and thus can be sold to recover some of its original cost. The final result from the June 72 transactions exactly offsets the original cost of the June 70, making the spread a wash. The focal point is 71.27. As the ending June cattle price moves below that level, small gains begin to accrue. Above 71.27, losses begin.

Although we haven't mentioned it before, this spread is technically known as a bearish *vertical* spread; the one for sugar was a bullish *vertical* spread. The name derives from the fact that the maturity months are the same for both options, so they appear in the same vertical column in a newspaper table.

There are also diagonal spreads, horizontal spreads, and many others. If the subject intrigues you, the books mentioned at the end of this chapter are excellent sources.

A Word About Commissions

There are many firms selling options to public customers. They range in size from major futures commission merchants to very small firms that deal only in options. Their commission rates also vary widely. The margin for profit in option spreads is not great. As we stated earlier, the option spreader accepts a limited gain in return for a limited risk. Commission rates that are unusually high may absorb most or all of this potential gain, making the spread transaction futile.

Hedging with Options

Greek letters are used to identify various aspects of option behavior. There are several, but we will mention only one—delta—because that is the one you hear most often. Delta is a decimal that stands for an option's reaction to a change in the futures price. If the option premium goes up 1 when the futures price goes up 1, the delta is 1.00. If the option goes up .47 when the futures price goes up 1, the option's delta is .47.

It follows, then, that in-the-money options have high deltas; out-of-the-money options have low deltas.

When we were talking about out-of-the-money options, we said that one of the problems with buying them is that the underlying futures price has to move a long way before the option's premium reacts very much. Another way of saying that is: The option has a very low delta. By the same token, an option that is deep into the money will have a delta approaching 1; the option premium will change virtually dollar for dollar with changes in the futures price. An option that is at the money will normally have a delta of about .50.

Option Hedge Example

You have probably deduced that a put option would make a good short hedge. Calls may likewise be used as long hedges. There would never be a margin call. The hedger's risk is limited to the premium paid and is fully known at the outset. Except for a fractional loss in time value as the weeks pass, the option provides the same degree of price protection as the futures hedge.

If it is to serve as a hedge, the option's premium must change when the price of the underlying asset changes. In other words, the option must have a high delta (be in the money). If the option premium doesn't change when the price of the underlying asset changes, the hedge offers no protection.

The greatest advantage of an option hedge over a futures hedge occurs when the hedge was, in hindsight, not really needed. For example, let's assume that your company manufactures copper tubing for industrial use. You have enough space to keep 150,000 pounds of copper metal on hand, which is enough for 2 months' production of tubing.

Your chief financial officer tells you that signs point to much higher copper prices in the next 6 months and recommends that you buy copper ahead now. Because you don't have the facilities to store the additional metal, you buy copper futures, thereby—except for changes in the basis—"locking in" today's cash price for the metal you will buy later.

You could have bought call options on copper futures instead. If the options are in the money, their premiums will move virtually in tandem with the price of the underlying futures, and losses on the cash side would be offset by gains in the call premiums.

A numerical comparison will make the differences between the two approaches apparent:

Long Futures versus Call Option as a Hedge in Copper			
Time	Cash Market	Futures	Calls
May 1	Copper 102.50 per pound	Buy 10 December copper at 104.30	Buy 10 December copper 100 at 8.50

Following is a comparison of the three possible outcomes from each transaction:

Outcome No. 1: As Expected, Copper Prices Rise

Time	Cash Copper	December Futures		December Copper 100 Call	
May 1	102.50 cents/pound	Buy 10 at	104.30	Buy 10 at	8.50
Later	118.80 cents/pound	Sell at	120.60	Sell at	20.80
	+16.30		+16.30		+12.30

Cash copper prices went up 16.30 cents per pound. Because there was no change in the basis, futures gained the same amount. The call options did not quite keep pace, because in the interim they lost 4 cents in time value. In retrospect, futures would have provided a better hedge.

Outcome No. 2: Copper Prices Unexpectedly Decline Sharply

Time	Cash Copper	December Futures		December Copper 100 Call	
May 1	102.50 cents/pound	Buy 10 at	104.30	Buy 10 at	8.50
				Expire	
Later	89.75 cents/pound	Sell at	91.55	worthless	
	−12.75		−12.75		−8.50

Cash copper prices fell from 102.50 to 89.75, a drop of 12.75 cents. Because there was no change in the basis, futures prices also fell 12.75 cents. The loss on the long futures position thus fully offsets the lower cash price, negating the potential windfall gain. The option, however, lost only 8.50 cents, as zero was as far down as it could go. Below that, further windfall gains (in the form of lower cash copper options) were no longer offset.

In this second outcome, the effective cost of the cash copper with the futures hedge is 102.50 cents per pound. With the option hedge, the effective cost of the cash copper is the actual cost of the metal (89.75) plus the money lost on the option (8.50), or a total 98.25 cents per pound. The option was the better hedge by 4.25 cents a pound.

Another relative benefit: Falling prices would have triggered margin calls in the long futures position. There is never a margin call in a long option position.

Outcome No. 3: Copper Prices Don't Change

Time	Cash Copper	December Futures		December Copper 100 Call	
May 1	102.50 cents/pound	Buy 10 at	104.30	Buy 10 at	8.50
Later	102.50 cents/pound	Sell at	104.30	Sell at	3.00
	0		0		−5.50

If cash copper prices stay flat, you can sell the futures for what you paid and break even. The option, however, would have lost some time value as the weeks passed. If you were able to sell it for only 3.00, say, you would sustain a loss of 5.50 cents per pound (8.50 − 3.00). Futures would be a better hedge in this instance.

Smart Investor Tip

An option hedge is more effective than a futures hedge when cash prices move sharply in the direction favorable to the hedger.

There's a rough rule in all this:

A futures hedge promises to be more effective if cash prices remain unchanged or move in an adverse direction. An option hedge promises to be more effective if cash prices move sharply in a favorable direction.

Although we have only scratched the surface, this is all we are going to say about hedging with options. For further information on hedging and other strategies for these versatile trading vehicles, please refer to the following Suggested Reading list.

Suggested Reading

Options on Futures: New Trading Strategies, John Summa and Jonathan Lubow. Wiley, New York, 2002.

Options on Futures: Essential Methods for Trading Success, Lawrence G. McMillan. Wiley, New York, 2002.

16

Rules and Regulations

I t would take both hands to pick up the books of rules and regulations surrounding futures trading. Most of the regulations are grist for lawyers. But there are some rules that you should be aware of, as they could one day concern you. The Web site listed at the end of this chapter is an excellent source for more information.

Broker Qualifications

The person most people refer to as their "commodity broker" is known technically as an *Associated Person*. He works for a brokerage firm. Historically, he is the person who takes your phone calls, places your orders, reports back to you when the order is filled, and generally handles your trading account. Before he can conduct public business, he is required to demonstrate his knowledge of the field by passing the National Commodity Futures Examination (Series 3). He must also be registered with the Commodity Futures Trading Commission and be a member of the National Futures Association, which conducts a check on his background.

Discretionary Accounts

Some customers give their brokers limited power of attorney to trade the customer's account entirely at the broker's discretion, without obtaining the customer's advance approval for trades. This authority must be given to the broker in writing.

Opening An Account

A customer opening a new commodity (or options) account will be asked to fill out and sign several forms. The main purposes of these forms are to inform the customer of the risks associated with futures trading; to determine the customer's net worth and whether he is financially suited to futures trading; and to give the brokerage firm advance authority to transfer the customer's funds within the firm or to close out the customer's positions if necessary to meet a margin call in the customer's futures account.

Of these, the last may need explanation. If you remember from our earlier discussion, original margin to support an open futures position is paid by the customer to the brokerage firm and by the brokerage firm to the clearinghouse. Additional margin is called for when the customer's equity falls below a certain level.

The brokerage firm has to meet its margin calls regardless of whether the customer meets his. The authority to close out positions or transfer funds is an emergency measure designed to protect the brokerage firm from having to absorb the customer's losses. It is used as a last resort when the firm has for some reason been unable to obtain the necessary additional margin from the customer.

Errors

Mistakes are unusual, but they do happen. Stop orders get placed at the wrong levels. An intended buy order gets entered as an order to sell. A broker forgets to advise his customer that an order was filled.

There are two broad principles that govern mistakes in trading. The first is that the transaction made between the floor brokers on the exchange trading floor stands. Any adjustments will be made elsewhere. The second is that any loss arising from a broker's trading mistake is taken by the futures commission merchant (FCM) or the broker personally; any windfall gains that might come out of the error belong to the customer.

We are talking here about relatively minor adjustments. If the amount involved is large, it is possible that the customer will get into the established processes for hearing and judging grievances. These are discussed in another paragraph.

Handling Your Money

Funds held in your name by a brokerage firm (FCM) are required to be segregated from the firm's money and separately accounted for. This segregation is intended to prevent the use of your money by another customer or the firm itself. Customer funds held by a brokerage firm in excess of those needed to fulfill margin requirements may be invested by the firm in interest-bearing obligations of the United States. Interest earned on these investments flows to the brokerage firm.

Risk Disclosure

When you first open a futures or options account, you will be asked by your broker to read and sign a risk disclosure document. The purpose of the document is to advise you of the risk of loss inherent in futures and options trading and to alert you to the possibility that such trading might not be financially suitable for you. It doesn't mention all the pitfalls but is just a warning.

Reports

A great deal of money moves by word of mouth in the futures markets. You give your order to your broker verbally, and he reports its execution back to you the same way. Transactions worth hundreds of thousands of dollars are consummated in the trading pits with the wave of a hand.

Confirmation of each futures trade is required to be made to you by the following business day. If you are online with your broker, you may receive the confirmation immediately. If you get your confirmations via USPS, it will not likely arrive in your mailbox for a few days.

In either case, when you get it, check it over to make sure the numbers are correct. You will also receive a monthly statement from the FCM carrying your account. It will show current open positions, net profit or loss from positions closed during the reporting period, and the equity in your account. You should compare these data with your own records also, to make sure that they jibe.

Reparations

If you believe you have been wronged by a commodity professional and are unable to settle the matter with your broker or his firm, there are two other avenues open to you. The Commodity Futures Trading Commission (CFTC) has a reparations procedure to settle disputes over money damages between private parties. A complaint must be filed with the CFTC within 2 years of the incident causing the complaint. The complaint is heard before an administrative law judge, and his ruling may be appealed by either party. If you receive an award and it is not paid within 30 days, the CFTC can suspend the registration of the commodity professional or prohibit him from trading in all contract markets.

The National Futures Association (NFA) has two grievance procedures. Mediation is a settlement process in which the parties work together to arrive at a mutually satisfactory solution. Arbitration is an adversarial process. Complaints must be filed within 2 years of the incident causing the complaint; they may be filed online. Arbitration proceedings are informal and are conducted in a location convenient to both parties; parties may be represented by counsel if they desire. Claims for any amount may be heard, and the ruling of the arbitrator or arbitration panel cannot be appealed.

Position Limits

There are speculative position limits on most commodities. These limits describe the maximum number of open futures contracts that may be owned or controlled by one person at one time. Bona-fide hedges are exempt from speculative limits. The CFTC sets the limits on several of the agricultural markets; the exchanges themselves set the limits on the rest.

An FCM must advise the CFTC when one of its speculative accounts exceeds the limit and must continue to advise the CFTC daily until the customer's position falls back below the limit.

Floor Brokers

A floor broker cannot execute a trade for his own account while he holds the same trade for a customer's account. This prevents him from taking a small position ahead of a large order that he knows will move the market favorably.

Unless you consent, a floor broker cannot fill your order by selling to you *from* his own account or buying from you *for* his own account.

He cannot prearrange trades to avoid making them by open outcry, except under special circumstances approved by both the CFTC and the exchange.

A floor broker is not permitted to disclose orders that he holds. This stops him from tipping off other floor brokers, who could benefit by buying or selling ahead of a large order and later splitting the gains with the broker who had held the order.

Guarantees

It is against the law for a commodity professional to say that he can guarantee you against loss in any commodity transaction. Except for joint accounts, pools, or partnerships where your written permission is given, it is also illegal for him to share in either the profits or losses from your futures transactions.

Attorneys

Commodity law is highly specialized. Today, more and more law firms are establishing separate departments to deal with this rapidly growing field. Law firms that are members of the Futures Industry Association would be presumed to have an interest. Information on these firms may be obtained directly by calling or writing the Futures Industry Association at 2001 Pennsylvania Ave. NW (Suite 600), Washington, DC 20006-1807. Telephone: 202-466-5460.

Taxes

You should seek professional tax advice if you are going to be involved with futures or options, as the rules are ever changing. However, the following general guidelines apply.

As was mentioned earlier in the book, futures contracts outstanding at the end of the year are marked to the market, and income taxes are paid on unrealized gains net of unrealized losses. The effect is as if each futures contract were sold for fair market value on the last business day.

It is also important whether you file as an investor or as a trader. An investor is someone with a paying job elsewhere who buys and sells for his personal account. A trader is someone whose buying and selling are more in the nature of his main business, of the way he makes a living. The two are treated quite differently under the income tax code.

Hedges are exempt from the mark-to-market rule. A hedge is defined as a normal business transaction intended to reduce the risk of change in the cash price of property or the risk of changes in interest rates or foreign currency exchange rates.

Most gains or losses from hedging transactions are ordinary. Hedges to protect inventory, receivables, or other assets in the normal course of business—

for example, a miller hedging in wheat futures—create ordinary income or loss. However, it is possible in unusual circumstances for a hedge to create capital gains or losses. A possible example would be a foreign currency futures hedge taken to protect an investment in an overseas subsidiary.

Suggested Reading

There are two Web sites with further information about the rules and regulations surrounding the futures and options markets.

The site www.freeadvice.com/financial_law/commodities_law is general in nature. The site www.greencompany.com/traders/guides is devoted specifically to taxes and accounting.

Chapter

17

Contracts in Brief

This chapter presents basic information on the major futures markets in the United States. The markets are presented alphabetically by commodity group. Within each group the individual markets are described. Included are technical data on the futures contract itself; information about where the actual commodity is produced, who uses it, and what causes its price to change; and a listing of sources for current supply and demand information.

The following abbreviations are used to identify the major exchange on which each futures contract is traded:

CBOT—Chicago Board of Trade

COMEX—Commodity Exchange, a division of the New York Mercantile Exchange

CME—Chicago Mercantile Exchange

IMM—International Monetary Market, a division of the Chicago Mercantile Exchange

IOM—Index and Option Market of the Chicago Mercantile Exchange

KCBT—Kansas City Board of Trade

MGE—Minneapolis Grain Exchange

NYBT—New York Board of Trade

NYME—New York Mercantile Exchange

The U.S. Department of Agriculture (USDA) is the fountainhead for fundamental information about the commodities that grow, including grains, cattle and hogs, cocoa, coffee, cotton, and orange juice. Cocoa and coffee are the purview of the Foreign Agricultural Service. Information on other USDA commodities can be found under the banner of the Economic Research Service or the National Agricultural Statistical Service (NASS). The Web site http://mannlib.cornell.edu is an entree to USDA historical reports, crop forecasts, and current market data. Fundamental information on metals, currencies, energy, and the financial futures is less localized.

Each of the following individual commodity write-ups contains specific sources for fundamental information on that particular commodity. These sources include materials published by the USDA, by the exchanges where the commodity is traded, in trade publications, and by private research organizations.

Currencies

Futures contracts are traded on the British pound, Japanese yen, Swiss franc, Australian dollar, Mexican peso, Canadian dollar, and the euro. All are traded on the International Monetary Market.

Factors affecting the prices of foreign a currencies on world markets include relative rates of inflation between nations, balance of trade, interest rates, government intervention, and economic growth rate.

A high inflation rate creates distrust of a currency. A nation experiencing severe price inflation will eventually suffer a weakening of its currency in relation to that of its world neighbors. If a nation is buying more than it sells, it has an "unfavorable" balance of trade. Capital is flowing out. As a result, the demand for its currency diminishes relative to the currencies of its customers, and that causes its value to decline.

Prices for a foreign currency also reflect comparative interest rates. If a nation's interest rates are high, foreigners will invest their money there. This creates demand for the currency and will cause its value to rise relative to the currencies of nations where lower interest rates attract fewer foreign investors. A country undergoing robust economic growth similarly attracts foreign investment.

Most government actions today are taken in the name of stabilizing foreign currency relationships. This does not rule out the possibility that they may one day exercise their greater powers to impose quotas, tariffs, or embargos, or take other actions that would have a significant and immediate effect on foreign currency value.

There is also some seasonality to the demand for some foreign currencies, caused by the ebb and flow of tourist activity and imports or exports of hard goods.

Where to Find More Information

Foreign currency prices are affected in some measure by almost every economic happening. Broad sources of information on the relationship between the U.S. dollar and foreign currencies include the U.S. Department of the Treasury and the U.S. Department of Commerce in Washington, DC.

In addition, there are three informative periodicals in the field: *The Economist* (111 W. 57th Street, New York, NY 10019), published weekly; *Financial Times* (1330 Avenue of the Americas, New York, NY 10019); and *Euromoney* (Nestor House, Playhouse Yard, London EC4V 5EX, England).

A helpful book is *Currency Forecasting*, by Michael R. Rosenberg (New York Institute of Finance, 1996).

Commodity: Australian Dollar	
Delivery months: March, June, September, December	
Price in dollars and cents per Australian dollar	Exchange: CME
Minimum tick: $.0001 = $10.00	Contract size: $100,000 (Aus)

The Australian economy is prosperous and well diversified. The broad goal of Australia's fiscal policy is full employment and stable prices. This combination, plus abundant resources and a sound currency, has enabled relatively fast economic growth, and the Australian standard of living is comparable to that of other advanced nations.

Some 65 percent of Australia's land is arable. A wide range of crops is grown, including wheat, barley, oats, rice, and sugar cane. Of that group, wheat is the most important, contributing 20 percent or more to total rural export income.

Australia has long been the world's largest producer and exporter of wool. Over 90 percent of the "clip" is sent overseas in raw form (greasy wool) for processing elsewhere. Other agricultural exports include barley, sugar cane, and beef.

Mining is equally significant in earning export revenues. Australian iron ore, coal, aluminum, and copper also find their way into the holds of departing ships.

Japan has historically been Australia's largest trading partner, accounting for about one-fourth of the two-way trade.

Commodity: British Pound	
Delivery months: March, June, September, December	
Price in dollars and cents per British pound	Exchange: CME
Minimum tick: $.0002 = $12.50	Contract size: 62,500 pounds

Great Britain is a major trading country and an international center for finance and business. London is the heart of the Eurodollar market. The Bank of England is the central bank and is responsible for issuing banknotes and managing the national debt. For the past several years, Great Britain has had an "unfavorable" balance of trade; that is, it has imported more than it has sold. The pound has been allowed to float in value since June 1972. Futures prices have ranged widely in the past 30 years, from just over $1.00 to $2.60.

Commodity: Canadian Dollar

Delivery months: March, June, September, December

Price in dollars and cents per Canadian dollar   Exchange: CME

Minimum tick: $.0001 = $10.00   Contract size: $100,000 (Can)

Canada is one of the world's leading trading nations. A major exporter of agricultural products, it is also the leader (in terms of value) in seafood exports. The nation is rich in minerals, leading all others in the production of zinc and nickel. The net flow of capital between Canada and the United States has been southerly. In the 1980s, Canadian-owned investments in the United States increased 68 percent; U.S. investments in Canada during the same period rose only 30 percent.

The Canadian dollar fell from a premium to a discount to the U.S. dollar in 1976 and has never recovered. Futures prices have ranged from 63 cents (U.S.) to 89 cents in the past 15 years.

Commodity: Euro FX

Delivery months: March, June, September, December

Price in U.S. dollars and cents per euro   Exchange: CME

Full-size Futures Contract

Minimum tick: $.0001 = $12.50   Contract size: 125,000 euros

E-mini Euro FX Futures Contract

Minimum tick: $.0001 = $6.25   Contract size: 62,500 euros

The European Union (EU) is the culmination of a move toward continental unity that began with the creation of the Economic Community in 1975. The Maastricht treaty, signed by 15 nations on November 1, 1993, provided the political, economic, and legal framework for the EU. As of May 1, 2004, there are 25 member nations of the EU.

The purpose of the EU is to increase cooperation among member nations. Goals include a common foreign policy, European citizenship, a single monetary policy, a European central bank, and a common currency.

Under the Maastricht treaty, most member nations have agreed to adopt the euro as their official medium of exchange. The holdouts—Denmark, Sweden, and the United Kingdom—still conduct business in their native currencies.

Euro banknotes are issued by the European central bank in denominations of 5, 10, 20, 50, 100, 200, and 500 euros.

Euro FX futures began trading on June 20, 1998. They joined the world at a 20-cent premium to the U.S. dollar and by 2000 had descended to their historic lows near 82 cents. In early 2005, the exchange rate is back up to near $1.20.

Although the economies of the member nations of the EU represent a broad spectrum of agricultural, manufacturing, and technological goods and services, the demand for their individual currencies has not always been strong enough to support individual futures markets. For the first time, the existence of a common currency will enable the direct hedging of foreign exchange risk in each of the member countries.

Economists hope that the euro will someday attain the status of the U.S. dollar as a worldwide store of value.

Commodity: Japanese Yen

Delivery months: March, June, September, December

Price in cents per yen   Exchange: CME

Full-size Futures Contract

Minimum tick: $ .000001 = $12.50   Contract size: 12,500,000 yen

E-mini Japanese Yen Contract

Minimum tick: $ .000001 = $6.25   Contract size: 6,250,000 yen

---

The Japanese economy is one of the strongest in the world. Only the United States has a larger gross national product (GNP).

Some 70 percent of the nation is forested, and the nation is self-sufficient only in rice. Industry is therefore dependent on the importation of raw materials to produce motor vehicles, steel, machinery, chemicals, and electrical equipment.

Japan's main exports are cars, electronic devices, and computers. Japan's most important single trade partner is the United States, which takes more than one-quarter of Japan's exports.

The historic high in Japanese yen futures was set in April 1995 at about $1.26. In early 2005, the yen is trading around 94 cents, a mirror image of weakness in the U.S. dollar.

Commodity: Mexican Peso	
Delivery months: March, June, September, December	
Price in dollars and cents per peso	Exchange: CME
Minimum tick: $.0025 = $12.50	Contract size: 500,000 pesos

Since 1940, the Mexican economy has expanded at an average annual rate of 6 percent. During the 1950s and early 1960s, agriculture fueled the growth. Since then, agricultural production has slipped, while the industrial sector has increased almost 40 percent. The North American Free Trade Agreement (NAFTA) has fueled further expansion.

Field crops grown in Mexico include cotton, wheat, and corn (maize). Corn is the most important, with about half of the nation's cropland devoted to it. Mexico is self-sufficient in beef, pork, sugar, and poultry. There is some mining of gold, silver, and copper, with silver predominating.

Tourism is important and is viewed as having enormous growth potential. It now accounts for about 10 percent of the total value of foreign earnings.

Petroleum is the centerpiece of the Mexican economy. As late as 1974, Mexico was a net importer of petroleum. New discoveries, deeper exploratory wells, and nationalization of the petroleum industry have brought new oil wealth, which has the potential of financing further broad economic development.

Commodity: Swiss Franc	
Delivery months: March, June, September, December	
Price in cents per Swiss franc	Exchange: CME
Minimum tick: $.0001 = $12.50	Contract size: 125,000 francs

Switzerland's well-ordered economy reflects an extended period of peace. With no important natural resources except water power, the Swiss economy is based on diversified industry and commerce and depends heavily on foreign labor from neighboring countries. Its perennial deficit in its foreign trade account is more than offset by surpluses in banking, insurance, and tourism.

Futures prices for the Swiss franc have ranged from 35 cents to 90 cents (U.S.) over the past 15 years, with the high set in the spring of 1995.

Energy

In terms of value of the product, petroleum is the largest business in the world. Crude oil is the most active futures contract traded on a physical commodity.

Petroleum futures markets were introduced in the mid-1970s, in response to the sudden price volatility caused by Organization of Petroleum Exporting Countries (OPEC) oil embargoes in 1973 and 1974. Crude oil is the basis for all petroleum products. Once pumped to the surface, water and gas are removed, and the crude is graded for density and sulfur content. It is then transported to refining centers.

Futures are traded on light sweet crude oil, heating oil No. 2, unleaded gasoline, and natural gas. E-mini contracts are traded on light sweet crude and natural gas. (The NYME refers to these as E-miNY).

Where to Find More Information

The New York Mercantile Exchange publishes an excellent magazine, *Energy in the News.* It contains current articles on pricing and production of petroleum, futures trading, and industry background. For further information, contact the marketing department of the exchange at One North End Avenue, World Financial Center, New York, NY 10282 (telephone: 212-299-2000).

A monthly newsletter published by the American Petroleum Institute (1120 L Street NW, Washington, DC 20005) provides analysis of recent developments in the production, imports, refining, and inventories of petroleum and petroleum products. The report is also available online at www.api-ec.api.org.

International Petroleum Statistics Report, available from the U.S. Government Printing Office (Washington, DC 20402), presents data on international oil production, consumption, imports, exports, and stocks. *Petroleum Marketing Monthly*, from the same source, provides current information about a variety of petroleum products. Both are available online: the first at www.eldis.org; the second at eia.doe.gov.

Commodity: Light Sweet Crude Oil

Delivery months: 30 consecutive months + long-dated futures

Price in dollar and cents per barrel   Exchange: NYME

Full-size Futures Contract

Minimum tick: 1 cent = $10.00   Contract size: 1,000 barrels

E-miNY Crude Oil Futures Contract

Minimum tick: 2½ cents = $12.50   Contract size: 500 barrels

Demand for crude oil derives mainly from refineries, which "crack" it into several different by-products. The most important of these are motor gasoline, heating oil, jet fuel (kerosene), diesel oil, and propane. In fact, the first three account for some 80 percent of all refinery output in the United States.

Because its demand is derived, price factors for crude oil are really those of its by-products. A series of cold winters, a significant increase in automobile use, or a new fuel-saving wide-body airplane would all influence crude oil prices in the long run. The most visible short-term price factors are OPEC efforts to reduce production and thereby raise prices.

Light sweet crudes are preferred by refiners because of their relatively high yields of high-value products such as gasoline, jet fuel, and heating oil.

Cash crude oil transactions may take place at several locations around the world. In the United States, the futures contract's delivery point is Cushing, Oklahoma.

Commodity: Gasoline (unleaded)

Delivery months: 12 consecutive months

Price in dollars and cents per gallon   Exchange: NYME

Minimum tick: $1/100$ cent = $4.20   Contract size: 42,000 gallons

---

Gasoline's principal use is as fuel for private automobiles, and its nature varies from one section of the country to another and from one season to another, to reflect driving conditions. The strongest seasonal demand is during the summer months. Prior to 1974, refiners added tetraethyl lead to their gasoline to improve octane ratings. Virtually no leaded gasoline is produced in the United States today.

The popularity of automobile travel is a major factor in the demand for gasoline. Retail gasoline prices are slow to respond to changes in its production costs. Likewise, gasoline demand is relatively inelastic; that is, even hefty increases in prices at the pump don't seem to have much effect on automobile use.

Gasoline futures are part of the "crack" spread, whereby a refiner buys crude oil futures, sells gasoline futures, and thus establishes in advance his profit margin for that part of the refining process.

Commodity: Heating Oil No. 2

Delivery months: 18 consecutive months

Price in dollars and cents per gallon   Exchange: NYME

Minimum tick: $1/100$ cent = $4.20   Contract size: 42,000 gallons

Heating oil accounts for 25 percent of the yield of a barrel of crude oil.

The principal use of heating oil is in furnaces to warm residential and commercial buildings. Ninety percent of heating oil supplies come from domestic refinery production; the remainder comes from imports and inventory.

There is a strong seasonal tendency in cash prices for heating oil. Stored supplies tend to build up in the fall and are depleted during the winter heating season. Prices tend to firm with the arrival of frost. Increases or declines in the price of the source—crude oil—also eventually pass through to the price of heating oil.

Demand for heating oil is relatively inelastic, although consumers will lower their thermostats when prices are extremely high. Persistent high petroleum prices encourage the development and use of alternate heating means, such as electricity or natural gas.

Because of its high positive price correlation with its by-products, crude oil futures provide effective cross-hedges for actual diesel fuel and jet fuel.

The heating oil futures contract on the New York Mercantile Exchange calls for delivery in New York harbor. Since futures began trading in late 1978, prices have ranged from a low of 30 cents a gallon to recent historic highs near $1.70 a gallon. Heating oil futures are part of the "crack" spread, whereby a refiner buys crude oil futures, sells heating oil futures, and thus establishes in advance his profit margin for that part of the refining process.

Commodity: Natural Gas

Delivery months: 72 consecutive months

Price in dollar and cents per MMBtu   Exchange: NYME

Full-size Futures Contract

Minimum tick: $\frac{1}{10}$ cent = $10.00   Contract size: 10,000 million MMBtu

E-miNY Natural Gas Futures Contract

Minimum tick: $\frac{1}{2}$ cent = $25.00   Contract size: 5000 million MMBtu

---

Natural gas is found throughout the world. Leading producers, in order of their importance, are the United States, the Russian republics, Canada, Romania, Mexico, Italy, and Venezuela. The United States accounts for about one-fourth of world production and use.

Natural gas is formed deep within the earth by the decay of organic matter under heat and pressure from many layers of overlying rock and sediment. It is obtained by drilling. Because of its relatively high transportation cost, most natural gas (78 percent) is consumed in the country where it is produced. In the United States, it is transported to end users through a network of intra- and interstate pipelines.

As it is found, natural gas is composed of several gases and water. The natural gas delivered to your home by the local gas company has been refined to 93 percent methane, which is colorless and odorless. Sulfur compounds called mercaptans are added to create an odor to warn of gas leaks.

Natural gas is used as a fuel to produce heat and light, and as a raw material in the making of antifreeze, detergents, pesticides, plastics, and other materials. The major benefits of natural gas as an energy source are that it burns cleanly, producing low levels of emissions and pollutants, and that it is in abundant supply. Recoverable reserves in the lower 48 states are estimated to be enough for 62 years at current rates of use and production.

Natural gas accounts for about one-fourth of total energy consumption in the United States. Its use is split fairly evenly between heating homes and offices and firing industry and electric utilities. Comparative demands between the two sectors are mirror images; residential use tapers off in warm weather, while consumption by electric utilities rises sharply to satisfy the needs of air conditioners.

Before 1978, the natural gas market was largely government controlled. Prices were stable and contracts were long term. In that year, the Natural Gas Policy Act was passed, deregulating the industry. That action freed natural gas prices, opened up active competition, and set the stage for a futures market that could be used by producers, pipelines, and end users of natural gas to hedge the new price risks.

The natural gas futures contract was launched by the New York Mercantile Exchange on April 3, 1990. Prices have ranged widely, from $1.00 to $11.90 per MMBtu. Deliveries against the futures contract are made at the Sabine Pipeline Company's Henry Hub near Erath, Louisiana.

Foods and Fibers

Included in the category of foods and fibers are cocoa, coffee, sugar, cotton, and orange juice. Futures contracts for all of these commodities are traded on the New York Board of Trade (NYBT).

Commodity: Cocoa	
Delivery months: March, May, July, September, December	
Price in dollars per metric ton	Exchange: NYBT
Minimum tick: $1.00 = $10.00	Contract size: 10 metric tons (22,046 pounds)

Cocoa production is centered in Africa, where the leading producer is the Ivory Coast. Cocoa is also grown in Brazil, Ghana, and Nigeria. About 75 percent of the world crop comes to harvest in the 5-month period from October to March. A smaller harvest occurs in the May–July period. The principal use of cocoa is the making of confections. The United States is the leading consumer; Germany is second.

Cocoa futures have traded in a broad range. Since 1965, prices have been as low as $500 per ton and as high as $5400 a ton, the latter an extraordinary peak reached in 1977. The International Cocoa Agreement (ICA), formed in 1980, attempted unsuccessfully to control prices by buying or selling buffer stocks.

Seasonal influences cause prices to set highs in summer and again in late fall. Prices are usually lowest in the first quarter. Real or rumored changes in supply caused by such incidents as price fixing, crop disease, hot and dry summer growing weather, or shipping disruptions have the most direct effect on price levels. However, the rugged terrain in which cocoa is grown and the fact that it is produced almost exclusively in developing nations make communications difficult. Information about the size of the crop, its welfare, and the level of stockpiles is hard to get and not always reliable.

One measure of consumption is the grinding of the processed cocoa beans to cocoa powder, which is widely reported. Over the longer term, changes in disposable income also affect the price of cocoa, as manufacturers generally respond to lower chocolate consumption by reducing the amount of chocolate in their confections.

Where to Find More Information

The NYBT publishes reports on the cocoa market. These include the level of warehouse stocks, spot prices, news that affects cocoa prices, and the overall economic outlook for cocoa. *Tropical Products*, published four times a year by the FAS, provides data on cocoa world production and the international supply and demand situation for this exotic crop.

Commodity: Coffee	
Delivery months: March, May, July, September, December	
Price in dollars and cents per pound	Exchange: NYBT
Minimum tick: $5/100$ cent = $18.75	Contract size: 37,500 pounds in about 250 bags

Although many nations grow coffee, Brazil and Colombia are the most important producers. Brazil's main coffee harvesting season is April to September; Colombia's is October to March. The United States is the world's largest single importer of the breakfast beverage, followed closely by Europe. The most popular are the mild coffees from Colombia, and they also usually top the price list. Robusta coffee from the Ivory Coast has been growing in importance in recent years, reflecting its use for instant coffees.

Coffee is a weather market. Winter in Latin America coincides with summer in the Northern Hemisphere, and the threat of tree-damaging frost in June and July has been known to send futures prices rocketing upward. Drought has also played a part. Since 1975, futures prices have ranged from 45 cents a pound to $3.40 a pound, a swing of some 755 percent.

Other factors influencing coffee prices are the quantities of green coffee on hand, labor unrest in exporting countries that leaves coffee sitting on the dock, overt steps taken by the governments of producing countries to control coffee production and prices, and insect damage to the growing crop.

On a longer-term basis, consumer preferences are also important. Although coffee consumption has a reputation of staying high in spite of sharp price increases from time to time, there has been a long-term trend toward less coffee drinking in the United States in recent years.

Where to Find More Information

The USDA publishes several sources of current information on coffee. They include *Foreign Agricultural Trade of the U.S.A.*, put out by the Economic Research Service (ERS), and *Foreign Agriculture*. Coffee production is estimated and reported by ERS in January and August each year. As with cocoa, the NYBT is a good source of up-to-date supply and demand information.

Commodity: Cotton	
Delivery months: March, May, July, October, December	
Price in cents per pound	Exchange: NYBT
Minimum tick: $\frac{1}{100}$ cent = $5.00	Contract size: 50,000 pounds = 100 bales

Cotton is grown in several countries, including China, India, Brazil, Pakistan, Egypt, Turkey, the United States, and the Russian republics. The United States and the former USSR have historically been the world's leading producers. Growing areas in the United States are, in order of importance, Texas, California, Mississippi, Arizona, and Arkansas. Planting starts as early as February, although the bulk of the U.S. cotton crop is planted in April. Harvesting is done mainly in October and November.

The United States is the largest cotton consumer in the world. About half of the cotton consumed in the United States is used to make apparel. The rest finds its way into sheets, pillowcases, towels, and other industrial and household uses. Cotton exports from the United States are a major factor in world markets and are highest in the first quarter. Consumption by cotton mills peaks in the fall as the new crop arrives, then tapers off toward spring.

Over the past 30 years, cotton futures prices have ranged from a low of 30 cents a pound to a high of $1.15 a pound. On a seasonal basis, spot prices for combed and cleaned cotton are usually highest in the spring. Nonseasonal factors would include the level of government stockpiles, the government loan level for cotton, and actions taken by foreign cotton producers to control prices or supplies. However, the overwhelming price determinants are the price of U.S. cotton relative to the prices of foreign cotton and synthetic fibers, and consumer preferences, such as the continuing popularity of all-cotton denim clothing.

Where to Find More Information

The USDA publishes the weekly *Cotton Market Review* and the *Cotton & Wool Situation*. USDA cotton production estimates are released monthly. The *Cotton and Wool Yearbook*, published each November, contains statistical information on domestic and world cotton production, consumption, exports, use, and prices.

Other sources comprise the reports of the NYBT and monthly data published by the U.S. Census Bureau on cotton consumption and mill margins.

Commodity: Orange Juice (Frozen Concentrated)	
Delivery months: January, March, May, July, September, November	
Price in cents per pound	Exchange: NYBT
Minimum tick: $\frac{5}{100}$ cent = $7.50	Contract size: 15,000 pounds

Florida is the home of citrus in the United States, and more than 75 percent of its orange crop is processed into frozen concentrated orange juice (FCOJ). The most important harvest periods are the month of January and the period from mid-April to mid-June; the latter is when the Valencia oranges, prized for their flavor, are gathered.

FCOJ is the quintessential weather market. Temperatures below 28°F damage the oranges; three degrees less, and the trees also start to suffer. Since

1900 there have been some 35 major cold spells (26°F for 2 to 3 hours) in the Florida Orange Belt. Most freezes have occurred in December and January, but they have come as early as November and as late as March. Damage has ranged from a slight loss of fruit to the destruction of a large number of trees. Even the threat of a cold spell in growing regions can start FCOJ futures prices climbing.

Price influences on the demand side include government buying of orange juice for distribution in school lunch programs and the popularity of substitute soft drinks or breakfast beverages.

FCOJ futures prices have at times reacted sharply to the first official estimate of the current Florida orange crop, issued by the USDA in October.

Where to Find More Information

The USDA provides two sources of current information: ERS reports of estimated orange production and juice yield, which are issued monthly (except in August), and NASS's *Citrus Fruits*, an annual report that summarizes acreage, yield, production, use, price, and the total value of the current and previous year's orange crop. Information on current orange inventory and processing is also published by the NYBT.

The Florida Citrus Processors Association (P.O. Box 780, Winter Haven, FL 33882), a voluntary organization of citrus growers and processors, provides an array of current statistical information on oranges, including weekly reports of FCOJ stocks on hand, the movement of FCOJ into food stores, crop estimates, and foreign imports of oranges.

Commodity: Sugar	
Delivery months: March, May, July, October	
Price in cents per pound	Exchange: NYBT
Minimum tick: $\frac{1}{100}$ cent = $11.20	Contract size: 112,000 pounds

Many countries produce sugar. Sugar cane, grown mainly in tropical regions, is a perennial. Sugar beets, which produce an identical sweetener, thrive in more varied climes and need to be replanted each year. Cane is the predominant source.

Brazil, China, India, and the European Union are the leading producers of sugar, accounting for more than 30 percent of total world output. Major importers of sugar are the United States, Japan, the Russian republics, South Korea, and the European Union member countries. In the United States, purchases for home use account for 25 percent of consumption. Bottlers of soft drinks, bakeries, and candy makers take the rest.

Factors affecting sugar prices include weather in growing regions, stockpiles of sugar on hand, and government actions taken to prop up prices. An International Sugar Agreement (ISA) was concluded between some of the producing nations in 1978, in an attempt to control sugar prices with quotas and stockpiling measures. It has been ineffectual.

Demand for sugar has grown consistently over the years, reflecting a growing world population and increasing standards of living in developing nations. Whether this increase in demand will continue depends in large part on the extent of use of artificial sweeteners in soft drinks and confections.

The NYBT lists two futures contracts: sugar No. 11, which is world sugar and trades actively, and sugar No. 14, which is based on the price-regulated domestic sugar market and seldom has much of a following. Only about 10 to 15 percent of the sugar produced enters the "free" world market, so relatively small changes in the supply of sugar can have a sharp impact on world sugar prices.

Where to Find More Information

The FAS publishes two annuals: *World Sugar Situation*, which shows levels and changes in world production and consumption of sugar; and *Situation and Outlook in Selected Countries*, which covers all major sugar exporting and importing nations.

The USDA publishes the monthly *Crop Production Reports* for sugar beets and cane. There's a *Prospective Plantings* report for sugar beets in March and an *Acreage* report for cane in June. They provide early indications of the forthcoming world supply of sugar.

A private statistical organization is F.O. Licht, a German firm. Licht's quarterly *International Sugar and Sweetener Report* presents data on the level of sugar stocks, trends in sugar prices, and the overall supply and demand situation in world sugar. It is available from F.O. Licht, 80 Calverly Road, Tunbridge Wells, Kent, TN1 2UN, England.

Grains

Active grain futures markets include corn, wheat, and oats. Though classified as oilseeds, soybeans and their by-products (soybean oil and soybean meal) are also generally included in this group. Grain futures are traded on the Chicago Board of Trade, the Kansas City Board of Trade, and the Minneapolis Grain Exchange. They are also traded on the Winnipeg (Canada) Commodity Exchange.

In addition to the data shown, the Chicago Board of Trade also trades mini-size contracts in corn, wheat, and soybeans. The mini-contracts comprise 1000 bushels, tick in one-eighths, and trade only by open outcry.

Full-size grain futures contracts also trade electronically after hours, from about 7:30 p.m. to 6:00 a.m. CST, Sunday through Friday.

Some USDA publications cover more than one agricultural field crop. *Crop Production* is a monthly publication and its coverage varies with the time of the year. Regular coverage of corn, soybeans, and wheat starts in August. *Prospective Plantings*, published on March 31 each year, reports expected plantings of corn, wheat, soybeans, cotton, sugar beets, and oats. These publications can be viewed online at http://usda.mannlib.cornell.edu.

In addition, there are four outlook reports: *Feed Outlook, Cotton and Wool Outlook, Oil Crops Outlook*, and *Wheat Outlook*. These are published monthly and are available by subscription from the National Technical Information Service (NTIS). The telephone for the order desk at NTIS is 1-800-999-6779. Its Web site is www.ntis.gov.

Commodity: Corn	
Delivery months: March, May, July, September, December	
Price in dollars and cents per bushel	Exchange: CBOT
Minimum tick: ¼ cent = $12.50	Contract size: 5,000 bushels

The United States is the world's largest corn producer. The leading states are Illinois and Iowa. Some corn is also grown in Indiana, Minnesota, and Nebraska. Corn is a summer crop, planted in the spring and harvested in the fall. Major consumers of the yellow grain are livestock, with hogs, cattle, and poultry accounting for most of the disappearance. The United States is also the world's largest exporter of corn, sending about 25 percent of each year's crop overseas.

Like most field crops, corn has a seasonal price pattern. Lows are set at harvest, when supplies weigh on the market. Prices tend to advance from these levels to a high in the spring, just before the new crop is planted.

Other factors influencing corn prices are the price and availability of substitute livestock feeds, which include soybean meal, milo, and wheat; the loan level and other government provisions for price or yield control; and the size of the corn crop in Argentina, Brazil, and other exporting nations. The principal price-making factor, however, is the number of poultry and livestock that comprise the market for corn.

An irregular but very potent price-making factor is weather, as was demonstrated by the 1996 crop, which rallied from $2.20 to $5.50 a bushel on the prospect of short supplies and dry growing weather. In fact, it has been said that the fate of the corn crop in the United States depends on whether it rains in the Corn Belt in June and July.

Where to Find More Information

The USDA is the best single source of supply and demand information.

A quarterly *Grain Stocks* report shows stocks of corn in on- and off-farm storage facilities and the capacities of those facilities. An annual summary, published in the second week of January, provides U.S. data for corn acreage, yield, and production. *Feed Outlook*, published monthly and available only electronically, discusses actual and forecast corn supply and consumption.

Demand for corn can also be inferred from USDA *Hogs and Pigs* reports, *Cattle on Feed* reports, and *Livestock and Meat Situation* reports, which show current projected numbers of four-legged corn consumers. *Feedstuffs*, a weekly agribusiness magazine (Miller Publishing Company), provides timely information on factors affecting feed demand.

Commodity: Wheat	
Delivery months: March, May, July, September, December	
Price in cents per bushel	Exchange: CBOT
Minimum tick: ¼ cent = $12.50	Contract size: 5,000 bushels
Delivery months: March, May, July, September, December	
Price in cents per bushel	Exchange: KCBT
Minimum tick: ¼ cent = $12.50	Contract size: 5,000 bushels
Delivery months: March, May, July, September, December	
Price in cents per bushel	Exchange: MGE
Minimum tick: ¼ cent = $12.50	Contract size: 5,000 bushels

The most important wheat-producing region in the world has historically been the land occupied by the Russian republics. The United States is second, followed at a distance by China, India, Canada, and France. Wheat production in the United States is centered in the Great Plains. The major producers are Kansas, Oklahoma, Nebraska, and Colorado.

Most wheat is winter wheat, planted in the fall and harvested in June and July. That which is planted in the spring and harvested in the fall is referred to as spring wheat.

There are three relatively active futures contracts. The most liquid is the contract on the Chicago Board of Trade; it is based on No. 2 soft red winter wheat, which is milled for making crackers, cookies, cakes, and pastries. Second in activity is the Kansas City contract; it calls for delivery of hard red winter wheat, which comprises our major wheat export. Hard red spring wheat traded on the Minneapolis Grain Exchange is a high-protein grain and is often mixed with lower-protein soft wheats. Despite the disparity in their growing periods and end uses, prices in the three wheat markets do not tend to diverge greatly.

Virtually all wheat that is not exported goes into foods. It takes about $2\frac{1}{2}$ bushels of wheat to produce 100 pounds of flour. However, on the rare occasions when wheat and corn prices are about the same, wheat has also been used as food for livestock and poultry.

Exports play an important role in wheat prices. The United States is the world's largest exporter, selling about half of its annual crop overseas. Major world importers of wheat include Brazil, China, Japan, Korea, and The Netherlands. The levels of wheat production in other nations also have an effect on our prices. Wheat grown in the Southern Hemisphere reaches world markets a half-year later than U.S. wheat.

Where to Find More Information

As with corn, the best single source of supply and demand information is the USDA. Its *Wheat Yearbook*, released annually in March, presents foreign crop news, wheat stock levels, prices, and disappearance. *Grain Stocks* is a quarterly publication that shows wheat on hand and disappearance during that quarter. *Wheat Outlook*, published each month, examines the current supply, use, demand, and prices for all U.S. wheat.

The Foreign Agriculture Service publishes the *Weekly U.S. Export Sales Report* that covers transactions of 100,000 tons or more.

Commodity: Oats	
Delivery months: March, May, July, September, December	
Price in dollars and cents per bushel	Exchange: CBOT
Minimum tick: $\frac{1}{4}$ cent = $12.50	Contract size: 5,000 bushels

Oats are grown in Minnesota, the Dakotas, Iowa, and Wisconsin. The crop is planted in the spring and harvested from late July to early August. The United States grows about one-quarter of the world's oats and consumes virtually all of it domestically.

The principal use for oats is livestock feed. Only a fraction finds its way into oatmeal for human consumption. Farmers who grow oats keep two-thirds or more of their production to feed their own animals.

Oat prices have ranged between $1.00 and $3.00 per bushel for most of the time over the past 15 years. Prices respond to a number of influences. There has been an ongoing decline in the amount of acreage being planted to oats, which will eventually cause higher prices. Drought or crop disease that threatens supply can send prices sharply higher, as was seen in the dry summer of 1988; oats rallied to just under $4.00 a bushel, the highest price ever registered.

Other supply aspects include the cost and availability of other animal feeds, especially corn. A bushel of oats weighs about half as much as a bushel of corn; if feeding values be the same, a bushel of oats should theoretically cost about half as much as a bushel of corn. In fact, oat prices generally run about 10 percent to 15 percent below corn prices, by weight.

On the demand side, the numbers of poultry and livestock are the overriding consideration.

Where to Find More Information

There is no single USDA publication devoted to oats. However, the planting, harvesting, progress, and overall condition of the oats crop are covered in USDA *Prospective Plantings*, *Small Grain Summary*, and the quarterly *Grain Stocks*.

Commodity: Soybeans	
Delivery months: January, March, May, July, August, September, November	
Price in cents per bushel	Exchange: CBOT
Minimum tick: ¼ cent = $12.50	Contract size: 5,000 bushels

The United States is the world's leading producer of soybeans, followed by Brazil and China. Soybeans vie with corn as the most important cash crop in the United States. They are grown in Illinois, Iowa, Indiana, Ohio, Missouri, and Minnesota—the Corn Belt. Soybeans are planted between mid-April and June, but they may be put in the ground somewhat later without harmful effects and are often used as an alternate crop when weather prevents the planting of corn or cotton. The soybean harvest is usually complete by October.

Although they are often grouped with grains for discussion, soybeans are an oilseed. They are grown for their yield of soybean oil and soybean meal. A 60-pound bushel of soybeans will produce 47 pounds of meal, which is the driving market, and 11 pounds of oil. About two-thirds of the U.S. crop are crushed at home. The balance is exported out of the Great Lakes and Gulf ports, bound primarily for Japan and Western Europe.

There is a seasonal tendency for cash soybean prices to rise from a low around harvest time to a peak the following spring. The supply of competing soybeans, such as those from Brazil, also affects U.S. soybean prices in world markets. Even the prices of corn and cotton have an indirect effect because corn and cotton compete with soybeans for growing space. However, the most significant factor for soybean prices is the crush margin, or the difference between the cost of the beans and the prices of their end products. If the prices for soybean meal and soybean oil are relatively high, crushers will bid for beans and drive bean prices up.

Where to Find More Information

The progress of the soybean crop is closely followed. The USDA's *Prospective Plantings*, published at the end of March, provides the first clues to production prospects. In July, the final figure for planted acreage is released, and monthly crop estimates are provided from August through November. Grain stocks are reported in January, March, June, and December.

Weekly FAS reports contain information on soybean export commitments and transactions. The monthly USDA *Oil Crops Outlook* (available by electronic means only) and the annual *Oil Crops Yearbook* present statistics and projections of supply and demand for the entire soybean complex. *Grain and Feed Weekly Summary and Statistics* reports on soybeans ready for export, prices, and a comparison of soybean prices with the prices of soybean oil and soybean meal.

Data on soybean crushing, stocks, and disappearance are also provided monthly by the U.S. Census Bureau. The National Oilseed Processors Association (1300 L Street NW, Washington, DC 20005; telephone: 202-842-0463) publishes a yearbook of trading rules relating the purchase and sale of soybeans, plus weekly and monthly statistical reports. Information on the cost and availability of these materials may be obtained by contacting the association directly.

Commodity: Soybean Meal	
Delivery months: January, March, May, July, August, September, October, December	
Price in dollars per ton	Exchange: CBOT
Minimum tick: 10 cents = $10.00	Contract size: 100 tons

Soybeans are crushed to obtain their oil and meal. Of the two, meal is considered the more valuable by-product; its price is also more volatile, because it cannot be stored for long.

Soybean meal is rich in protein (40 to 45 percent) and is a major ingredient in high-quality feed for hogs, cattle, and poultry in the United States. Meal in the United States is produced in some 100 processing plants. About three-fourths of the meal is consumed domestically; the remaining fourth is exported, mainly to Western Europe, Canada, and Japan. The most important competitors for soybean meal in the world market are fish meal and peanut meal. The former comes primarily from Peru, the latter from India.

There is some seasonality to meal prices, which tend to be lowest in the fall and to peak out in the winter when demand is heaviest.

The supply of soybean meal is determined by the amount of crushing, and that is a function of the crush margin, or the profitability of crushing beans. If beans are relatively inexpensive, crushers will continue to operate, and meal prices will fall.

Demand for meal depends on the price and availability of competing products; the level of stocks on hand; the rate of disappearance; and, most important, the number of high-protein feed-consuming animals in the United States and other nations around the world.

Where to Find More Information

The supply of soybean meal depends largely on the supply of soybeans. For information on soybean production, see page 193.

Commodity: Soybean Oil	
Delivery months: January, March, May, July, August, September, October, December	
Price in cents per pound	Exchange: CBOT
Minimum tick: $\frac{1}{100}$ cent = $6.00	Contract size: 60,000 pounds

The United States is the major world producer of soybean oil and accounts for 90 percent of all soybean oil exports. One 60-pound bushel of soybeans gives up 11 pounds of this golden liquid, the most important vegetable oil in world trade. Virtually all of the soybean oil produced is consumed by the food industry, where its major uses are in shortening, salad dressings, cooking oils, and margarine.

The long-range supply of soybean oil is dependent on the size of the soybean crop plus any carryover from previous seasons. The new supply can be estimated by assuming that a normal 60 percent of the new crop will be crushed. Unlike soybean meal, soybean oil stores well. About 80 percent of the soybean oil produced goes into domestic use, with 20 percent going to exports.

Because other fats and oils can be used in place of soybean oil in many products, the prices of substitutes are important. Lard, cottonseed oil, and butter prices all have an effect on domestic soybean oil demand. On a broader scale, soybean oil also competes with palm oil, coconut oil, rapeseed oil, groundnut oil, and sunflower seed oil. The most important of these have historically been the first two; however, concerns about cholesterol have reduced the demand for tropical oils. Palm oil, from Malaysia and Indonesia, is used in shortening. Coconut oil comes from the Philippines and is used primarily in candy and bakery goods.

Where to Find More Information

As with soybean meal, the supply of soybean oil is dependent on the supply of the source commodity and the extent of crushing activity. The *World Production, Market, and Trade Report,* published by FAS, shows current supply, demand, and trade estimates for soybean oil and soybean meal for the United States and major foreign countries.

Indexes

Indexes comprise a relatively new category of futures markets. The asset underlying the futures contract is not a tangible commodity but the value of the index itself. Settlement is by transfer of cash at the maturity of the futures contract.

There are active futures markets in seven indexes: the Dow Jones Industrial Average, Goldman Sachs Commodity Index, NASDAQ 100 Index, Nikkei 225 Index, S&P 500 Index, S&P MidCap 400 Index, and the U.S. Dollar Index.

In addition to their normal daytime trading hours, all of these futures contracts trade electronically after hours.

E-mini futures index contracts are smaller in size and trade only electronically. They have proved to be very successful. The e-mini S&P 500 was the fifth most active futures market in the world in 2004.

A good general reference source for futures on stock indexes is *Stock Index Futures: A Guide for Traders, Investors and Analysts,* by Neil S. Weiner (Wiley, New York, 1984).

Commodity: GSCI (Goldman Sachs Commodity Index)	
Delivery months: each month	
Price in index points and hundredths	Exchange: CME
Minimum tick: .05 index points = $12.50	Contract size: $250 × GSCI

The GSCI is an index of the prices of 24 actively traded physical commodity futures contracts. The GSCI was developed by Goldman Sachs to represent the performance of these commodities as a group. The commodities in the index include energy, metals, meats, grains and oilseeds, and foods and fibers.

The difference between the GSCI and other commodity indexes is that each commodity in the GSCI is weighted in the calculations to reflect the relative amount of its world production.

The GSCI has a positive correlation with inflation and a negative correlation with bond and stock returns, important criteria for portfolio diversification. Academic studies have shown that by adding exposure to physical commodities, portfolio managers can increase the return of a traditional U.S. stock and bond portfolio without increasing its volatility.

GSCI futures are traded side by side at the CME—both by open outcry and electronically.

Where to Find More Information

Like all other indexes, the GSCI reflects the balance of price changes among its constituent commodities: cattle, hogs, wheat, corn, soybeans, natural gas, crude oil, unleaded gasoline, heating oil, gold, silver, aluminum, nickel, copper, zinc, lead, tin, sugar, cotton, coffee, and cocoa.

A comprehensive source of information on the GSCI futures contract is the *GSCI Information Guide*, published by the Chicago Mercantile Exchange.

Commodity: S&P MidCap 400 Stock Index

Delivery months: March, June, September, December

Price in index points and hundredths   Exchange: CME

Full-size Futures Contract

Minimum tick: .05 index points = $25.00   Contract size: $500 × index

E-mini S&P MidCap 400 Stock Index Futures Contract

Minimum tick: .10 index points = $10.00   Contract size: $100 × index

---

Standard & Poor's MidCap 400 Index measures the group performance of the stocks of 400 moderately sized U.S. companies. Like the S&P 500 Index, the MidCap 400 is capitalization weighted. The predominant industry groups in the index are technology, finance, utilities, and consumer cyclicals.

To be a member of the S&P MidCap 400, a stock must be traded on the New York Stock Exchange, the American Stock Exchange, or NASDAQ. Foreign companies whose stocks trade as American Depositary Receipts or American

Depositary Shares are ineligible, as are mutual funds, limited partnerships, and real estate investment trusts (REITs). No stock can be a member of both the S&P 500 and the S&P 400.

Other criteria for admission to the 400 include a good liquidity/turnover ratio and a review by the Index Committee at Standard & Poor's, which takes care to ensure that the index accurately represents the aggregate economic performance of middle-sized companies in the United States.

Where to Find More Information

Investigate the CME's Web site at www.cme.com.

Commodity: Nikkei 225 Stock Average	
Delivery months: March, June, September, December	
Price in index points	Exchange: CME
Minimum tick: 5 index points = $25.00	Contract size: $5.00 × the Average

Nikkei 225 futures are based on the Nikkei 225 Stock Average, a price-weighted index of 225 actively traded Japanese stocks on the Tokyo Stock Exchange.

Japanese equity markets are highly volatile. During the past 10 years, the Nikkei 225 Stock Average has moved between a low of 7,600 and a high of 22,795, a swing of more than 300 percent.

Nikkei 225 futures can be used by U.S. pension funds, mutual funds, money managers, and institutional traders to protect diverse portfolios of Japanese equities against price risk. The futures contracts are dollar denominated; that is, there is no need to make any conversions between U.S. dollars and yen. Settlement is by cash.

Nikkei 225 futures are traded both by open outcry and electronically, side by side.

Where to Find More Information

The *2004 GSCI Information Guide*, published by the CME, is a good reference. It can be found at www.cme.com, where it can be read online or printed out.

The *Guide* shows the commodities in the Index and how they are weighted, how the Nikkei 225 Stock Index is calculated, a trading calendar, a list of frequently asked questions, and how the Nikkei has correlated with other stock indexes since 1990.

Commodity: NASDAQ 100 Stock Index

Delivery months: March, June, September, December

Price in index points and hundredths   Exchange: CME

Full-size Futures Contract

Minimum tick: .50 index points = $50.00   Contract size: $100 × index

E-mini NASDAQ 100 Stock Index Futures Contract

Minimum tick: .05 index points = $10.00   Contract size: $20 × index

---

The 100 is the first index futures contract on NASDAQ stocks. Like the S&P 500, the NASDAQ 100 is capitalization weighted; that is, each stock affects the value of the index in direct proportion to the dollar value of its shares outstanding. The index is rebalanced annually to ensure that it remains an accurate surrogate for the NASDAQ Stock Market as a whole.

To join the index, a stock must meet certain criteria. Only one class of stock per issuer is permitted. A stock must be listed on the NASDAQ for a minimum of 2 years before it is considered for inclusion in the index.

The sector breakdown of the stocks in the index is: computers, 52 percent; industrials, 28 percent; telecommunications, 12 percent; biotechnology, 7 percent; and transportation, 1 percent. Though it is one-fifth the size of the S&P 500, the total value of the stocks in the NASDAQ 100 is only one-tenth the value of the larger index, reflecting the fact that the NASDAQ 100 contains more lower-priced issues.

Where to Find More Information

The *CME Equity Index Manual*, published by the Chicago Mercantile Exchange, contains a section on the NASDAQ 100. It explains how the index is calculated, what stocks it contains, and how it behaves relative to other stock indexes.

NASDAQ 100 Investors Guide 2002–2003, by Michael P. Byrum, is available from the New York Institute of Finance. This excellent source tells you how to use stock market volatility to your advantage. It profiles each stock in the index, provides historical charts and graphs, and describes trading strategies.

Commodity: Dow Jones Industrial Average	
Delivery months: March, June, September, December	
Price in index points	Exchange: CBOT
DJIA ($10) Futures Contract	
Minimum tick: 1 point = $10.00	Contract size: $10 × index
Mini-DJIA ($5) Futures Contract	
Minimum tick: 1 point = $5.00	Contract size: $5 × index

The Dow Jones Industrial Average (DJIA) is probably the most closely watched stock index in the world. Developed by Charles Henry Dow in 1884, the first DJIA was the arithmetic average of 11 principal U.S. companies, then mostly railroads.

There are 30 stocks in the DJIA today. The companies represented are large-cap market leaders like General Electric, IBM, and Home Depot. Combined, the 30 stocks in the DJIA have a total market value of more than $3 trillion and represent one-fifth of the market value of all U.S. stocks.

Although the number of stocks remains at 30, the composition of the DJIA changes from time to time to stay in step with waxing and waning of company fortunes and advances in technology.

Futures contracts are cash settled.

Where to Find More Information

The CBOT Dow Complex Reference Guide is available online at the CBOT Web site: www.cbot.com. It describes how the Index is compiled, how to conduct arbitrage using the Index, and the benefits of electronic access.

The Stock Market Barometer, by William Peter Hamilton, can be found at www.alibris.com. The author is the midwife of the Dow Theory; in 1882, along with Edward Jones, he established the Dow Jones Financial News Service. The book explains the Dow theory's principles, its affinity for market cycles, and its performance in predicting where the stock market is headed. The book was first published in 1937 and is now in its 14th edition.

Commodity: Standard & Poor's 500 Stock Index

Delivery months: March, June, September, December

Price in index points and hundredths   Exchange: IOM

Full-size Futures Contract

Minimum tick: .01 index points = $25.00   Contract size: $250 × Index

E-mini S&P 500 Futures Contract

Minimum tick: .25 index points = $12.50   Contract size: $50 × Index

The Standard & Poor's 500 Stock Index comprises 500 listed and over-the-counter stocks. About three-fourths of the stocks are industrials. The balance, in decreasing order of representation, are utilities, financial institutions, and transportation companies.

The Index reflects about 70 percent of the nation's big business.

In calculating the value of the S&P 500 Index, the individual constituent stocks are weighted according to their market capitalization. A price movement in a high-priced stock will therefore have a greater effect on the Index than the same price move in a lower-priced stock.

The S&P 500 futures contract is traded both by open outcry during the day and electronically when the trading floor is closed. E-mini S&P 500 futures are traded only electronically.

Where to Find More Information

The brochures *2004 Equity Information Guide* and *E-mini Stock Futures* both address the S&P 500 futures contracts. They are published by the CME and are available online at www.cme.com, where they may be perused or downloaded. An introductory book that might also be helpful is *How the Stock Market Works* (2nd edition, 1993) by John M. Dalton. It is published by the New York Institute of Finance.

Commodity: U.S. Dollar Index

Delivery months: March, June, September, December

Price in index points and hundredths   Exchange: NYBT

Minimum tick: .01 = $10.00   Contract size: $1000 × U.S. Dollar Index

The U.S. Dollar Index represents a fixed basket of the currencies of the 10 major U.S. world trading partners, weighted according to each country's share of world trade. The original index comprised the currencies of Germany, Japan, France, the U.K., Canada, Italy, The Netherlands, Belgium, Sweden, and Switzerland.

When some of these nations began their transition to the euro, the composition and weighting of the U.S. Dollar Index were modified. The current weighting is: euro, 57 percent; Japanese yen, 14 percent; British pound, 12 percent; Canadian dollar, 9 percent; Swedish krona, 4 percent; and the Swiss franc, 4 percent. The U.S. Dollar Index is a trade-weighted geometric average of these six currencies.

Potential hedgers in U.S. Dollar Index futures include U.S. individuals or businesses with economic interests in an array of developed nations, as they would be exposed to multiple foreign-exchange-rate risks.

Where to Find More Information

The exchange publishes two comprehensive information sources: *U.S. Dollar Index (USDX) Futures and Options* and *USDX Brochure*. Both are available online at www.nybot.com.

Inasmuch as the index is the obverse side of the foreign currency values, information on the currencies themselves is germane. Broad sources of information on the relationship between the U.S. dollar and these six currencies would include the U.S. Department of the Treasury and the U.S. Department of Commerce in Washington, DC.

In addition, there are three informative periodicals in the field: *The Economist* (527 Madison Avenue, New York, NY 10022); *Financial Times* (1330 Avenue of the Americas, New York, NY 10019); and *Euromoney* (Nestor House, Playhouse Yard, London EC4V 5EX, England).

Other Index Futures

The following index futures contract is still traded, but trading volume is relatively low and open interest is a fraction of what it once was.

Value Line Stock Index.   The Value Line, inaugurated in 1982, was the first index futures contract to be traded. It is based on the 1650 stocks contained in the *Value Line Investment Survey*.

Each stock receives equal weight in the calculation of the Value Line index. No allowance is made for capitalization or price. As a consequence, the index tends to be more sensitive than other stock indexes to fluctuations in lower-priced stocks and the stocks of smaller companies.

Value Line futures are traded on the Kansas City Board of Trade. Contract size is $100 × the index; the minimum tick is .05 index points, which equals a $5 change in equity. Open interest in Value Line Stock Index futures as of this writing is essentially zero.

Interest Rates

Forecasting the course of interest rates is complex. Some of the domestic factors to be taken into consideration include demand by business for funds to construct new plants, carry inventory, or retire debt; government spending for public works, social welfare, and military personnel and hardware; changes in income tax; operations by the Federal Reserve Board to control inflation; changes in the money supply; and the level of consumer personal income, debts, and savings.

Interest rates are also affected by interest rates in other nations, balance of trade, the availability of other sources for money, interest rates on other short-term instruments such as CDs and commercial paper, and general economic conditions.

Futures contracts are traded on U.S. Treasury 2-, 5-, and 10-year notes, U.S. Treasury bonds, Eurodollar, 1-month London Interbank Offered Rate (LIBOR), 30-Day Federal funds, and Euroyen.

Treasury bonds and 10-year Treasury notes represent long-term interest rates; 2- and 5-year Treasury notes reflect medium-term interest rates; Eurodollar, Euroyen, LIBOR, and 30-day Fed funds are considered to represent short-term interest rates.

All of these futures markets also trade electronically after hours. In some cases, trading by open outcry and electronic trading overlap.

Where to Find More Information

Most of the how-to brochures previously published by the CME have been moved to its Web site, where they may be read online or downloaded. The list of brochures and booklets is extensive, covering the futures markets in general and CME's futures contracts in particular. At the Web site, look under the heading "Education."

For questions, call the CME at 1-800-331-3332 or e-mail its marketing department at info@cme.com.

A good general reference source is *Forecasting Interest Rates*, by John B. Schwartzman (McGraw-Hill, New York, 1992).

Commodity: Eurodollar	
Delivery months: March, June, September, December	
Price = 100 minus annual yield, expressed as a percent	Exchange: IMM
Minimum tick: .01% = $25.00	Contract size: $1 million

A Eurodollar is a U.S. dollar on deposit outside the United States. Most Eurodollars reside in the London branches of major world banks. They are the basis for dollar loans made by European banks to commercial borrowers. There are also fixed-income securities denominated in Eurodollars.

Eurodollars are part of what is known as the "money market." Their price reflects short-term interest rates in Europe, specifically, the 3-month London Interbank Offered Rate. The factors that affect short-term interest rates are many. They include actions taken by central banks to raise or lower the money supply, interest rates in other nations, balance of trade, the current level of demand for short-term loans, the availability of other sources for money, interest rates on other instruments such as CDs and Treasury bills, and general economic conditions.

Eurodollar futures are part of the CME's mutual offset system with the Singapore Exchange (SGX), under which a position taken on one exchange may be offset on the other.

Commodity: Euroyen	
Delivery months: March, June, September, December	
Price in percent of par (100%)	Exchange: CME
Minimum tick: .005% = 1250 yen	Contract size: 100 million yen

The asset underlying the Euroyen futures contract is a 3-month time deposit of 100,000,000 yen. Settlement is by cash.

Like Eurodollars, the Euroyen futures price is expressed in terms of an index that is derived by subtracting the implied interest rate from 100. For example, if the implied Japanese 3-month interest rate for a given period is 5.65 percent, the corresponding Euroyen futures price would be 94.35 (100 − 5.65). Euroyen futures are also part of the CME's mutual offset system with the SGX, under which a position taken on one exchange may be offset on the other.

Euroyen futures can be employed in a variety of ways. The most basic use would be to control the vulnerability to changes in yen interest rates, such as would be sustained by a fiduciary who has yen on deposit in a Japanese bank or has a fixed requirement to borrow yen in the coming months. There are more sophisticated uses, most of which are beyond our scope here.

Initial and maintenance performance bonds (and profits) for Euroyen futures are denominated in yen; the CME has a mechanism that enables its clearing members to transfer and receive funds in yen.

Commodity: 1-Month LIBOR	
Delivery months: consecutive months out 12 months	
Price in percent of par (100%)	Exchange: CME
Minimum tick: .005% = $12.50	Contract size: $3 million

LIBOR is an acronym for London Interbank Offered Rate, the interest rate at which the biggest London banks are willing to loan Eurodollar deposits to each other. It is similar to the prime rate in the United States.

Eurodollars make an excellent benchmark for short-term interest rates. The annual market is well in excess of $1 trillion and is dispersed throughout Europe and the Caribbean.

Like Eurodollar futures, LIBOR contracts are priced in terms of an index. A price futures of 92.26, for example, would reflect an underlying interest rate of 7.74 percent (100 − 92.26). The asset underlying the futures contract is a 1-month time deposit of $3 million. Settlement is by cash and is based on the average spot market value of LIBOR at that time.

Both Eurodollar and LIBOR futures markets allow a hedger or lender to lock in an interest rate for a specified period of time. The time horizon for Eurodollar futures is 3 months; for 1-Month LIBOR futures, it is 1 month. The shorter time horizon for LIBOR futures enables a market participant to fine-tune his risk exposure by allowing him to reevaluate the situation every month and, if desired, adjust his position. LIBOR futures have proven to be effective for cross-hedging commercial paper and other short-term credit instruments.

Commodity: 30-Day Fed Funds	
Delivery months: consecutive months to 24 months ahead	
Price: 100 minus monthly average overnight Fed funds rate	Exchange: CBOT
Minimum tick: .005% = $20.835	Contract size: $5 million

Each business day, U.S. banks trade about $100 billion in deposits among themselves. These deposits have a term to maturity of 1 day and are known as "overnight Fed funds."

The rates these banks charge each other for these 1-day loans are averaged and published daily by the Federal Reserve Bank of New York. This average serves as an accurate benchmark for the spot cost of short-term credit.

A close correlation exists between the 1-month term rate for Fed funds and rates for CDs, commercial paper, LIBOR, and Eurodollars. Money managers can use 30-Day Fed Funds futures to manage risk in these and other short-term credit instruments.

For a basic example, a fiduciary who intends to borrow money under a fixed rate 1 month hence could protect against rising interest rates (and subsequent opportunity loss) during the interim by selling short 30-Day Fed Fund futures now.

Settlement is in cash and calls for delivery of the interest paid on $5 million in overnight Fed funds held for 30 days.

Commodity: Treasury Bonds

Delivery months: March, June, September, December

Price in percent and $\frac{1}{32}$% of par	Exchange: CBOT
Minimum tick: $\frac{1}{32}$ = $31.25	Contract size: $100,000

Until October 2001, U.S. Treasury bonds were sold through the Federal Reserve to domestic and foreign investors to meet long-term obligations of the federal government. T-bonds are coupon bearing; they pay a fixed dollar amount of interest semiannually. T-bond maturities extended out to 30 years. The secondary (dealer) market for T-bonds is still extremely broad and liquid.

U.S. Treasury bonds have been the international flagship for long-term interest rates, and their cash and futures prices are sensitive to changes in the interest rate picture.

Commodity: Treasury Notes (10-year)

Delivery months: March, June, September, December

Price in percentage and $\frac{1}{32}$% of par	Exchange: CBOT
Minimum tick: $\frac{1}{2}$ of $\frac{1}{32}$ = $15.625	Contract size: $100,000

Commodity: Treasury Notes (5-year)

Delivery months: March, June, September, December

Price in percentage and $\frac{1}{32}$% of par	Exchange: CBOT
Minimum tick: $\frac{1}{2}$ of $\frac{1}{32}$ = $15.625	Contract size: $100,000

Commodity: Treasury Notes (2-year)

Delivery months: March, June, September, December

Price in percentage and $\frac{1}{128}$% of par	Exchange: CBOT
Minimum tick: $\frac{1}{4}$ of $\frac{1}{32}$ = $15.625	Contract size: $200,000

Treasury notes are midrange on the yield curve, maturing in from 2 to 10 years. They are sold to public investors by the Federal Reserve to fund ongoing government operations and refinance the national debt. There is also an active secondary (dealer) market.

As shown above, there are three active T-note futures contracts. They differ in the maturity of their underlying cash instruments and their pricing.

Meats

Futures contracts are traded on cattle, feeder cattle, lean hogs, and pork bellies. All four contracts are traded simultaneously by open outcry and electronically. The Chicago Mercantile Exchange is the home of all of these futures contracts and has published a wealth of information on them over the years. Most of the information is available online at www.cme.com.

Current data on the supply of and demand for these commodities is provided by both private research sources and the U.S. Department of Agriculture. A USDA publication that covers sales, prices, and slaughter in all of the meats is *Livestock, Meat and Wool*, published weekly. Pertinent publications for each individual market are listed at the end of each briefing sheet.

Commodity: Cattle (Live)	
Delivery months: February, April, June, August, October, December	
Price in cents per pound	Exchange: CME
Minimum tick: $2\frac{1}{2}$ cents = $10.00	Contract size: 40,000 pounds

Cattle raised for beef comprise the largest single segment of American agriculture. Fresh beef cannot be stored; prices will adjust to sell all the beef that is in the supply pipeline. In the past 30 years, cattle futures prices have ranged from a low of 35 cents to a high of $1.04 cents a pound.

Cattle are fed on grass or corn. They are placed on feed at a weight of about 700 pounds and marketed some 8 to 10 weeks later at weights of 1000 to 1200 pounds. Most fed cattle come from the feed grain areas of the Midwest. More calves are born in the spring than any other time of the year, so most yearlings are put on feed in the fall. Cattle prices tend to be seasonally lowest at this time and highest in early spring.

Cattle prices are affected by several factors. These include the weather during the feeding season, the condition of range and pasture land, government buying programs, and the prices of competitive meats like chicken and pork. From a larger perspective, consumer preferences also play a significant role.

Average per capita consumption of beef peaked in 1975. It declined about 30 percent in the next 15 years, and since 1990 has held steady.

Cattle have an irregular long-term price/production cycle of about 8 years, in which the numbers of animals available for slaughter respond to changes in the prices of cattle and feed, rising gradually when cattle prices remain relatively high and falling when cattle prices are low.

Commodity: Feeder Cattle

Delivery months: January, March, April, May, August, September, October, November

Price in cents per pound	Exchange: CME
Minimum tick: 2½ cents = $12.50	Contract size: 50,000 pounds

Feeder cattle are yearling steers. They comprise the input for cattle feeders, who fatten them up and sell them for beef. Feeder cattle futures have been traded since 1971; their prices have ranged widely, from 25 cents to near $1.20 a pound. The futures contract is cash settled.

The demand for feeder cattle reflects prices for finished cattle. Finished cattle prices are affected by several factors (see page 207).

Where to Find More Information

The USDA is the primary source for information on the supply and demand situation in live cattle and feeder cattle. USDA publications include weekly, monthly, and quarterly releases. The weekly reports contain summaries of market news. There are monthly reports on the placement of cattle on feed, numbers on feed by weight group, and marketing of cattle in the major feeding states. The USDA also publishes a comprehensive monthly *Cattle on Feed* report; and in February and July, the USDA report *Cattle* shows, among other data, the number of potential feedlot cattle available.

A historical analysis of the *Cattle on Feed* reports and booklets explaining live cattle and feeder cattle futures are available online from the CME.

Commodity: Hogs (Lean)

Delivery months: February, April, June, July, August, October, December

Price in cents per pound	Exchange: CME
Minimum tick: 2½ cents = $10.00	Contract size: 40,000 pounds

Most hogs are raised where their food is grown: in the Corn Belt. Iowa is the leading hog producer by a large margin. Other hog-producing states are Illinois, Minnesota, Ohio, and Wisconsin.

Although the pattern has been modified recently by confined hog raising, sows tend to farrow (give birth) in the spring and the fall. The time from farrowing to a market weight of 220 pounds is about 6 months. Slaughter of mature animals is lowest in midsummer, and prices tend to firm then. Demand also peaks during the summer barbecue season. Prices are seasonally lowest in the November–December period, when slaughter is at its highest.

One factor that affects the supply of hogs is the hog/corn ratio, which is the number of bushels of corn it would take to buy 100 pounds of live hog. When corn prices are high relative to hog prices (the ratio is low), hog production is discouraged. A high ratio (cheap corn, high-priced hogs) acts as a spur to hog production.

There is also a long-term "cycle" to hog production, as producers respond to the ups and downs in hog prices: High hog prices lead to increased production; this pushes hog prices down, and that causes production to slow, which pushes prices back up again. In the past, the hog cycle has had an average length of about 4 years.

Demand for hogs reflects consumer demand for pork products, which include bacon, ham, roasts, chops, and frankfurters. This demand, in turn, reflects pork prices, the prices of other red meats, consumers' levels of disposable income, and dietary preferences.

Hog futures contracts are cash settled.

Where to Find More Information

The quarterly USDA *Hogs and Pigs* report is a comprehensive source of information about hog inventory numbers, the pig crop, and farmers' farrowing intentions. Other pertinent USDA publications include *Livestock Slaughter*, published monthly and annually; *Livestock, Dairy, and Poultry Monthly*; and *Livestock and Meat Situation*, published monthly.

Commodity: Pork Bellies (Frozen)	
Delivery months: February, March, May, July, August	
Price in cents per pound	Exchange: CME
Minimum tick: 2½ cents = $10.00	Contract size: 40,000 pounds

A pork belly is uncured bacon. One hog yields two pork bellies of from 12 to 14 pounds each. Pork bellies tend to accumulate in freezers from October to April, reflecting both low demand and high hog slaughter during the period. Net movement of frozen bellies is out of storage during the summer months.

Demand for bacon does not change much when the price of bacon changes. As a consequence, the principal price-making factor for pork bellies is their supply, and a relatively small change in supply can have a great effect on price. The forthcoming supply of fresh pork bellies can be approximated by projecting hog farrowings forward for six months and multiplying the resulting number of hogs by 26 pounds. This number would be added to known supplies of bellies on hand to derive the total projected supply for any particular period.

Longer term, the supply of pork bellies depends on the number of hogs that are slaughtered. This brings the hog/corn ratio and the hog cycle into the equation.

Where to Find More Information

The USDA publishes information on the bacon slice, which reflects demand for the end product. The supply of pork bellies is largely a function of hog fundamentals, sources for which are described under that topic.

Metals

The major metals futures markets comprise copper, gold, platinum, and silver. The last three are generally looked on as precious metals, whereas copper is considered to be an industrial metal.

The futures markets for copper, gold, and silver are on the Commodity Exchange (COMEX) division of the New York Mercantile Exchange. Platinum futures are traded on the New York Mercantile Exchange. All four metals futures contracts are traded both by open outcry and electronically.

Where to Find More Information

The U.S. Geological Survey in Washington, DC periodically releases information based on the level of metal imports, secondary recovery in the United States, and stocks of the metal held by importers, dealers, and fabricators of this country. It also publishes the *Minerals Yearbook* and the *Mineral Industry Surveys*, which provide timely data on production, distribution, stocks, and consumption of mineral commodities. General information on metals supply and demand may also be found in the *Statistical Abstract of the U.S.*, which may be obtained from the Superintendent of Documents, Government Printing Office, Washington, DC 20402. The USGS Web site is http://minerals.usgs.gov.

A helpful book is *Portable Wealth: The Complete Guide to Precious Metals Investment* by Adam Starchild (Paladin Press, Boulder, CO, 1998). Magazines devoted to the subject include *Engineering and Mining Journal* and *Modern Metals*.

Commodity: High-Grade Copper	
Delivery months: 23 consecutive months	
Price in dollars and cents per pound	Exchange: COMEX
Minimum tick: $^5/_{100}$ cent = $12.50	Contract size: 25,000 pounds

Most of the world supply of copper is produced in the United States. Other leading world producers are Zambia, Chile, Canada, Zaire, and Peru. Mine production in the United States is centered in Arizona. The United States is also the world's largest consumer of copper, accounting for about 25 percent of total world usage. CIPEC, a trade organization comprising major world producers, accounts for about 70 percent of international trade in copper.

Copper is an excellent conductor of heat and electricity and virtually does not oxidize. Its principal uses are in electric and electronic equipment, building construction, and engines. However, it is found in almost every product in an industrialized nation.

Because of its international nature, copper prices are directly affected by supply-reducing strikes or political unrest in foreign producing countries. Foreign exchange rates influence the effective price of copper to an importing nation. Other price factors include government embargos, production curtailments because of water shortage or other environmental considerations, overt efforts by CIPEC to control prices, and the amount of stockpiled copper, particularly at the London Metal Exchange (LME), a major world repository.

From a longer perspective, copper prices also reflect changes in the level of economic activity in consuming countries, and the prospect of another metal (aluminum) or a man-made material substituting for it in some uses.

Commodity: Gold	
Delivery months: Current 3 months plus any February, April, August, and October out to 23 months; and any June and December within 60 months	
Price in dollars and cents per troy ounce	Exchange: COMEX
Minimum tick: 10 cents = $10.00	Contract size: 100 troy ounces

Commodity: Gold

Delivery months: First 3 consecutive months

Price in dollars and cents per troy ounce   Exchange: CBOT

Minimum tick: 10 cents = $10.00   Contract size: 100 troy ounces

Mini-gold Contract

Delivery months: Consecutive months
out to 1 year

Minimum tick: 10 cents = $3.32   Contract size: 33.2 troy ounces

Both contracts are traded only electronically

Traditional supply/demand analysis of gold is difficult because of the psychological factors involved. Gold is a charismatic metal that was once thought to have magical powers. It has historically been considered a hedge against inflation and a safe haven for wealth when paper currencies fall into disrepute.

The largest producer of gold is South Africa, which accounts for about half of annual world production. The former USSR has been the next largest, with about 15 percent. Gold is also generated by the melting down of scrap. This secondary supply is more difficult to gauge than gold refined from ore, but about one-quarter of annual supplies are estimated to be derived from this source.

As an industrial metal, gold also has unique properties. It does not rust or corrode. It is an excellent conductor of heat and electricity and is the most malleable of all metals. It finds its way into a variety of products, including jewelry, electrical and electronic components, dentistry, coins, and medals and medallions.

The demand for gold has several facets. An important one is the demand for jewelry, which, in turn, reflects the level of world discretionary spending power. The prospect for lower interest rates may cause gold buying in anticipation of business expansion and a general increase in economic welfare. Sales of gold by central banks to raise foreign exchange would put pressure on gold prices. An increase in gold production would also have a depressing effect. Changes in inflation pressures, as measured by popular indexes, may cause investor demand for gold to rise or fall.

Topical information about gold can be found at the National Mining Association, 101 Constitution Avenue NW, Washington, DC 20001 (it absorbed the Gold Institute in 2003). The National Mining Association Web site is www.nma.org.

Sources for historical or background information include *The Gold Book* by Pierre Lassonde (Penguin Books, New York, 1993).

Commodity: Platinum	
Delivery months: January, April, July, October	
Price in dollars per troy ounce	Exchange: NYME
Minimum tick: 10 cents = $5.00	Contract size: 50 troy ounces

Production of platinum is dominated by South Africa, which accounts for the lion's share of world supplies. South African ores are as much as 10 times richer than anywhere else in the world. Canada, a distant second, produces platinum as a by-product to its nickel and copper mining operations.

Demand for platinum is three-pronged: in jewelry, as a catalyst in the refining of crude petroleum, and for use in automotive catalytic converters. Forty percent of the annual production of platinum goes into emission control devices on gasoline-driven cars and light trucks in the United States. Changes in this aspect of demand would derive from relaxed Environmental Protection Agency (EPA) emission standards, the discovery of a substitute for platinum in catalytic converters, or increasing concern with automotive air pollution in Japan and Western Europe.

The largest consumer of platinum for jewelry is Japan, where for centuries the metal has been preferred by women over gold for necklaces and wedding and engagement rings. However, gold has been making inroads into the Japanese jewelry market in recent years. Platinum's role in the petroleum cracking process is as a catalyst for certain necessary chemical reactions.

Like gold, the metal also is used by investors as a store of value, and its price from time to time has been higher than the price of gold. Platinum prices are also more volatile than gold prices, for two reasons: the platinum futures market's relatively small size and low liquidity, and the fact that above-ground holdings of investment platinum in the form of bars and wafers are small.

Commodity: Silver	
Delivery months: Current 3 months plus any January, March, May, and September out to 23 months, and any July and December within 60 months	
Price in cents per troy ounce	Exchange: COMEX
Minimum tick: ½ cent = $25.00	Contract size: 5,000 ounces

Commodity: Silver

Delivery months: First 3 consecutive months

Price in dollars and cents per troy ounce   Exchange: CBOT

Minimum tick: .001 = $5.00   Contract size: 5000 troy ounces

Mini-silver Contract

Delivery months: Consecutive months
out to 1 year

Minimum tick: .001 = $1.00   Contract size: 1000 troy ounces

Both contracts are traded only electronically

Silver comes from three sources. Primary production comes from the refining of newly mined ore and consistently falls short of world silver demand. Secondary production fills the gap; it comprises silver that is recovered from melted art objects and flatware, used photographic film, and scrap electrical connectors. The third source is world silver stocks held in such repositories as COMEX, the London Metal Exchange (LME), and government coffers.

Mexico is the world's largest producer of silver, followed by Peru, Canada, Australia, and the United States.

Demand for silver arises from several sectors of the economy. Silver is an excellent conductor of heat and electricity, is resistant to corrosion, and has beauty. Its most consistent use has been in photographic film and solutions, which historically have taken about 120 million ounces annually. Electronic components consume another 60 to 80 million ounces each year, and this amount is likely to rise with increasing world industrialization. Silver is the favorite metal of European jewelry makers. The demand for silver in jewelry is responsive to changes in the metal's price. For example, jewelry demand is estimated to have fallen more than half during the silver bull market of 1979–1980, when prices soared to $41.50 cents per ounce.

Other uses are dentistry, the making of storage batteries, and as a hedge against inflation or currency unrest, like gold.

The Silver Institute (1200 G Street NW, Ste. 800, Washington, DC 20005, telephone: 202-835-0185) publishes a free quarterly newsletter (*Silver News*) as well as several written reports (some free, some not) on silver mining, fabrication, and usage. The reports may be ordered online at www.silverinstitute.org.

Wood

There is only one wood futures contract actively traded today. It is lumber, traded on the Chicago Mercantile Exchange. For some years there was also a futures market in plywood, but it fell to a lack of trading activity.

Commodity: Lumber	
Delivery months: September, November, January, March, May, July	
Price in dollars and cents per 1000 board feet	
Minimum tick: 10 cents per 1000 board feet = $11.00	Exchange: CME Contract size: 110,000 board feet

Most of the lumber produced in the United States comes from the Pacific Northwest. Douglas fir is the leading lumber and is grown primarily in Oregon, Washington, and northern California.

The bulk of the lumber produced goes into the construction of new residential homes, so the actual and anticipated housing starts are important influences on prices. There is also a seasonal price movement; sawmills tend to acquire a large inventory of logs at the end of the warm-weather cutting season, and cash lumber prices tend to hit annual lows then. Prices are usually highest in the spring, as the building season gets under way. Prices are also affected by the level of logging and mill operation; and any strikes, fires, drought, or heavy precipitation that would slow operations will reduce supply and have a positive effect on prices.

In addition to the level of housing starts, demand for lumber is also indirectly influenced by interest rates, the availability of mortgage credit, and weather during the building season.

Where to Find More Information

The U.S. Department of Commerce makes monthly reports on housing starts and building permits. These reports are widely published and are followed closely by lumber interests. There is also a large amount of trade literature available. The WWPA organization (522 SW 5th Avenue, Yeon Building, Portland, OR 97204) publishes *Western Lumber Facts*, a monthly overview of the lumber industry from housing starts to U.S. Forest Service timber sales; *Statistical Yearbook*; and the semiannual *Economic Forecast*, which covers supply, imports, usage, and the overall lumber market outlook. Random Lengths Publications, Inc., Box 867, Eugene, OR 97440, publishes *Random Lengths*, a weekly, and *Yardstick*, a monthly compilation of key lumber data.

Chapter 18

Discover Electricity

The personal computer and the Internet have electrified futures trading in every sense of the word.

Waiting for you at the touch of a few computer keys is a treasure trove of futures market information, much of it free. Waiting just over the hill is electronic futures trading, in which your personal computer can be used to communicate directly with the exchange trading floor.

This chapter will deal with the vast amount of futures market information that is available on the Internet. The next chapter looks at electronic trading.

Birth of the Internet

The seeds for the Internet were planted in the late 1960s, when the U.S. government sponsored the development of electronic links between itself and various research computers at major universities. The principal purpose of the network was to speed the movement of scientific and technical information. However, the government also envisioned the network as a possible means of emergency communication if the national telephone system were ever knocked out.

As time passed, the network grew. Schools, businesses, libraries, and individuals joined in. And the messages changed. The network's normal diet of official reports and research data began to be interlaced with news and entertainment.

The personal computer triggered an Internet explosion. Suddenly any person's desk could become a window on the world. The addition of movement, color, sound, and photographic images enhanced the view.

In its most elemental use, the Internet is a huge library. However, unlike bricks-and-mortar libraries, the information on the Internet is literally at your fingertips.

The Web numbers more than 200 million pages. Buried in those millions of pages are a great deal of data and information about the futures markets. Like gold nuggets in a mountain stream, the problem is finding them.

Sources

This chapter deals with sources of reading material about the futures markets: books, magazines, newspapers, government organizations, the futures exchanges, and some of the private organizations that make it their business to collect and distribute futures market information.

Books

At the end of most chapters, we have listed a few selected books that are good sources for readers who want to delve further into the subject at hand. More information about them (and the publisher's other offerings) can be found at each publisher's Web site. Following are the major publishers of books on futures.

John Wiley & Sons   www.wiley.com/

The Wiley bookstore offers a large selection of books on futures and options. Books may be ordered online with a credit card over a secure, encrypted browser; or by telephone, fax, or U.S. mail. Books are shipped from Wiley's book distribution center in New Jersey.

Wiley also publishes *Journal of Futures Markets*, an academic quarterly.

New York Institute of Finance   www.nyif.com

The NYIF bookstore sells financial books of all publishers, but the number of books offered is limited. Its catalog may be searched by subject, author, or a specific word or phrase. The last works best. A search link is provided on the home page. Shown for each book are its title, price, number of pages, year of publication, and an extensive synopsis of the book's contents. There's an online order form for a NYIF catalog. Individual books can be ordered by e-mail or telephone.

McGraw-Hill   www.mcgraw-hill.com

Books of all publishers are sold at McGraw-Hill's online bookstore, which you can reach at:

www.bookstore.mcgraw-hill.com

Inasmuch as there are almost 2000 book titles listed under the heading of finance and investing, the most effective approach is to search the catalog. To do so, click *Search Catalog* and type in the book's category, subject, or a keyword (e.g., "futures"). If you are looking for a specific book, you can also search the catalog by author, ISBN, or title.

For most books, the information given is relatively scanty. Others, ostensibly books that the publisher is promoting, get fuller treatment, including a synopsis of the book's contents.

Books can be ordered online, by fax, or by telephone.

Wall Street Directory   www.wallstreetdir.com

The Wall Street Directory Web site is almost in a category by itself. It contains many links to financial sources, including current financial news, information on bonds and derivatives, lists of day-trading and online brokerage firms, names of money management companies, data on market prices and technical indicators, risk management, proprietary trading systems, books—and more.

Topical Information

Futures Magazine   www.futuresmag.com

Futures magazine is an excellent resource. Feature articles in this monthly magazine deal with commodity fundamentals, new approaches to technical analysis, money management, and specific trading systems.

The Web site shows the current issue of *Futures* in capsule form, although selected feature articles and editorial columns in the current issue can be read online in their entirety.

The Web site also presents the company's commercial products and services. These include weekly futures price charts (by mail or online), daily market technical commentary, market trend analysis, a telephone hotline with recorded market analytical messages, a chat room, a bookstore, and a compendium of mathematical technical indicators. There are free short-term trial subscriptions to some of the services.

Also presented are links to allied Web sites that are not affiliated with *Futures* magazine. These links include accounting services, futures brokers, educational services, historical market technical data, simulated trading, and trading contests.

Futures publishes special issues three times a year. Their annual *Source Book* contains a comprehensive listing of participants in the business of futures, from FCMs to purveyors of computer software to a complete list of the previous year's feature articles and columns. The *Guide to Computerized Trading* lists Internet and computerized services, and a special issue in September is devoted to the ways and means of trading.

Commodity Research Bureau (CRB)   www.crbindex.com

CRB's oldest publication is *Futures Market Service* (FMS), a weekly fundamental analysis of 35 commodities. Known as the "Blue Sheet," FMS has been published continuously since 1934. FMS is available by subscription via U.S. mail or by e-mail.

CRB Futures Perspective, a weekly printed chart service, provides its subscribers with price charts and other technical indicators for all major futures markets. A CRB bookstore has a limited number of futures titles that can be ordered by mail or online.

The CRB Data Center offers online access to open, high, low, and closing futures prices, a daily FMS, a daily electronic futures trend analyzer, and COMMODEX, a proprietary futures trading system. The CRB Market Center provides the wherewithal for online trading, including global news affecting futures, fundamental analysis, summaries of technical market studies, and real-time price quotes. CRB Data Center and CRB Market Center services are available by subscription.

Government Organizations

Certain agencies of the federal government gather and disseminate information that can be used in the fundamental analysis of individual futures markets.

Chief among these are the Commodity Futures Trading Commission (CFTC) and the U.S. Department of Agriculture (USDA). Also worth investigating are the U.S. Department of Commerce, the U.S. Geological Survey, and the Federal Reserve Board.

The CFTC publication of most interest to futures traders is the *Commitments of Traders Report*, which summarizes weekly data on the open interest holdings of commercial and noncommercial futures trader and includes changes from the previous report. The report is available directly from the CFTC via the Internet, and from intermediaries by several means.

The USDA (www.usda.com) has three divisions that provide futures data and information: Economic Research Service (ERS), National Agricultural Statistical Service (NASS), and Foreign Agricultural Service (FAS).

Economic Research Service. ERS analyzes current world agricultural situations and forecasts market conditions. It publishes *Situation and Outlook Reports* throughout the year, analyzing the economic outlook for all agricultural commodities. Some reports are available in print; others are not. Each report is devoted to a single commodity or commodity group.

A comprehensive calendar of ERS reports is free and can be ordered from the Web site (www.econ.ag.gov/) or by e-mail (service@econ.ag.gov). Electronic copies of the reports can be obtained online at a Web site maintained for ERS by Cornell University. The address of the Cornell Web site is

usda.mannlib.cornell.edu/

National Agricultural Statistical Service. NASS estimates and reports on the production, stocks, inventories, disposition, utilization, and prices of agricultural commodities. Its reports are widely followed and anticipated by traders. Some of its reports are prepared behind closed doors—for example, *Hogs and Pigs*, *Cattle on Feed*, *Crop Production*—and their releases have been known to move commodity prices dramatically.

Individual NASS reports examine stocks on hand of a particular commodity, farmers' growing intentions, progress of unharvested crops, expected crop yields, and probable prices.

A calendar of NASS reports can be obtained via the Web (www.econ.ag.gov/), by e-mail (service@econ.ag.gov), or by calling the NASS Information Hotline at 1-800-727-9540.

NASS's Web site (www.usda.gov/nass/pubs/pubs.htm) has links to an online NASS reports calendar, a list of NASS reports by commodity, reports on crop weather, agricultural graphics, a monthly agricultural newsletter, and a NASS yearbook entitled *Statistical Highlights of U.S. Agriculture*. There's also a search function that allows you to search the NASS site by keyword.

Foreign Agricultural Service. FAS collects, analyzes, and disseminates information about global supply and demand, trends in world trade, and overseas markets for U.S. agricultural products. Included are lists of foreign buyers; a summary of agricultural conditions in individual foreign countries; and satellite imagery to determine weather, growing conditions, and crop progress overseas.

The U.S. Geological Survey (www.usgs.gov), which took over the responsibilities of the U.S. Bureau of Mines in 1996, offers information about the production and worldwide usage of gold, silver, platinum, and copper.

The Federal Reserve Board Web site (www.bog.frb.fed.us) gives you access to the minutes of Federal Open Market Committee meetings; the "Beige" book of commentary on current economic conditions in each Federal Reserve district; and current data on money stocks, foreign exchange rates, interest rates, industrial production and capacity, and consumer installment credit.

The U.S. Department of Commerce (www.doc.gov) provides information on international trade conditions, the importing of goods and services into the United States, and the business climate in other nations around the world. Specific data include recent U.S. Treasury auction results, statistics on energy usage, and economic indicators that you hear mentioned on the evening news from time to time—housing starts, inventory levels, consumer prices, building permits, leading and lagging indicators, and the index of industrial production.

One-Stop Shopping. If you're wandering government hallways looking for commodity information, there are two Web sites that exemplify the value of the Internet.

www.fedstats.gov

www.usda.gov/nass/pubs/pubs.htm

The FedStats site is operated by the Department of Commerce and provides instant links to the Web sites of more than 100 government agencies that produce data of interest to the public. The site can be searched alphabetically or by subject. (Figure 18.1 shows the FedStats home page.)

The second Web site is called "USDA—National Agricultural Statistical Service Publications." It provides you with an online USDA reports calendar, individual USDA reports, crop weather, agricultural graphics, and the ability to search the entire USDA Web site by individual commodity or by keyword.

Example

Suppose that you were interested in cattle fundamentals. On the FedStats home page, type "cattle" and click *Search*. The result is a list of ERS and NASS Web sites that deal with cattle. Each entry on the list shows a summary of the site's contents.

Available is an ERS report entitled "U.S. Beef Industry: Cattle Cycles, Price Spreads, and Packer Concentration." Individual pages discuss the characteristics of the cattle cycle, explain how the cattle cycle affects cattle prices, and compare the current cattle cycle with past cattle cycles.

Also available is an online copy of *Agricultural Outlook Magazine*.

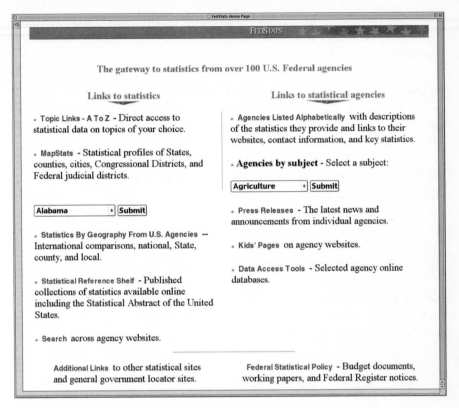

Figure 18.1 The FedStats Web site home page. Operated by the U.S. Department of Commerce, the site provides shortcuts to government data and information that a futures trader may find useful.

Another site lists all ERS publications devoted to livestock, dairy, and poultry production. It tells you what each publication is about, what it costs (if anything), when it is published, and how you can get a copy.

Current information includes color charts and graphs of all-cows inventories from 1980 to the present time, cattle on feed for the last 3 years, and the total U.S. cattle inventory each year since 1870.

Example

You suspect there might be a cold snap in Florida this winter, so you're looking for fundamental information about oranges and FCOJ.

You open the "National Agricultural Statistical Service Publications" location. On the Web site's home page, you click on *Reports by Commodity*. Then scroll down the list of commodities to *Oranges*. Click there and you'll have access to the monthly USDA *Crop Production* reports, providing the current status and forecasts for the orange crop and FCOJ production; and, the six most recent annual summaries of orange acreage, fruit yield, FCOJ production, imports, orange prices, and the value of the current and the previous 2 years' orange crops.

Futures Exchanges

The exchanges are the greatest single fount of information about themselves and the futures contracts they trade.

The list of what each exchange offers to Internet browsers is changing constantly. The best way to find out what's available is to key into the source yourself and explore the site.

The exchanges offer a number of features on their Internet pages:

Futures and options price quotes: Intraday quotes; daily opening, high, low, and closing prices; and time and sales data.

Market commentary: Remarks, recorded or live, focusing on individual futures markets and the fundamental forces currently affecting them. Included, if applicable, are levels of deliverable stocks and an account of actual deliveries of physical commodities made during the period.

Volume and open interest: Volume and open interest levels for each contract month and each futures market.

Technical analysis: Commentary on significant technical factors in each market. Presentations discuss price support and resistance levels, current trends, and projected price turning points. Analysis may include bar charts, point-and-figure charts, candlestick charts, on-balance volume, relative strength, moving averages, and stochastics.

Background information on each futures market: Where the commodity is produced, its major users, the factors that affect its supply and demand, the substitutes it has, the importance of hedgers, and how crop yields are determined.

Current cash prices for each commodity: Prices based on actual cash transactions at exchange-designated geographic locations that day.

Export data: Quantity and destination of commodities shipped overseas.

Current crop data: Planting, progress, condition, value, and expected yield.

Contract specifications: Detailed description of exchange specifications for each futures contract, including contract quantity, delivery months, last notice day, last trading day, exchange-designated delivery points, grades acceptable for delivery, and premiums or discounts for substitute grades.

USDA crop reports: Report data and analytical commentary, provided soon after the report is officially released by the U.S. Department of Agriculture.

CFTC data: Most recent *Commitments of Traders Report.*

Education: A listing of the books, brochures, pamphlets, and videotapes the exchange makes available about its products and services. Date, location, and tuition for domestic and foreign classroom sessions on futures and options.

Membership: Data about the number and diversity of members, membership history, and the most recent price at which a seat on the exchange was sold.

News: Newsworthy information about the exchange, its members, and the futures contract it trades.

Here are the URLs for the major U.S. futures exchanges:

Chicago Board of Trade	www.cbot.com
Chicago Mercantile Exchange	www.cme.com
New York Board of Trade	www.nybot.com
New York Mercantile Exchange	www.nymex.com
COMEX (a division of NYME)	www.nymex.com
Kansas City Board of Trade	www.kcbt.com
Minneapolis Grain Exchange	www.mge.com

Other Roads

There are other Internet avenues to explore, depending on how far you want to travel.

Virtually every commodity has its own trade association; its site will have a great deal of information about that commodity, including its price, production, usage, supply, and demand.

A full directory search of the individual commodity name will lead you to many related sites. Some may not be germane, but others will. And it's likely to be information or data that you couldn't readily find elsewhere.

Suggested Reading

The following titles can be previewed and ordered at www.alibris.com.

How the Internet Works, Preston Galla. Que, 1999.

Sams Teach Yourself the Internet in 24 Hours, Ned Snell. Sams, 2001.

Chapter 19

Trading Futures Electronically

Trading futures electronically is not black magic. Even though information moves at the speed of light, success in the market still requires discipline, knowledge, and patience.

There are several benefits to electronic trading:

- *Convenience.* The financial information you need for your trading decision—your current holdings, the amount of free cash in your account, how much margin money the trade will require—can be found on your computer screen.

- *Speed.* Electronic orders are filled and reported instantly. Speed of execution can be important in a fast-moving market.

- *Lower commissions.* Because fewer of their resources are tied up in executing your trade, futures brokerage firms typically charge less for handling an electronic transaction.

- *Independence.* When you trade electronically, you decide what to do and when to do it. No one else has an input into your trading decision, unless you want them to.

Electronic trading also holds a potential pitfall. When you're acting alone, you have no backstop. Electrons don't think for themselves, and they can sometimes run amok.

Terry Wooten, in his book *The Almanac of Online Trading* (McGraw-Hill, 2000), tells of a London trader who, after making an electronic trade in bonds, inadvertently leaned his elbow on his computer keyboard. The key he touched sent a wave of 145 separate sell orders for bonds.

In another incident, a trader meant to type a limit price of $12.40 into an online buy order. Instead, he mistakenly typed in $21.40, reversing the first two digits, and hit the "submit" button. He was fortunate. His order was filled at $12.42, the going price at the time; but it could legally have been filled at any price up to $21.40.

History

The history of electronic trading has several milestones. The first, already behind us, is the use of the personal computer and the Internet to obtain quotes, price charts, research reports, and other futures market information.

The second milestone is *online trading*, where the trader's personal computer is used to enter a trade directly at the broker's Web site. The broker verifies the order and sends it to the exchange trading floor or to the exchange's electronic trading platform, where the order is executed.

Although some online trading has taken place since 1969, when Instinet first introduced a private electronic trading platform, the real breakthrough was the Chicago Mercantile Exchange's (CME) Globex electronic trading system, introduced in 1992, which enabled worldwide computerized futures trading.

The final milestone is *direct access* to the exchange, in which order entry, order verification, and the matching of the best bid and offer are done by computer. Marking the advent are e-mini S&P 500 futures, the first only-electronic futures contract, introduced by the CME on September 9, 1997.

Business on exchange trading floors has been done by human beings in open outcry for some 150 years. But this is changing. Virtually all of the new overseas futures exchanges trade only electronically. The percentage of electronic trading on the two major Chicago exchanges, the CME and the Chicago Board of Trade (CBOT), passed the halfway mark in early 2004.

Getting Started

What does it take to set yourself up for online trading? First is a relatively powerful home computer. Then you'll want online access to futures price quotes. You'll also probably want some online analytical software to help you interpret current market action and forecast price movements. And, finally, you'll need a futures brokerage firm with a good electronic presence, one that accepts orders and reports fills electronically.

Access

For online trading, you will want high-speed Internet access. Several ways to acquire it include cable TV modem, a telephone digital subscriber line (DSL), and space satellite. The two most common are cable TV and DSL. Both preclude the need for a second phone line, and each is capable of increasing your modem speed 20 times or more. In a 2000 survey of cable modem and DSL subscribers conducted by *Consumer Reports*, 90 percent said that their new service was superior to their old dial-up online connections.

Cable TV uses your existing coaxial TV cable to deliver Internet information to your computer. The information is handled by a special modem that is separate from the cable converter box. DSL connects you to the Internet over your existing telephone line while still leaving the line free for normal calls. It uses a special high-speed telephone modem designed specifically for DSL.

Cable modem and DSL are not available everywhere. Some local cable television companies are not set up for cable modems. The availability of DSL depends on the potential subscriber's distance from the telephone company's switching station.

The quality of service of cable modem and DSL differs. Initially, at least, cable modems are faster than DSL. They are also easier (and cheaper) to install. But cable modem service can suffer from popularity. You are the only one on your DSL telephone line. Cable modem is, in effect, a party line; the more local cable modem users there are on the system, the slower is the downloading speed for everybody.

The price of high-speed Internet access is declining. For noncommercial subscribers, the effective monthly cost of cable modem or DSL is now little more than what you would pay for a conventional dial-up service.

Placing Orders Online

Your online brokerage firm will provide you with computer screens showing your open positions, your present account balance, and any orders that you have resting. There is also an order screen where you can place a new order by typing in the futures contract that you want to trade, the quantity, any contingencies, and clicking the "submit" button. The order screen also allows you to get a quick quote or a peek at a current price chart, and you can choose to temporarily delay entering your order (i.e., to "park" it).

Price Quotes

There are many sources for futures price quotes.

Brokerage firms. Most brokerage firms that offer online futures trading also provide real-time price quotes for their clients. Some firms also provide streaming quotes. These may come with conditions, like a minimum account size or a certain minimum number of trades per month. Firms may also provide a look at the "book": the size and price for standing bids and offers away from the current price.

Futures exchanges. The futures exchanges provide price quotes for their own futures contracts. Delayed quotes are free, and the delay is usually 10 minutes. The futures exchanges also provide an array of market information by subscription. Depending on the exchange, this can include real-time streaming quotes, interactive price charts, news, real-time intraday time and sales, and delayed quotes from other major futures exchanges.

Commercial vendors. Several commercial firms specialize in selling futures market information to their subscribers. The most familiar names are probably Reuters and Bloomberg.

Reuters (www.online.reuters.com) has a long history of reporting global financial information. Its *Commodities 2000* service provides real-time price quotes on 150 commodities and 42 options. It also offers market news. Some of the information is free, but you have to register to gain access to it. Cost of the service varies, depending on the coverage selected.

Bloomberg Financial Markets (www.bloomberg.com) delivers data, breaking news, and market analysis to private and institutional investors via the Internet 24 hours a day. Bloomberg also has a television channel where you can find market analysis and interviews with market gurus.

TraderWire is an online package provided by OsterDowJones Commodity News (www.osterdowjones.com). It offers fundamental information, technical analysis, weather impact reports, market sentiment indicator, shipping reports, and other market coverage by subscription.

CRB Market Center Plus (www.crbindex.com) provides real-time quotes, charts, and news to its subscribers. Dow Jones News Service delivers current financial news. Its Web site is www.dowjonesnews.com.

QCharts (www.oners.ims.ca) and ASCTrend (www.ablesys.com) offer to their subscribers real-time prices, customizable charts, buy/sell signals, and technical trading tools like Bollinger Bands, Donchian channels, and Fibonacci counts. QCharts offers a 30-day free trial. ASCTrend has a 30-day trial subscription.

Direct Access

As of this writing, there are some 30 futures brokerage firms that provide a trader with direct access to the exchange for electronic trading. Their names and Internet addresses are listed in Appendix H.

Some firms also offer direct access for open-outcry trades. They include the following:

Cannon Trading Co., Inc.	www.e-futures.com
Farr Financial, Inc.	www.fardirect.com
Iowa Grain Company	www.iowagrain.com
Lind-Waldock & Co.	www.lind-waldock.com
NetFutures	www.netfutures.com
PFG Direct	www.pfgbest.com
Rand Financial Services, Inc.	www.rand-usa.com
SMART futures	www.smartfutures.net
TradeStation 8	www.tradestation.com/8225
York Electronic Services	www.yorkbe.com

These firms differ in the commissions they charge and the additional services they offer, such as free real-time quotes, interactive price charts, or Internet links to market research sources. They also differ in where your order lands. With some, online orders can bypass the exchange floor trading desk altogether and go straight to a hand-held electronic device in the pit.

Trading Arcades

The efficiency and low cost of electronic trading have spurred the growth of trading arcades, where a private trader can pay to gain access to a full array of the tools he needs to conduct electronic trading for his own account.

The trader leases a seat in the arcade and typically deposits $10,000 to $50,000 of his own money for use as margin. The arcade provides him with computer access to the Internet, reduced trading commissions, a fast order-entry system, sophisticated price forecasting tools, and current market data and news. The owner of the arcade may also supply additional working capital.

The arcade owner is paid in two ways: seat rent, which ranges from $2000 to $6000 a month and a split of the trader's profits, commonly 50/50.

An allied operation is known as a "prop shop." The difference is that in the prop shop experienced professional traders receive a salary or wages to trade someone else's money.

The Downside

Larry Williams, a well-known speaker and futures market guru, tells about the time, some years ago, when he put on a relatively big futures position, placed stop orders above and below his entry price, and went camping in the wilderness for 10 days. He says that it was the most comfortable futures position he ever had, because he couldn't worry it. He had no price quotes, no telephone, no newspaper.

It's possible to get too close to markets. If you start reacting to every price tick, your objectivity is going to go down the drain.

Online trading puts market price action in your lap. It is the ideal environment for acting on impulse, which, as we have seen earlier, is not a prescription for success.

A study reported in the May 22, 2000 issue of *Business Week* analyzed the trading results of 1067 traders who switched from telephone to online trading. According to the study, after the switch, the group's trading activity went up and their trading results went down (falling from plus 2 percent to minus 3 percent). Granted, these were stock traders, but human nature is the same everywhere.

If you have to call your local futures broker to place a trade, you have a natural buffer. He will (if he's doing his job) discuss with you your reasons for choosing the trade. He may offer his firm's technical or fundamental outlook for that particular futures market. He may even try to talk you out of the trade.

When all you have to do to place an order is touch a key on your personal computer, you have to be your own buffer.

We've talked elsewhere in this book about planning, about deciding beforehand—even commiting to writing—the profit goal in the trade you are considering, the amount of money you are willing to risk, and the specific reasons why you believe the trade will be a success.

Such planning is even more important for online trading. Deliberate planning defers the impulse. It creates, at least in part, the buffer that online trading lacks.

Suggested Reading

The Almanac of Online Trading, Terry Wooten. McGraw-Hill, New York, 2000.
e-investing: How to Choose and Use a Discount Broker, Rob Carrick and Guy J. Anderson. Wiley, New York, 2000.
The Art of Electronic Futures Trading, William R. Kaiser and James E. Green. McGraw-Hill, New York, 2003.

20

Day Trading

Futures positions can be divided into two broad categories: position trades and day trades.

A futures position that is held overnight is generally referred to as a position trade. Position traders keep their eyes on longer-term price trends; they may hold the same futures position for several days or weeks. Day trading is what it sounds like: the opening and closing of a market position within the same day or trading session. The object is to capture quick trading profits from relatively small intraday price moves.

Day traders end each business day flat, with no positions. They are therefore immune to any adverse economic news that might break while the markets are closed, and this immunity is deemed one of the advantages of day trading.

Because fundamental market factors—weather, crop yields, the total number of grain-consuming animals, interest rates, consumer preferences—change very slowly, day trading decisions are invariably based on technical analysis. Especially important are price support and resistance levels, as they can be established with just a few days of price action.

The requirements for successful day trading are (1) a liquid, volatile futures market; (2) a futures brokerage firm that offers online order entry, low commissions, and good trade executions; (3) access to up-to-the-second market and price information; (4) a willingness to spend a large part of the business day tracking price movements and placing buy or sell orders; and (5) a strong stomach.

Market Selection

Volatility

To provide a good venue for day trading, futures prices must be active; they must cover a lot of ground during the day. There's no point in buying a ticket on a train that never leaves the station.

There are several ways to measure a market's volatility. The simplest way is by eyeball. One look at a daily price chart will tell you whether prices in that particular market have been traversing wide daily trading ranges.

A more accurate way is to measure price volatility mathematically. The values needed for these calculations are the average daily price ranges in that market for the past several days. These are derived by subtracting the daily low price from the daily high price for each day, adding up these daily ranges, and dividing that total by the number of days. (For days that have large price gaps or days that open and remain at the limit, the previous day's closing price can be used as the opposite benchmark.)

The average daily price range is divided by the maximum possible daily range in that market. The answer is that market's present volatility index.

Let's take an example, and to keep it simple, we'll use corn futures on the CBOT. The present daily price limit for corn is 20 cents, so the maximum daily price range is 40 cents (from limit up to limit down).

The number of trading days to use in your calculations is up to you. Some consider 14 days to be the optimum number—long enough to provide a good representation, yet short enough to give adequate weight to the most recent trading days.

Now, suppose that the actual daily ranges in corn futures prices over the past 14 days have been as shown in Figure 20.1. These daily ranges add up to 85½. If you divide that total by 14, the number of days in your calculations, you get an average daily price range for September corn futures of 6.11 cents. This number is converted to a percentage of the maximum range by dividing 6.11 by 40, yielding an answer of .15275 or 15.3 percent.

So, the average daily price range for September corn futures over the past 14 days has been about 15 percent of the maximum allowable limit-to-limit daily range. Fifteen percent is the volatility index for September corn futures.

Volatility indexes can be similarly derived for other futures markets, and the indexes compared to identify the markets that are, from the standpoint of volatility, the most suitable for day trading.

If only one market is under your microscope, there's no hard and fast rule for the required minimum volatility index, but any market with a volatility index of 20 or more should provide adequate opportunities for day trading.

Day Number	Daily Price Range (cents per bushel)
1	6
2	7½
3	8
4	5¼
5	6¾
6	5
7	6½
8	4¾
9	6
10	3¼
11	5½
12	7¾
13	7
14	5¼
Total	85½ ÷ 14 = 6.11

$$6.11 \div 40 = .15275 \text{ or } 15.3 \text{ percent}$$

$$\text{Volatility Index} = 15$$

Figure 20.1   Calculating the volatility index.

Liquidity

A market's liquidity is a function of its trading volume. In fact, the lack of trading volume in a futures market can be the cause of price volatility. If a market is so thinly traded that your order tends to influence the price level, any resulting price movement will be against you.

This effect can be readily avoided by restricting your day-trading activity to futures markets that have a large following. Volume data for each futures market are presented in Web information pages, price charts, and newspaper price tables.

Ongoing Trends

Trending markets contain strong undercurrents. A day trade taken against the present trend—for example, a long position in an established downtrend—is unnecessarily exposed to countervailing forces, even though the position is expected to be on for only a matter of minutes.

The possibility of adverse price movement increases if your short-term price objective is not reached immediately, and you decide to leave the position in place for a while longer.

When day trades are placed in consonance with the apparent underlying price trend in that market, the odds, however slim, are on your side.

The algorithms presented by Eugene Nofri and Jeanette Nofri Steinberg in their slim volume, *Success in Commodities . . . the Congestion Phase System*, should be of interest to day traders. The Nofri thesis is simple: When prices are within a congestion phase, there is a high probability (approaching 75 percent, according to the authors) that a 2- or 3-day move in one direction will be immediately followed by a close in the opposite direction. A congestion phase is defined by the authors as a recent high and low with at least 2 days of pullback from the high and 2 days of rally from the low.

Losses

Losses are magnified in day trading because there is limited amount of time for you to recover from a setback.

Recovering from a loss is not as straightforward as it might seem. Getting back to where you started requires a greater percentage gain than the percentage lost. It's like walking along a slippery slope; it's easier to slide down than to climb back up.

This effect is shown as follows:

Percentage Loss	Percentage Gain Needed to Recover
5	5.3
10	11.1
15	17.6
20	25.0
25	33.3
30	42.9

For example, if you have an equity of $1000 in a position and lose 20 percent, your equity drops to $800. To get back to your original equity level of

$1000, you have to earn $200 profit, which is a 25 percent return on your current $800 equity (200 ÷ 800 = .25).

Number of Positions

Seasoned day traders recommend against having more than one futures position on at any one time. If you are juggling two or more day trades, you won't be able to give any one of them the attention it requires.

Choosing a Conduit to the Futures Market

The brokerage firm you use for day trading will be online. It will provide you with real-time prices and market information and offer fast, reliable order execution and relatively low trading commissions.

Orders that are not handled properly or filled efficiently (slippage) can eat up a large part of your potential day-trading gains. The same goes for commissions. Because your intraday profit goals are nominal, commissions represent a relatively large percentage of your risk/reward.

Online Order Entry

Another important element is time. The conventional order process, involving the telephone, is much too slow and cumbersome for day trading. For effective day trading, you need a firm that is hard-wired, that routes your online orders directly to the trading floor for execution, and that reports fills back to you electronically.

Price Quotes

Up-to-the-second price quotes are of vital importance to day traders. Sources for real-time quotes are discussed in the preceding chapter.

Commissions

It wasn't too long ago that big futures commission merchants charged three-digit commissions for a single-lot futures trade.

That's changed. The economies of e-commerce and the heightened competition among specialized futures trading firms have driven futures trading commissions down to bedrock. There are online brokerage firms today that will handle a round-turn e-mini futures trade for $7 or less.

Trading Help. Some online firms offer proprietary software for their clients to use. The software enables traders to review past price history, recognize price trends, identify price support and resistance levels, generate buy and sell signals, back-test home-grown trading algorithms, and more.

Firms vary in the nature and price of the trading system software they offer. A list of firms and their trading software would include:

Software	Company	Web Site
Amibroker	amibroker.com	www.amibroker.com
CQG	CQG, Inc.	www.cqg.com
eSignal	Interactive Data Corp.	www.esignal.com
Metastock	Reuter/Equis Intern'tl	www.metastock.com
ProTA Gold	Beesoft	www.beesoft.net
TradersStudio	TradersStudio	www.tradersstudio.com
TraderXL Pro	AnalyzerXL LLC	www.analyzerxl.com
TradeStation	Trade Station Technologies, Inc.	www.tradestation.com
Wealth-Lab	Wealth-Lab, Inc.	www.wealth-lab.com

Some firms also offer training or education for new traders. One is Ira Epstein and Company Futures. Their Futures Academy offers a three-part course that includes a written textbook, an accompanying CD-ROM, and a "Train to Trade" segment with a live broker. The course comes with access to Epstein hotlines, charting software, streaming price quotes, paper trading, and 60 days of mentoring.

Among other firms offering similar curricula are Peregrine Financial Group's E-academy of Trading and the nonprofit Institute for Financial Markets.

So, where do you start? Chapter 19 gives you a limited selection of online futures brokerage firms to choose from. There are others listed in the book *The Complete Guide to Electronic Futures Trading*, referenced at the end of this chapter.

Because the landscape is ever-changing, it may require some electronic window-shopping for you to find the brokerage firm and online services that meet your requirements.

Keep Your Head Down

Day trading is serious business. Traders who approach it as a lark or a hobby will soon join the reputed 90 percent who fail.

Ultrashort-term buying and selling of futures contracts require extra discipline. It's even more important that you have a specific trading plan, and that you stick to it. The plan, preferably in writing, should answer the questions: How much money will I commit to trading? Which markets will I trade? Which positions? Why? What is the maximum acceptable loss for each position? What is the profit goal for each position?

Because day trading is a fast track, the use of stop orders and the immediate taking of small losses are basic to survival. It's also a good idea to review your trades at the end of each day to see what worked and what didn't, and to see how you might learn from any mistakes that you made.

Then there's the matter of time. Occasionally it might be possible for you to set your positions early in the day, place your protective stop orders, and direct your attention to other matters. But that would be contrary to human nature. You will wonder if your stops have been hit, whether there has been new market information that affects your holdings, if a situation is developing that calls for you to take a new tack.

If you are going to day trade, you should plan to be wed to your computer screen for a large part of the day.

The Right Stuff

A recent newspaper article concerned a stock market investor who, after day-trading stocks full time for several months, quit and went back to his previous 9-to-5 job. He said that he felt as if he had been paroled from prison.

Day trading of futures is no less stressful.

We all differ in our willingness to accept risk. Some seek a chance to bungee-jump; others believe that anyone who jumps off a 300-foot tower with a rubber band around his ankle must have a few screws loose. That's physical risk, of course, but financial risk is much the same. The financial bungee jumper bets $1000 on a 30-to-1 shot at the racetrack. At the other end of the range is the person who is quite content with a 4 percent annual return on a bank CD.

Your tolerance for risk could be genetic. According to Robert Deel, writing in *The Strategic Electronic Day Trader*, listed in the Suggested Reading at the end of the chapter, there is evidence that the presence of one particular gene marks the risk taker. If the gene is absent, you are naturally less disposed to seek or tolerate risk.

If you're considering trading futures, you are certainly not one to keep your money under a mattress. But even futures trades vary widely in risk. A net position in S&P 500 futures is much more hazardous than a long-term spread in one of the grain markets.

Only you can assess your tolerance for risk. And even that introspection might be too subjective. The only sure way is to day trade for a while and see how you handle it. If day-trading literally gives you a stomachache, it's likely not for you.

Suggested Reading

The Complete Guide to Electronic Futures Trading, Scott Slutsky and Darrell Jobman. McGraw-Hill, New York, 2000.

The Strategic Electronic Day Trader, Robert Deel. Wiley, New York, 2000.

Technical Analysis for Short-term Traders, Martin Pring. Marketplace Books, Columbia, MD, 2000.

How to Start Day Trading Futures, Options and Indices, Jeffry Katz and Donna McCormick. McGraw-Hill, New York, 2001.

Technical Trading Online, Robert Roth. Wiley, New York, 2001.

More Chart Patterns and What They Mean

Triangles

Triangles come in more than one variety. The *symmetrical* triangle looks like the equilateral triangle you probably first met in freshman math, with all three sides and all three angles equal. It has some of the qualities of a rectangle. The difference is that the top and bottom sides of the pattern are not parallel but converge to a point at the right.

If the rectangle signifies a standoff between the bulls and the bears, the symmetrical triangle represents a pitched battle between them. With each rally, the sellers step in at a lower point to turn prices back. Each decline is met with buying at a higher level. The battle is over when one side finally prevails and prices break out of the triangle. Figure A.1 (p. 242) shows an example.

When a symmetrical triangle interrupts a swift price move, it often marks the middle of that move. That is, the travel of prices beyond the triangle will be about equal to the travel of prices before the triangle.

The symmetrical triangle in Figure A.1 turned out to be a reversal pattern, marking a major top in wheat futures.

There are two other kinds of triangles, and each contains a built-in indication of where prices are likely to go next. They are both right triangles. They are called *ascending* and *descending* triangles.

An ascending triangle has the flat side on the top. The rising line at the bottom of the triangle indicates that buyers are becoming increasingly aggressive, as

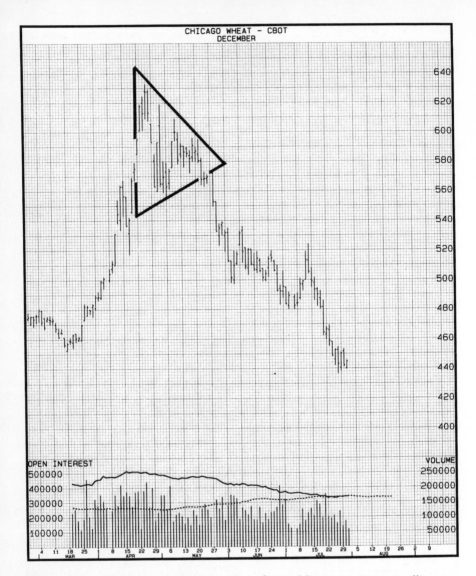

Figure A.1   The symmetrical triangle is formed by two minor trendlines, one upward and one downward. Prices are typically squeezed toward the apex before breaking out of the pattern. This particular symmetrical triangle formed a market top.

Chart courtesy of *CRB Futures Perspective*, a publication of Commodity Research Bureau.

they are stopping each decline at a successively higher level. Sellers are not stepping up their activities; rallies meet resistance and are turned back at about the same price each time. The pattern holds the promise that the confrontation will be won by the more aggressive bulls, when overhead resistance is finally overpowered.

Figure A.2 shows a descending triangle pattern. Here the bears are the aggressors, as rallies are turned back at a lower price each time. When the reservoir of buying power at about $1.70 a pound was tapped out, coffee prices fell through the floor of the triangle and headed lower.

Figure A.2   The descending triangle indicates that the bears are becoming increasingly aggressive; they are stopping each rally at a lower level than the previous one. The buyers, in the meantime, are just holding their own. The pattern presages a downside breakout, as was demonstrated in this weekly chart for coffee futures.

Chart courtesy of *CRB Futures Perspective*, a publication of Commodity Research Bureau.

Triangles may mark either price reversal points or areas of price consolidation. As with rectangles, there are clues. A descending triangle at the end of a long upward price move would carry the presumption of a reversal pattern. An ascending triangle in an extended bear market would have a good probability of marking the bottom.

Double Tops and Bottoms

A double top occurs when an ongoing rally fails in an attempt to make a new high. The pattern is a harbinger of change. It symbolizes diminished buying power. After pushing prices to a succession of new peaks, the bulls have suddenly lost some of their strength. If, in the ensuing decline, prices should close below the intervening low, it would indicate that not only are the bulls getting weaker, but the bears are getting stronger. It is at that point that the topping pattern is considered complete.

A double bottom is the same pattern, inverted. After pushing prices relentlessly down to a series of new lows, the bears are unable to do it again. Prices stop instead at about the same level as the immediately previous decline. From that point they rally. When the intervening high is surpassed, the bottoming pattern is confirmed and a new uptrend begun. Double bottom patterns are not seen as often as double tops.

Figure A.3 (p. 245) provides an example of a double top.

Expanding Tops and Bottoms

An expanding top marks a major turning point. The price pattern looks like an unstable boat in rough water. Each new high is higher, and each new low is lower, until the market finally capsizes. There are generally five clearly visible turning points, starting with the first high. The pattern is considered completed when prices close below the low of the day on which the last high was made. On occasion there will be a sixth and seventh point before prices finally turn downward.

Figure A.4 (p. 246) shows an example of an expanding top.

In an expanding bottom, the pattern is inverted. Expanding bottoms are rare.

Gaps

A gap is a price range on the chart where no trading took place. If tomorrow's low price is higher than today's high price, the two price ranges will not overlap; white space would be left on the chart, and an upside gap would be formed. If

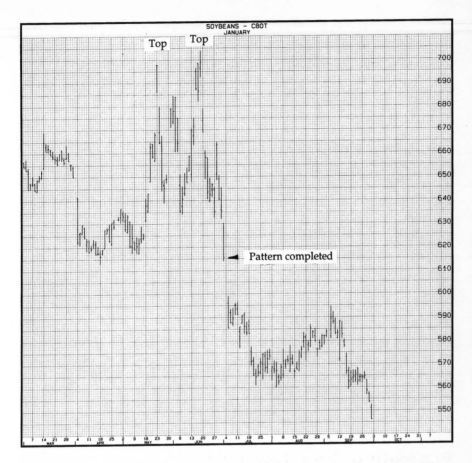

Figure A.3   A double top. Soybean prices peaked on May 23 at about $7.00 a bushel. When prices rallied back to the area 4 weeks later, they were unable to register new highs. The close below $6.35, the intervening low, completed the double top reversal pattern and ushered in a major decline.
Chart courtesy of *CRB Futures Perspective*, a publication of Commodity Research Bureau.

today's high price is lower than yesterday's low, a downside price gap would be created.

Gaps are formed on the opening of trading. They are caused by the overnight buildup of orders in the pit and are not unusual. However, most of them are "closed" later in the day, as subsequent trading activity eventually moves through the empty price range, and the gap never appears on the chart.

Gaps that are not closed symbolize powerful forces. Look at Figure A.5 (p. 247). The momentum in feeder cattle prices was clearly downward in the

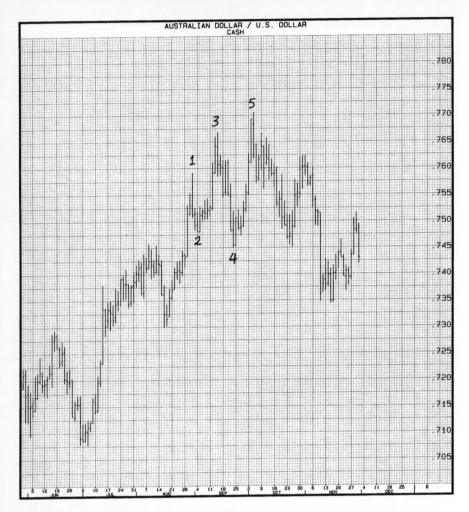

Figure A.4   Expanding tops generally have five waves, but a sixth and seventh wave may occur before the market reverses course. The top is completed when prices close below the low of the day on which the high was registered. In this example, that was on October 5, at a price near .7580.

Chart courtesy of *CRB Futures Perspective*, a publication of Commodity Research Bureau.

spring of that year. On April 29, an abrupt change in market psychology occurred. The bulls suddenly awoke. Prices gapped sharply upward and never looked back.

What causes the change in market psychology? It could have been any one of a number of factors: a report that indicated higher feed grain prices, indications of an increased demand for beef at home or abroad, an outbreak of disease among cattle.

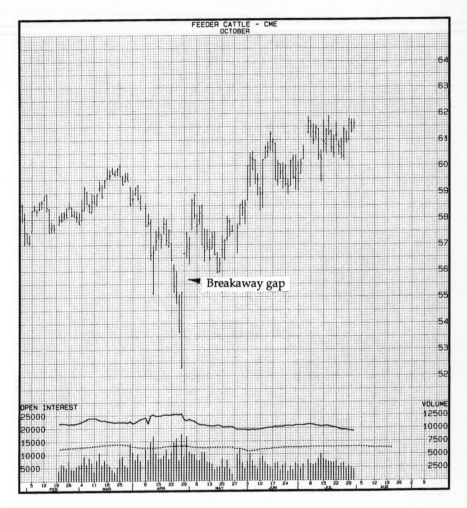

Figure A.5   This wide "breakaway" gap in feeder cattle signaled a sudden awakening of bullish market forces.

Chart courtesy of *CRB Futures Perspective*, a publication of Commodity Research Bureau.

Whatever the cause, it was not ephemeral; the ensuing rally lasted 3 months and carried all the way to 62 cents a pound.

It is not unusual for prices to create a gap when leaving an established chart pattern. It's as if they need the extra inertia to break clear, like a rocket leaving the earth's gravity. A gap in this position is referred to as a *breakaway* gap (Figure A.5).

Figure A.6 (p. 248) shows a different kind of gap. From June to mid-August, prices for March cotton were in an established downtrend. Then there

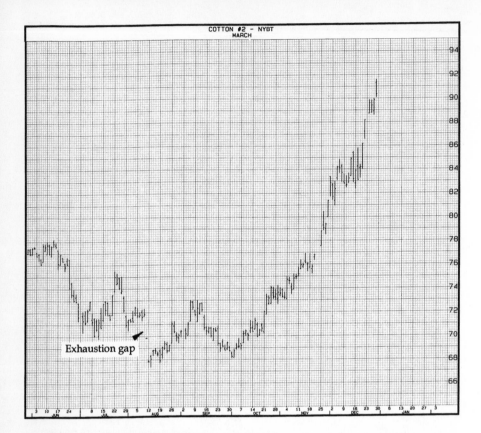

Figure A.6 Consecutive limit-down days in mid-August created a wide "exhaustion" gap, a sign that the bears were tiring. The small gains that followed led eventually to a double-bottom reversal pattern and a 3-month rally to new contract highs.

Chart courtesy of *CRB Futures Perspective*, a publication of Commodity Research Bureau.

was sudden blowoff. On August 15 and 16, prices gapped sharply downward on extremely high trading volume.

It was the bears' last lunge. The following day, the market began to inch upward. Within 4 months, prices had advanced 33 percent from their August lows.

Appropriately, these are called *exhaustion* gaps. An exhaustion gap has two special qualities: It is usually found at the end of a relatively sustained price move, and it is the widest gap on the chart.

The final category comprises gaps that are formed near the middle of extended price moves. Called *measuring* gaps, they are not as common or considered as reliable as breakaway or exhaustion gaps. Figure A.7 is an example of a

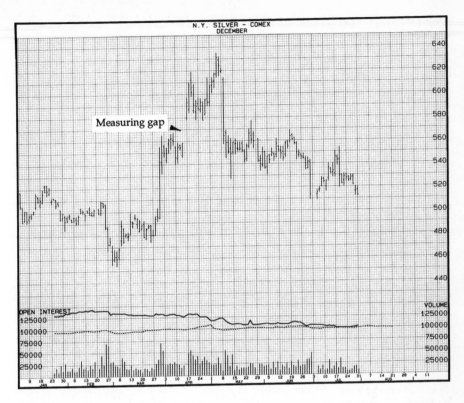

Figure A.7 The upside price gap that formed in silver futures in mid-April turned out to be of the "measuring" kind. That is, it occurred almost exactly in the middle of the sharp rally from $5.00 to $6.35 per ounce.

Chart courtesy of *CRB Futures Perspective*, a publication of Commodity Research Bureau.

measuring gap that kept its promise. The upward move in silver began in late March at a price of $4.80. The big gap formed on April 17 embraced a price level of $5.65, the halfway point in a sharp rally.

Some other incidental intelligence: For a gap to be significant, its presence must be unusual; charts of thinly traded markets are full of gaps that mean nothing. The gap should also be unusually wide. The price action immediately following the gap is also important. If the gap is closed in the next day or two, it's a sign that the buyers or sellers who created the gap may not have sufficient numbers to keep the price move going, and the gap's significance would be reduced. As we mentioned earlier, gaps may also provide support and resistance, but their performance in this regard is erratic.

Unusual Reversals

Among the annals of price chart patterns, island reversals may well be the most dependable. Unfortunately, they are quite rare. The island is formed by a pair of price gaps. Prices gap to new highs or lows, trade in that area for a day or two, then immediately gap sharply in the other direction. The day or two of intervening price action is left floating in white space, an island that marks a market turning point.

Figure A.8 shows a 1-day island reversal that marked the summit in February heating oil. The stage was set on August 1, with an upside (exhaustion) gap. The next day, falling prices left a downside gap in their wake, and the island reversal was formed. The ensuing decline was still intact at Christmas.

Some trends end not with a bang but with a whimper. An example can be seen in July natural gas (Figure A.9, p. 252). After a quiet descent over a period of 8 months, downward momentum eased in early January. Prices moved sideways for a couple of months, then gradually bent around to the upside. The result is a saucer-shaped pattern, sometimes called a "rounding bottom" by technicians.

Another seldom-seen chart phenomenon is the "head-and-shoulders" reversal pattern, which can be found at market tops or market bottoms.

An example of a head-and-shoulders top is shown in Figure A.10 (p. 253). Prices form the left shoulder and head with what look like just two more new highs and normal pullbacks in an ongoing uptrend. The first suspicion of a reversal is raised when the rally in early January fails to reach a new high. When prices break down through the "neckline" drawn across the pattern's lows, suspicions are confirmed; the reversal formation is completed.

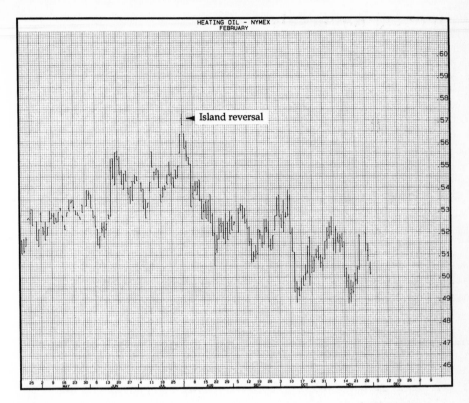

Figure A.8   Although the earlier price action doesn't show on this chart, the 1-day island reversal on August 1 ended a sustained 5-month rally in heating oil futures.

Chart courtesy of *CRB Futures Perspective*, a publication of Bridge Commodity Research Bureau.

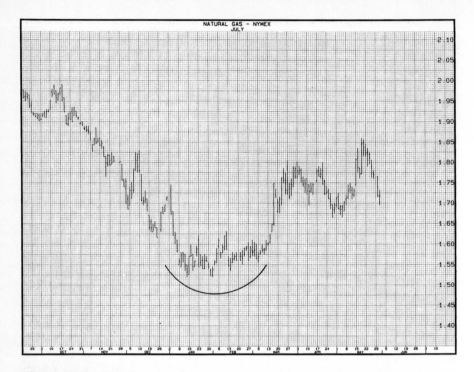

Figure A.9   Found more often in conservative stocks than in futures, the so-called rounding bottom signals a gradual change in momentum from bearish to bullish.

Chart courtesy of *CRB Futures Perspective*, a publication of Commodity Research Bureau.

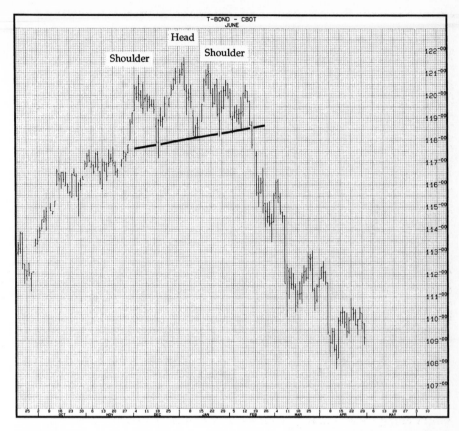

Figure A.10 The head-and-shoulders top is completed when prices break down through the neckline drawn across the pattern's consecutive lows. This one, which also marked an all-time high in T-bond future prices, provided the jumping-off point for a major downtrend.

Chart courtesy of *CRB Futures Perspective*, a publication of Commodity Research Bureau.

More About Point-and-Figure Charts

To give you a better idea of how a point-and-figure chart works, let's build an actual point-and-figure chart from scratch. We'll use Eurodollar futures, a box size of 10 points, a three-box reversal, and the following prices:

Day	High	Low	Close
1	91.20	90.96	91.00
2	91.55	91.10	91.30
3	92.02	91.78	91.95
4	91.95	91.72	91.87
5	91.63	90.92	91.41
6	91.23	91.02	91.03
7	91.18	90.92	91.05
8	91.63	91.22	91.47
9	91.44	90.84	91.12
10	90.84	90.65	90.71

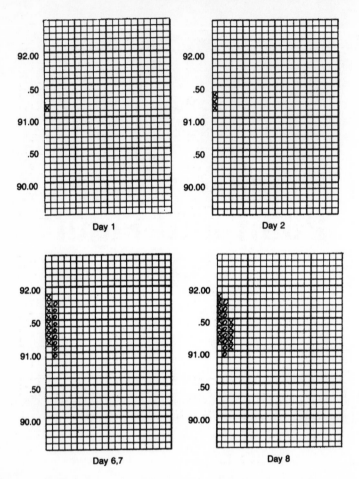

Figure B.1 Ten days in the life of a point-and-figure chart. Prices are in the table on the previous page. The arrow on Day 9 marks a point-and-figure "sell" signal—when the present column of Os drops one space below the immediately previous column of Os.

We'll begin our chart with Day 1. Looking back over the price action of the previous few weeks, we see that an advance is under way; so we'll start by plotting Xs. We put an X in the 91.20 box, the high on Day 1 (see Figure B.1).

After the close the next day (Day 2) we update our chart, using that day's low and high prices. The first thing we look for is a possible reversal. There was none. The low on Day 2 was 91.10. That's only one box below yesterday's high of 91.20. According to the rules we set up ourselves for this chart, the daily low must be at least three full boxes below the most recent high before it is consid-

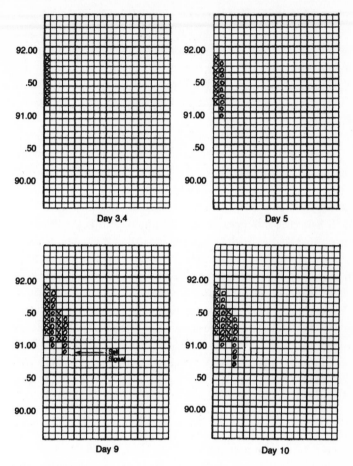

Figure B.1 *(Continued)*

ered a reversal. We then check to see if there was a new high. There was, at 91.55. Staying in the same column, we put an X in the 91.30 box and an X in the 91.40 box. We do not put an X in the 91.50 box because it was not completely "filled"; that is, prices did not completely traverse the 91.50 box but stopped in the middle of the box at 91.55.

The rally continues. After the close on Day 3 we again update our chart. We look first for a possible reversal. Again, there was none. We next check the day's high price. It was 92.02, a new peak. To record the advance, we add five Xs to the chart: in the 91.50 box, the 91.60 box, the 91.70 box, the 91.80 box, and the 91.90 box. We make no mark in the 92.00 box because prices did not reach the upper boundary of that box at 92.10; they stopped at 92.02.

The next day (Day 4), the high and low prices are 91.95 and 91.72. We check for a possible reversal. The low of 91.72 is only one box below 91.90, the highest X. There was no reversal. The high of 91.95 is below yesterday's high, so no X is added to the column. As a result, *nothing* is added to the point-and-figure chart this day.

The following day (Day 5), the high and low are 91.63 and 90.92. The low of 90.92 is nine boxes below our highest X at 92.00. That more than meets our three-box criterion for a price reversal. We move one column to the right and, starting with the 91.80 box, we add Os down to and including the 91.00 box. We don't put an O in the 90.90 box, because the decline stopped at 90.92; approaching it from the top, prices didn't completely "fill" the 90.90 box.

Our point-and-figure chart has just recorded a change in the price trend from up to down.

On Days 6 and 7, the lower trend continued. However, no entry was made on either day because there was no new low. On Day 8, the high price was 91.63. That exceeds our three-box reversal criterion, so we move one column to the right and put Xs in the 91.10 box, 91.20 box, 91.30 box, 91.40 box, and 91.50 box. For an X in the 91.60 box, prices would have had to reach 91.70 or beyond; the rally stopped at 91.63, so we leave the 91.60 box empty.

Prices turn down again on Day 9, creating a reversal to the downside and causing Os to be placed in the boxes for 91.40, 91.30, 91.20, 91.10, 91.00, and 90.90. The decline continues on Day 10, when the 90.80 and 90.70 boxes receive Os.

We would continue to plot Os in this column until we observe a daily high that is at least three full boxes above the lowest O. That would be an indication that the trend had reversed back to the upside; we would move to the next column to the right and start to plot Xs.

Adjusting Values

Because you select the box size and reversal criterion yourself, it is possible for you to fine-tune the point-and-figure chart. The smaller the box size, the more sensitive the chart is to price changes. The smaller the reversal criterion, the greater the number of trend changes that will be signaled. For volatile markets, you would use relatively large box sizes and reversal criteria, so the chart would ignore jittery short-term price fluctuations. In a quieter market, you would use smaller values, to pick up the more subtle price movements.

The key is to strike a happy medium. What you want your point-and-figure chart to do is to send you a signal when the underlying price trend has changed but ignore as much as possible the minor price changes that do not affect the present trend. Selecting the values to be used in a point-and-figure chart is as much art as science and is accomplished mainly by trial and error.

Trading Signals

Point-and-figure charts have another attribute not found in bar charts: Point-and-figure charts can give "buy" and "sell" signals. A simple point-and-figure sell signal occurs when the column of Os currently being plotted falls below the immediately preceding column of Os, as shown on Day 9 in Figure B.1. A buy signal is given when an ongoing column of Xs tops by at least one box the immediately preceding column of Xs, as in Figure B.2. Point-and-figure chartists recognize and use several other price patterns in making their trading decisions, but most are a variation on these simple buy and sell signals.

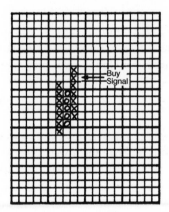

Figure B.2   A point-and-figure "buy" signal occurs when a column of Xs rises one box above the immediately previous column of Xs, as in this chart excerpt.

Optimizing

Technical analysts use computers to reconstruct past market activity and test trading theories. The underlying assumption is that a trading system that worked well in the past will work well in the future. Some analysts sell their findings in the form of proprietary trading methods, providing specific point-and-figure box sizes and reversal criteria that have worked well in certain markets over recent months. The process is called "optimizing" because it seeks the optimum balance between the values that produce the greatest profit and the values that produce the smallest loss.

The problem is, of course, that today's price behavior may not resemble yesterday's price behavior at all. Factors that affect prices are almost countless and in constant change. The conditions that caused a $7/32$ box and five-box reversal to work well for T-bonds last month, for example, may not be repeated this month or ever again.

Appendix

More About Moving Averages

Weighted Moving Averages

All prices are not all of equal importance. Yesterday's price is likely to be a better indication of current market sentiment than last week's price, and last week's price more indicative than the price a month ago. On this thesis, some technicians weight the various closing prices, assigning higher values to more recent prices. A typical weighting system for a 5-day moving average would be:

1 . . 2 . . 3 . . 4 . . 5

That is, today's closing price would be multiplied by 5, the previous day's closing price multiplied by 4, the day before that multiplied by 3, and so on back to 5 days ago. The totals are then summed and divided by the sum of the weights.

To take an example, suppose the "prices" for the last 5 days were 17, 20, 22, 23, and 24. The simple average would be the sum of those numbers (106) divided by 5, or 21.2. The weighted average, using the weighting system described before, would be:

Day	Price	×	Weight	=	Weighted Daily Value
5	24	×	5	=	120
4	23	×	4	=	92
3	22	×	3	=	66
2	20	×	2	=	40
1	17	×	1	=	17
			15		335 ÷ 15 = 22.3

The weighted 5-day average (22.3) is higher than the simple 5-day average (21.2) because the more recent prices are higher, and by design they have a greater influence on the outcome.

This is only one example. Weights may be assigned to any number of days and in any amounts.

The ultimate in weighting is called an *exponential* moving average. The recent days still get the most emphasis, but every day back to the start of the calculations is given some mathematical recognition. The technique was developed for use in antiaircraft fire control during World War II, to forecast the position of a moving target.

To get an exponential moving average started, you need an initial value. For this you could use the simple average of closing prices over the past several days; say, 10 days. This value is plugged into the formula:

$$MN = MO + C(P - MO)$$

where

MN = the new moving average

MO = yesterday's moving average

P = today's closing price

C = a smoothing constant

Each day the calculation is made again, using the previous day's exponential moving average for MO.

The key is C, the smoothing constant. It is always a number between 0 and 1. The smaller it is, the more days are included in the exponential moving average. For example, if a constant of .05 is used, the past 44 days have about 90 percent of the total weight. With a smoothing constant of .20, the past 10 days have about 90 percent of the total weight, and with a constant of .40 the past 4 days have 90 percent of the total weight. The value of the constant must be chosen by the technical analyst to fit the character of that particular market.

Trading With Moving Averages

The simplest approach to trading with a single moving average is:

When the daily closing price is about the moving average, be long.
When the daily closing price is below the moving average, be short.

For example, suppose you had just begun to keep a 3-day moving average, and the prices of the past several trading days were as shown in the table:

Day	Closing Price	Three-Day Moving Average	Position
1	89.50		
2	88.70		
3	87.25	88.50	
4	86.40	87.25	Go short
5	86.10	86.58	Stay short
6	85.90	86.13	Stay short
7	85.70	85.90	Stay short
8	86.30	85.97	Stay short
9	86.75	86.25	Cover short; go long
10	87.30	86.78	Stay long

On Day 3, the first day that you can calculate a value for the moving average, the closing price is below the moving average value. Following the two rules previously mentioned, you take a short position on Day 4.

On Day 5 the closing price is still below the moving average, so you keep your short position. The same is true for Days 6 and 7. On Day 8, after the close, you see that a switch has occurred; the closing price has moved above the 3-day moving average. Following the rules, you close out your short position and take a new long position on Day 9. You keep the long position until the daily closing price drops back below the moving average.

These two simple trading rules keep you always in the market. There are other moving average methods that allow more time for the price trend to change. For example, some traders use two moving averages: one short term (e.g., a 5-day moving average) and one long term (e.g., a 20-day moving average). A long position is held when the price is above both moving averages. A short position is held when the price is below both moving averages. At all other times the trader is out of the market.

As with point-and-figure charts, technical analysts have identified the moving averages that worked best in certain markets in the past. Many have published their conclusions. These trading criteria suffer from a problem we have talked about before: They assume that today's markets will closely resemble yesterday's markets, and that may not be the case.

More About Stochastics and Relative Strength

We promised to tell you how the Relative Strength Index is calculated: The formula for finding relative strength is:

$$\text{Relative strength} = 100 \times \left(\frac{RS}{1 + RS} \right)$$

where

$$RS = \frac{AU}{AD}$$

AU = the total number of days in the last 14 trading days with higher closes

AD = the total number of days in the last 14 trading days with lower closes

To begin, you need 15 days of closing prices for the market you're interested in. To take a specific example, suppose that the most recent closing prices for December T-bond futures were:

101-11, 101-28, 101-20, 102-02, 102-21, 102-10, 103-05, 103-16,
102-30, 103-12, 103-29, 104-04, 103-20, 104-10, 104-18

Starting with the second price, we count the days in which prices closed higher than the immediately previous day. There are 9; that's the value for AU. The days in which prices closed lower than the immediately previous day total 5; that's the value for AD.

Now we can figure out the current relative strength of this market:

$$RS = \frac{AU}{AD} = \frac{9}{5} = 3.6$$

We go back to the first formula and plug the value of 3.6 in for RS:

$$\text{Relative strength} = 100 \times \left(\frac{RS}{1 + RS}\right), \text{or}$$

$$\text{Relative strength} = 100 \times \left(\frac{3.6}{1 + RS}\right) = 100 \times \frac{3.6}{4.6}$$

$$100 \times \left(\frac{3.6}{4.6}\right) = 100 \times .782 = 78.2$$

The relative strength of December T-bonds futures at the moment is 78.2. That's a high value, but it could be expected; prices had an obvious upward bias during the last 14 trading days.

To continue with the process, you would add the next day's closing price to the list, drop the oldest closing price off, and recalculate.

The data may be used in different ways. Many analysts consider a divergence between the direction of prices and the direction of the Relative Strength Index to be particularly significant. They plot daily relative strength values on a chart of daily prices for the same market, so any divergence between the two is immediately apparent.

When he introduced his Relative Strength Index in 1978, J. Welles Wilder chose a period of 14 trading days as the basis for his calculations because he considered that that period represented the normal distance between commodity price peaks and valleys, or half of the natural price cycle.

But that number is not sacred. It's possible that 14 days is not the half-cycle in the market you're studying and that, as with moving averages, factoring a larger or smaller number of days into the calculations would produce more accurate values for relative strength. The best number of days to use must be determined by the market analyst on a case-by-case basis.

Generally, if the actual half-cycle of prices is greater than the number of days chosen, RSI values will tend to be too high, and vice versa.

Stochastics

We said earlier that closing prices in uptrends tend to cluster near the days' highs, and that in downtrends closing prices tend to cluster near the days' lows. As an ongoing trend loses its vigor, this behavior may change subtly. When a market is ready to turn from up to down, for example, the highs may still be higher, but closing prices often settle nearer to the lows of the day.

There are several stochastic indicators designed to determine market strength or weakness by evaluating the position of closing prices in the daily range. One of the earliest was the A/D (accumulation/distribution) oscillator, first published by Jim Waters and Larry Williams in an article in the May 1975 issue of *Commodities* magazine.

They began with two values, which they called *buying power* (BP) and *selling power* (SP). These are defined as:

BP = the day's high price minus the opening price
SP = the day's closing price minus the low price

These two values are plugged into the equation, where DRF means daily raw figure:

$$DRF = \frac{BP + SP}{2 \times (high - low)}$$

The maximum value for DRF is 1, which occurs when trading opens at the day's low and closes at the day's high. When the opposite happens—trading opens at the day's high and closes at the day's low—the value of DRF for that day is zero. All other cases will fall somewhere between zero and 1.

Suppose that the market we're looking at had on this day an opening price of 36.50, a high of 37.20, a low of 36.40, and a closing price of 36.85.

The DRF would be:

$$DRF = \frac{.70 + .45}{2 \times .80} = \frac{1.15}{1.60} = .718$$

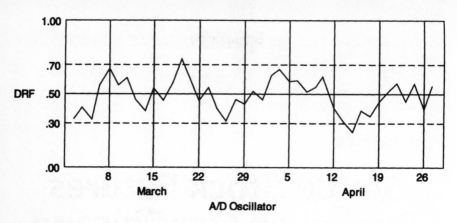

Figure D.1   A typical A/D stochastic oscillator.

When you have figured out the DRF for several days, the numbers can be plotted on a horizontal scale that runs from 0.00 to 1.00. Two horizontal lines are then drawn to cut off the extreme peaks and valleys. These lines will often fall near DRF values of 30 percent and 70 percent. The area above the top line is considered "overbought" territory. When prices fall below the lower line, the market is deemed to be "oversold" or poised for a rally. (See Figure D.1.)

A simple set of trading rules based on the A/D oscillator would be to close out all long positions and go short the day after DRF crosses above the top reference line, and to maintain these short positions until the day after the DRF falls below the lower reference line, at which time your position in the market is again reversed.

Single-Stock Futures Traded on OneChicago

3M Co.

Advanced Micro Devices Inc.

Alcoa Inc.

Allstate Corp.

Altera Corp.

Altria Group Inc.

Amazon.com Inc.

American Express Co.

American International Group

Amgen Inc.

Applied Materials Inc.

AT&T Corp.

Bank of America Corp.

Bed Bath & Beyond Inc.

Best Buy Company Inc.

Biogen Idec Inc.

Boeing Co.

Boston Scientific Corp.

Bristol-Myers Squibb Co.

Broadcom Corp.—CLA

Brocade Communications Sys

Caterpillar Inc.

Cephalon Inc.

Check Point Software Tech

ChevronTexaco Corp.

Chicago Mercantile Holdings Inc.

Cisco Systems Inc.

Citigroup Inc.

Coca-Cola Co.

Comcast Corp.

Computer Associates Int'l Inc.

Comverse Technology Inc.

Consolidated Edison

Dell Inc.

Dow Chemical Co.

Dreamworks Animation SKG Inc.

DuPont (E.I. Du Pont de Nemours)

Eastman Kodak

eBay Inc.

Elan Corp. PLC

Electronic Data Systems Corp.

Eli Lilly and Co.

EMC Corp.

Emulex Corp.

Exxon Mobil Corp.

Federated Department Stores Inc.

Ford Motor Co.

General Electric Co.

General Motors Corp.

Genzyme Corp.—Genl Division

Goldman Sachs Group Inc.

Google Inc.

Halliburton Co.

Hewlett-Packard Co.

Home Depot Inc.

Honeywell International Inc.

Intel Corp.

International Business Machines Corp.

International Paper Co.

J.P. Morgan Chase & Co.

JetBlue Airways Corp.

Johnson & Johnson

Juniper Networks

KLA-Tencor Corp.

Kohl's Corp.

Linear Technology Corp.

Lennar Corp.

Limited Brands Inc.

Maxim Integrated Products Inc.

McDonald's Corp.

Merck & Co. Inc.

Merrill Lynch & Co. Inc.

Micron Technology Inc.

Microsoft Corp.

Morgan Stanley

Motorola Inc.

Newmont Mining Corp Hldg Co.

News Corporation Ltd.

Nextel Communications Inc.

Nokia Corp. ADR

Northrop Grumman Corp.

Novellus Systems Inc.

NVIDIA Corp.

Oracle Corp.

PeopleSoft Inc.

PepsiCo Inc.

Pfizer

Phelps Dodge Corp.

PMC Sierra Inc.

Procter & Gamble Co.

QLogic Corp.

QUALCOMM Inc.

Research In Motion Ltd.

Reynolds American Inc.

SanDisk Corp.

SBC Communications Inc.

Schering-Plough Corp.

Schlumberger Ltd

Siebel Systems Inc.

Starbucks Corp.

Sun Microsystems

Symantec Corp.

Target Corp.

Tenet Healthcare

Texas Instruments Inc.

Tibco Software Inc.

Time Warner Inc.

Tyco International Ltd

U.S. Bancorp (New)

United Technologies Corp.

United Parcel Service Inc.

VERITAS Software Corp.

Verizon Communications Inc.

Viacom Inc.

Wal-Mart Stores Inc.

Walt Disney Co.

Wells Fargo & Co.

Williams Companies Inc.

Xilinx Inc.

Yahoo! Inc.

F

Single-Stock Futures Traded on LIFFE CONNECT

Abertis Infraestructuras SA

ABN AMRO Holdings NV

Accor SA

Aegon NV

Air Liquide SA

Akzo Nobel NV

Alcatel SA

Allianz AG

Altadis SA

American Express Co.

Amgen Inc

Arcelor

ASML Holding NV

Assicurazioni Generali SpA

Assurances Generales de France

Axa SA

Banca Intesa SpA

Banco Bilbao Vizcaya Argentaria SA

Banco de Sabadell SA

Banco Popolare Di Verona E Novara

Banco Popular Espanol SA

BASF AG

Bayer AG

Bayerische Hypo-und Vereinsbank AG

Bayerische Motoren Werke (BMW) AG

BNP Paribas SA

Bouygues SA

Capitalia SpA

Carrefour SA

Cisco Systems Inc

Citigroup Inc

Commerzbank AG

Compagnie de Saint Gobain

Compagnie Financiere Richemont AG

Compania Espanola de Petroleos SA
   (CEPSA)

Credit Agricole SA

Credit Suisse Group

DaimlerChrysler AG

Danske Bank A/S

Deutsche Bank AG

Deutsche Post AG

Deutsche Telekom AG

Dexia

DSM NV

E.ON AG

Endesa SA

Enel SpA

Eni SpA

European Aeronautic Defence and
   Space Company

Exxon Mobil Corporation

Fiat SpA

Fortis

France Telecom SA

Gas Natural SDG SA

General Electric Company

Groupe Danone SA

Heineken NV

Hennes & Mauritz AB

Hypo Real Estate Holding AG

Iberdrola SA

Industria de Diseno Textil SA
   (Inditex)

Infineon Technologies AG

ING Groep NV

Intel Corporation

Inbev SA

International Business Machines
   Corporation

Johnson & Johnson

KBC Bankverzekeringsholding

Koninklijke Ahold NV

Koninklijke KPN NV

Koninklijke Philips Electronics NV

Lafarge SA

Lagardere SCA

L'Oréal SA

LVMH Moet Hennessy Louis
   Vuitton SA

Mediaset SpA

Mediobanca SpA

Merck & Co. Inc

Metro AG

Microsoft Corporation

Münchener Rückversicherungs
   Gesellschaft AG

Nestlé SA

Nokia OYJ

Nordea AB

Norsk Hydro ASA

Novartis AG

Novo Nordisk A/S

Pernod Ricard SA

Peugeot SA

Pfizer Inc

Pinault-Printemps-Redoute SA

Porsche AG

Reed Elsevier

Renault SA

Repsol YPF SA

Riunione Adriatica di Sicurta SpA

Roche Holding AG

Rodamco Europe NV

Royal Dutch Petroleum Company

RWE AG

San Paolo-IMI SpA

Sanofi-Aventis SA

Santander Central Hispano SA

SAP AG

SBC Communications Inc

Schering AG

Schneider Electric SA

Siemens AG

Société Générale SA

Societe Television Francaise (T.F.1)

Sodexho Alliance SA

Solvay SA

Statoil ASA Physical

STMicroelectronics NV

Stora Enso Oyj

Suez SA

Svenska Handelsbanken AB

Swiss Reinsurance AG

Swisscom AG

Telecom Italia Mobile SpA

Telecom Italia SpA

Telecom Italia SpA (saving shares)

Telefonaktiebolaget LM Ericsson AB

Telefonica Moviles SA

Telefonica SA

TeliaSonera

Terra Networks SA

ThyssenKrupp AG

Time Warner Inc

Total SA

TPG NV

UBS AG

UniCredito Italiano SpA

Unilever NV

Union Fenosa SA

UPM-Kymmene Oyj

Verizon Communications

Vivendi Universal SA

VNU NV

Volkswagen AG

Wal-Mart Stores Inc

Wolters Kluwer NV

Zurich Financial Services AG

G Appendix

Overseas Futures Markets

Several active interest-rate futures contracts are traded on exchanges outside the United States. They include:

Euro bund. A Euro bund is a government bond issued by the Federal Republic of Germany. It carries a 6 percent coupon and has a maturity of from 8½ to 10½ years. Euro-bund futures are traded on Eurex, an electronic futures exchange located in Frankfurt, Germany. Euro-bund futures are also traded on the Chicago Board of Trade.

Euro bobl and *Euro schatz.* Euro bobl and Euro schatz are German government bonds of shorter maturities than the Euro bund. Both have coupons of 6 percent. The bobl has a maturity of from 4½ to 5½ years; the schatz has a maturity of from 1¾ to 2¼ years. Both are traded on Eurex and on the Chicago Board of Trade

Euribor. Euribor stands for Euro Interbank Offered Rate, the rate at which eurobank term deposits within the euro zone are offered by one prime bank to another. Euribor futures are traded electronically on Euronext.life, the derivatives side of Euronext.

TIIE 28. TIIE 28 stands for 28-day Mexican Interbank Equilibrium Interest Rate, the rate at which the supply of and demand for 28-day Mexican bank loans are in equilibrium. Futures contracts on the TIIE 28 are traded on the Mexican Derivatives Exchange, a subsidiary of the Mexican Stock Exchange.

KOSPI 200. The KOSPI (Korea Composite Stock Price Index) is an index of 200 major stocks listed on the Korea Stock Exchange. KOSPI 200 futures are traded electronically on the Korean Futures Exchange.

Interest rates. Bolsa de Mercadorias & Futuros in Brazil trades futures contracts on 1-day interbank deposits, long-term interbank deposits, and several financial intermarket spreads.

Firms with Direct Access for Electronic Trading

The following futures brokerage firms currently provide direct online access to the exchange for electronic trading. Most offer access to all U.S. and major international exchanges.

Alaron Trading Corp.	www.alaron.com
ANCO Discount Futures	www.ancofutures.com
ChicagoEFutures.com	www.chicagofutures.com
Carlin Futures LLC	www.carlinfutures.com
efutures.com	www.efutures.com
Fox Investments	www.foxinvestments.com
Ira Epstein & Co.	www.iepstein.com
Interactive Brokers	www.interactivebrokers.com
Lehman Brothers Inc.	www.lehman.com
Lind-Waldock	www.lind-waldock.com
Man Financial	www.manfutures.com
MBF Clearing Corp.	www.mbfcc.com
Merrill Lynch	www.mlx.ml.com
Merchant Capital	www.merchantcapitalinc.com
National Futures	www.nationalfutures.com

O'Connor & Co. LLC	www.eoconnor.com
PFG Inc.	www.pfgbest.com
Pioneer Futures	www.pioneerfutures.com
PreferredTrade Inc.	www.preferredtrade.com
Rand Financial Services	www.randfinancial.com
RB&H Financial Services LP	www.webvestor.com
Robbins Trading Co.	www.robbinstrading.com
Smart Futures	www.smartfutures.net
Terra Nova Trading LLC	www.terranovatrading.com
TradeStation Securities	www.tradestation.com
Vision LP	www.tradewithvision.com
EXRESSTRADE LLC	www.xpresstrade.com
Zaner Group LLC/NetFutures	www.zaner.com
	www.netfutures.com
ZAP Futures LLC	www.zapfutures.com

Index